TERRORISM, HOT SPOTS AND CONFLICT-RELATED ISSUES

IN PURSUIT OF THE LONE WOLF TERRORIST

INVESTIGATIVE ECONOMICS AND NEW HORIZONS FOR THE ECONOMIC ANALYSIS OF TERRORISM

Terrorism, Hot Spots and Conflict-Related Issues

Additional books in this series can be found on Nova's website under the Series tab.

Additional e-books in this series can be found on Nova's website under the e-book tab.

Criminal Justice, Law Enforcement and Corrections

Additional books in this series can be found on Nova's website under the Series tab.

Additional e-books in this series can be found on Nova's website under the e-book tab.

TERRORISM, HOT SPOTS AND CONFLICT-RELATED ISSUES

IN PURSUIT OF THE LONE WOLF TERRORIST

INVESTIGATIVE ECONOMICS AND NEW HORIZONS FOR THE ECONOMIC ANALYSIS OF TERRORISM

PETER J. PHILLIPS

nova publishers
New York

For permission to use material from this book please contact us:
Telephone 631-231-7269; Fax 631-231-8175
Web Site: http://www.novapublishers.com

Library of Congress Cataloging-in-Publication Data

In pursuit of the lone wolf terrorist: investigative economics and new horizons for the economic analysis of terrorism / editor, Peter J. Phillips (University of Southern Queensland, Queensland, Australia).
pages cm
Includes index.
ISBN: 978-1-62618-988-1 (hardcover)
1. Terrorism--Economic aspects. 2. Terrorism--Prevention. I. Phillips, Peter J.
HV6431.I47719 2013
363.325'165--dc23

2013017758

Published by Nova Science Publishers, Inc. † New York

CONTENTS

PREFACE

This is a book about two things. First it is a book about the opportunities confronting terrorists, especially lone wolf terrorists, and the choices that they make from those opportunities. I imagine that this will be useful to those people whose task it is to think about and analyse the terrorism context, whether it be researchers in terrorism studies or analysts associated with governments or law enforcement agencies. Terrorism has, up til now, been studied with the assistance of frameworks built on the basis of ideas that do not fit the context of lone wolf terrorism very well. Those ideas sit too far removed from the violent actions perpetrated by terrorists and terrorist groups. This book refocuses our analysis on the actions of terrorists that are of most concern to citizens and governments. These are the terrorist's violent actions, the biographies of violence, and the methods that were used to perpetrate them. An analysis of terrorism that treats its most tragic outcomes as its most heinous objectives not only refocuses terrorism studies on the thing that matters most, preventing human tragedy and pursuing those who inflict it, but in the process it presents a clear and operationally relevant picture of what the terrorist may be able to do and what he may be likely to choose to do.

The first part of this book is about opportunities and choices and pre-emption, the second part of this book is about the pursuit of the lone wolf terrorist. Once the lone wolf terrorist has chosen to attack he reveals his preference for risk. It is the advantage of the framework of opportunities and choices that is developed in the first part of this book that it is built upon both a precise definition and measurement of the risk associated with each attack method category. A choice from a particular category such as assassination, bombing, armed attacks or hostage taking, reveals the lone wolf terrorist's preference for risk. This alone would contribute to the work undertaken by law enforcement agencies, especially offender profilers, which at the moment depends upon a qualitative or logical assessment of the risk that the offender has taken rather than a quantitative assessment of the terrorist's choice versus his alternative opportunities. However, a robust assessment of the lone wolf terrorist's risk preference leads to other aspects that may be important in the development of a profile of the offender. It is in this way that the economic analysis developed in this book is operationally relevant to an actual law enforcement agency pursuing a real individual offender.

The origins of this work date to the day in the early 2000s when I first saw the Rand Corporation's terrorism data. I saw the data through the eyes of a 'financial economist' and, in particular, through the lens of one of the most clearly developed and useful economic-theoretical frameworks. This framework was Markowitz's mean-variance analysis. I wrote a paper that was published in Defence and Peace Economics in 2009[1] that contains the first expression of these ideas and, as it seems, the first application of this type of analysis to terrorist choice. In it, as in this book, I took the view that terrorists perpetrate violence and they choose attack methods with which to perpetrate it. It seemed to me then, and I believe it more strongly now that I have studied both the words and deeds of terrorists, that we should prepare for the possibility that terrorists attempt to inflict as much human tragedy as they can given the resources available to them and the amount of risk they wish to bear. I did not know this was actually an iconoclastic position that would be at odds with the received wisdom of terrorism studies.

I also did not expect that the theoretical framework I was using, mean-variance analysis, would be the target of simplistic counter-arguments long since resolved within modern finance theory. In the 1960s and 1970s, the idea that we could obtain an individual's 'preference ranking' over a set of opportunities on the basis of each opportunity's average payoff and the variability of its payoffs, was championed by at least two Nobel Prize winners in James Tobin and Harry Markowitz. The problem, highlighted by critics at the time, was that such a preference ranking would not be consistent with the famous von Neumann and Morgenstern axioms of rational choice unless the individual making a choice was described by a quadratic expected utility function *or* the payoffs were normally distributed. The latter is sometimes not observed and the former comes with some implications that were deemed undesirable. In particular, quadratic utility implies that a person may one day 'have had enough' and, in fact, this point of satiation may occur over a relatively narrow range of payoffs. Given, however, that mean-variance analysis provided a preference ranking that could be computed easily on the basis of two observable statistics, its proponents defended their approach with vigour.

Of course, the same two problems, quadratic utility and normally distributed payoffs, have been mentioned to me a few times since I first began arguing for the adoption of the method as the one most likely to produce plausible computable results in a terrorism context. My position is the same as that taken by Markowitz and Tobin three decades ago. The von Neumann and Morgenstern axioms do not tell us anything about the actual choices a person might make and mean-variance preference rankings approximate a 'full' expected utility analysis even in the absence of quadratic utility or normally distributed payoffs and, even if quadratic utility did need to be applied, it too approximates the results obtained from other utility functions. What is more, quadratic utility might not be desirable in finance where more money might always be preferred to less but it might be very useful in terrorism where a terrorist may decide that he has perpetrated enough violence, at least for now. It might have problems, but mean-variance analysis has significant advantages over the full expected utility analysis that has usually been applied to the analysis of terrorist choice and the old 'objections' to the approach cannot be brought to bear against its application to the analysis of terrorism because they never identified critical logical flaws in the first place.

I did not write anything further on terrorism until late 2009 after receiving some encouragement from a well-known economist who highlighted the innovative nature of my approach. In 2010, I wrote a paper that applied the same sorts of ideas to lone wolf terrorism[2]. Again, I was surprised. When this paper was published in Peace Economics, Peace Science

[1] Phillips (2009).
[2] Phillips (2011).

and Public Policy in 2011, it quickly attracted more than its share of downloads. Apart from its analysis of lone wolf terrorism and the choices of lone wolf terrorists, this paper contains glimpses of what might be an operational or investigative manual for law enforcement agencies in pursuit of a particular lone wolf terrorist. This only occurred to me some months after its publication at which point a colleague and I delved into the investigative psychology and offender profiling literature in an attempt to find out how an economic analysis may be applied to the development of behavioural investigative advice. The results of this research were published in 2012 in the Journal of Applied Security Analysis[3]. We reported the outlines of an approach that would use a combination of mean-variance analysis and the standard models of criminal behaviour as a framework within which an investigator could place a particular lone wolf terrorist based on the lone wolf's actions and choices. A final piece of the overarching analytical vision was put in place in late 2011 when I wrote a paper about the actions of 'spree' lone wolf terrorists or those individuals who engage in short sprees of violence, usually shooting sprees. This was presented at a conference on peace science held in Berlin in mid-2012 and published as a very concise short 'letter' in Peace Economics, Peace Science and Public Policy in late 2012[4].

In each case, however, the journal articles contain work that was developed intuitively and quite quickly and fortunately without any substantial slips. The ideas needed more refinement and more consideration. In 2011 I decided to start work on this book. After many revisions along the way, I am pleased to present an approach to the analysis of terrorist opportunities and choices that is operationally relevant and will be of utility to law enforcement agencies seeking to pre-empt and pursue the lone wolf terrorist. It is an approach that defines and measures the outcomes and risk associated with each attack method category and allows law enforcement to develop a clearer picture of the opportunities and choices of a violent lone wolf offender. The economic logic of choice and the models that have been developed both within orthodox economics and behavioural economics provide many more opportunities to develop insights into terrorist behaviour that are not only relevant to broader policy and strategic decisions but to the operational decisions that must be made by law enforcement agencies pursuing particular individual offenders. In writing this book, I have benefited from insights provided by Gabriela Pohl, whose own work is an analysis of the choices of the Federal Republic of Germany's Red Army Faction (RAF). Our sometimes opposite views on terrorist objectives and motivations have sharpened my focus on more than one occasion.

University of Southern Queensland
March 2013

---

[3] Phillips and Pohl (2012).
[4] Phillips (2012).

ANALYTICAL SUMMARY

CHAPTER 1

The provision of behavioural investigative advice that is directly relevant to law enforcement efforts to apprehend a lone wolf terrorist represents the new horizon for the economic analysis of terrorism. Economic analysis is concerned with the lone wolf's opportunities and choices. These can be delineated on the basis of 'risk' and 'reward'. When the investigative economist delineates the terrorist's opportunities and choices, the lone wolf terrorist is encompassed within an economic framework. Before the lone wolf strikes, no-one knows who he is or what 'type' of lone wolf terrorist he is. When he makes his choice to attack, he reveals his preference for risk. Because we have delineated the lone wolf's opportunities and choices on the basis of risk and reward, his choice reveals a preference for a particular level of risk. This revealed risk preference allows us to draw inferences about the lone wolf. A profile of the lone wolf can be sketched on the basis of economic analysis.

CHAPTER 2

The traditional economic analysis of terrorism evolved from the application of expected utility theory to a variety of different choice scenarios, especially the choice to engage in criminal behaviour or some combination of criminal behaviour and legitimate behaviour. From there it was a logical step to the construction of an economic model of terrorist behaviour. Important results have been derived from this. Economists have a good theory to explain the ways in which payoffs and penalties affect terrorist choice, the ways in which changes in payoffs and penalties lead terrorists to substitute one activity for another and the ways in which the risk and rewards available to different terrorist activities affect terrorist choice. This work provides the foundations for an economic analysis of terrorism that is capable of providing investigative advice relevant to the pursuit of a particular lone wolf terrorist.

CHAPTER 3

The lone wolf faces a trade-off between risk and reward. The attack methods that are available to the lone wolf terrorist have expected payoffs. The payoffs are risky and the actual payoffs may diverge from those which were expected. The expected payoffs and risk that characterises the attack methods may be measured by the statistics: mean and variance. This statistical measurement provides an essential part of the foundation for the economic analysis of the lone wolf's choice of attack method. Indeed, an economic analysis may be constructed on the basis of mean and variance. This mean-variance expected utility analysis captures the idea that the lone wolf faces a trade-off between risk and reward and allows computable results to be generated rather than purely logical-theoretical conclusions. This is exactly what we need if we are to generate operationally relevant investigative advice.

CHAPTER 4

The first step towards encompassing the lone wolf terrorist within the economic framework is to identify the categories of attack methods from which the lone wolf may choose. The RAND-MIPT categories for transnational terrorist attack methods are: armed attacks, arson, assassination, hostage, bombing, hijacking, kidnapping, unconventional and 'other'. Lone wolves have usually selected armed attacks and bombings as their attack methods of choice. These attack methods are also the most commonly selected attack methods of the transnational terrorists. The payoffs that the lone wolf can expect are reflected in the historical time series of injuries and fatalities that have been inflicted by the transnational terrorists. The lone wolf cannot escape from the statistical structure that describes the injuries and fatalities associated with each of the attack methods and combinations of attack methods.

CHAPTER 5

Each attack method has an expected payoff and a risk. Additional expected payoffs are available only by bearing additional risk. But there is a special property embedded within the statistical structure which emerges because expected payoffs of each of the attack methods are imperfectly correlated. The lone wolf terrorist may obtain 'gains from combination'. By combining attack methods, additional expected payoffs are available without additional risk. Imperfect correlation of attack methods produces a concave set of risk-reward pairings and the opportunity for gains from combination. Law enforcement must consider the 'concavity' of the risk-reward trade-off. Providing some insights into the nature of the lone wolf terrorist's risk-reward trade-off is one of our main contributions to law enforcement efforts designed to pre-empt the lone wolf.

CHAPTER 6

Statistical structure enables an economic analytical framework to be constructed and allows the lone wolf terrorist's opportunities to be determined. Mean-variance expected utility analysis takes the statistical structure of the attack methods and builds an economic framework of opportunities and choices around that structure. The result is that the lone wolf terrorist confronts opportunities characterised by a statistical structure of risks and rewards. His optimal—and most dangerous—choices within this statistical structure may be determined.

CHAPTER 7

All of the lone wolf's opportunities are contained within the opportunity set. This contains every possible pair of expected payoff and risk associated with every possible combination of attack methods. The lone wolf terrorist will prefer those opportunities that provide the highest expected payoffs at each level of risk. The constituents of this 'efficient' set of opportunities are found by determining the combination of attack methods that produces the maximum expected payoff at a given level of risk. The solution of this problem reveals that combinations of assassination and bombing dominate other combinations at low levels of risk while combinations of bombing, hostage taking and unconventional attacks dominate other combinations at high levels of risk. If law enforcement knows what the lone wolf's opportunities are, they are better positioned to anticipate his choices and actions.

CHAPTER 8

The lone wolf's preferences for risk play a critical role in determining which attack method or combination of attack methods he will choose. If he is not very risk averse, he will choose combinations of armed attacks, bombing, hostage taking and unconventional attacks. If he is more risk averse, he will choose combinations that include bombing, hostage taking and unconventional attacks but allocate relatively more resources to bombing and relatively less resources to the riskier attack methods. If he is very risk averse, he will choose combinations of attack methods that include assassination and bombing. If he is very risk averse but cannot combine attack methods, he will choose assassination. If we know the lone wolf's preference for risk, we know what type of attack method combination he is likely to choose. Risk preference forms the basis for our profile of the lone wolf terrorist.

CHAPTER 9: SUMMARY

At this point, we pause to summarise our analytical work before moving on to part two of the book. An approach to the analysis of the lone wolf terrorist from the perspective of economic science deals with the lone wolf's opportunities and choices. Fundamentally, the lone wolf's opportunities consist of expected payoffs and risks. To reach the point where the lone wolf's opportunities are laid bare in this manner we categorise his possible attack methods and work out the expected payoffs and risks that characterise each attack method category. The trade-off that the lone wolf faces emerges as a clearly defined risk-reward trade-off. The nature of this trade-off depends on the extent to which the lone wolf can combine different attack methods. For different cases, including the case where no combination is possible, we can determine the lone wolf's most dangerous choices. This represents the contribution that economic analysis can make to the delineation of the lone wolf's opportunities and choices. Once the lone wolf makes a choice, this delineation or framework may form the basis for the drawing of inferences about the unknown offender.

CHAPTER 10

Offender profiling is the activity of drawing inferences about the offender from evidence left at the crime scene. To do this, the profiler usually makes use of some typology or classification scheme. The evidence at the crime scene allows the profiler to classify the crime as being of a certain type. The offender will have characteristics associated with that type. This allows a profile of the offender to be sketched on the basis of the evidence left at the crime scene. For example, a crime scene that may be classified as 'organised' will suggest an organised offender. An organised offender will have an organised life outside of his criminal activities. He will have at least average intelligence, be socially competent and in skilled employment. A disorganised crime scene will suggest a disorganised offender and law enforcement will be instructed to look for an individual who leads a disorderly lifestyle.

CHAPTER 11

Crime scenes are classified as organised or disorganised. An organised crime scene may be one where the offender plans the crime, restrains the victim and carries a weapon to and from the crime scene. A disorganised crime scene may be one where the crime scene is left in disarray, a murder weapon or other evidence is left at the scene and the victim's body is left in the open. The two different types of crime are presumed to have been committed by two different types of individual. Furthermore, the crime scene is reflective of their character. An organised crime scene suggests and organised character and vice versa. The weaknesses inherent within the organised/disorganised typology include the provision that the organised or disorganised offender will continue to commit organised or disorganised crimes over time. Perhaps more significant is the reliance of the organised/disorganised typology on personality trait based models of behaviour. The weakness of personality trait based models has long been recognised by psychologists.

CHAPTER 12

Before a lone wolf terrorist strikes, no-one knows who he is. No-one knows what type of lone wolf he is. No-one knows his preference for risk. When he strikes, he reveals something about himself. He reveals his existence and he reveals his preference for risk. Like the offender profilers and investigative psychologists who try to build a sketch of the offender from the evidence available at the crime scene, the investigative economist may take that crime scene evidence and use it to determine the 'type' of lone wolf that might have been responsible for a terrorist action. The investigative economist allocates the lone wolf a place within a risk preference typology: very risk averse (less risk seeking), moderately risk averse (or moderately risk seeking) or very low risk aversion (more risk seeking). On the basis of this classification, which is analogous to the approach applied by offender profilers, the investigative economist draws inferences about the lone wolf. The inferences that can be drawn include the lone wolf's likely proximity to the scene of the attacks, the likelihood that he specialises in terrorism, the likelihood that he will be found engaged in other forms of non-violent expression and the likelihood that he will increase the intensity of his attacks or simply drift away for an indefinite period of time. These are aspects of the operational advice that economics may provide to law enforcement.

Chapter 13

To show how the drawing of inferences from 'revealed risk preference' may work in practice, we examine three prominent cases of lone wolf terrorism: the cases of George Metesky (the Mad Bomber), Franz Fuchs and Theodore Kaczynski (the Unabomber). Each of these cases attracted considerable law enforcement attention and profiles were constructed in each case by investigative psychologists. The application of the framework developed in the earlier part of this book illustrates more clearly the additional inferences that may be drawn about the offender when his actions and his crime scenes are looked at from the perspective of economic analysis.

Chapter 14

Up to this point in the analysis, we have concentrated on serial lone wolf terrorists. These are terrorists who strike time after time, just like a serial killer. During our discussion, however, we come across a number of 'spree' lone wolves. These are terrorists who strike suddenly with a spree of violence, usually a shooting spree. We ask, "What 'type' of terrorist is the lone wolf spree shooter?" He is not easily classified as 'risk averse' or 'risk seeking'. Rather, he is a 'plunger' who decides to suddenly and all at once plunge all of his resources into terrorism. The particular characteristics of the spree lone wolf are explored and the implications of these characteristics for law enforcement are discussed.

Chapter 15

The pursuit of the lone wolf terrorist is a law enforcement operational matter. The investigative economist, operating in a manner analogous to the investigative psychologist and offender profiler, assesses the evidence at the scene of the attack. Of most importance is the type of attack method or combination of attack methods that the lone wolf has used. Each attack method and combination has an expected payoff and risk. A lone wolf reveals his preference for risk by choosing a particular attack method or combination. From this revelation, the investigative economist makes further inferences about the lone wolf. These inferences represent investigative advice that may contribute to the management of the law enforcement efforts directed towards apprehending the lone wolf. Further development of the capabilities of economics to provide such operationally relevant advice is the new horizon for the economic analysis of terrorism.

Part One

Chapter 1

THE INTRODUCTION

> The multiple stabbings and blitz-style attacks from the rear told me that we were dealing with an asocial type (though not necessarily antisocial) who'd be withdrawn, unsure of himself, and unable to engage his victims in a conversation, develop a good line, or con or coax or trick them into doing what he wanted. These were not the crimes of someone who knew his victims. The [killer] was non-preferential, like a spider waiting for a bug to fly into his web.... I expected this guy to have a bad background.... There would have been a precipitating stressor before it began. I certainly expected him to be white since all of the victims were, and I thought he'd have some blue-collar mechanical or industrial job. Because of the efficiency of the murders and his success in evading police thus far, I pegged his age at low to mid-thirties. I also thought he'd be pretty bright. If they looked into his IQ it would be well above normal....[1]

This is an offender profile of the 'Trailside Killer' constructed by FBI agents working out of the Behavioural Science Unit at Quantico. When serial killers have killed two or three times, law enforcement agents can usually determine that the murders are the work of a single individual. At this point, when it is clear that a single individual is responsible for the murders and a pattern of evidence has emerged through the analysis of the multiple crime scenes, it becomes possible for the profiler to develop a 'picture' of the unidentified subject (UNSUB) based on the evidence that has been left at the crime scenes. The offender profile is a list of characteristics that the UNSUB might have, including employment status, age, intelligence and education. The offender profile is an attempt to narrow down the pool of potential suspects and assist law enforcement's pursuit of the serial killer.

Like the serial killer, the lone wolf terrorist plans and executes his criminal activities alone, outside of a command structure and without accomplices. Some lone wolves have operated for almost twenty years before finally being captured. Others have engaged in 'sprees' of murder lasting just a few hours. The fact that they operate independently makes them extremely difficult to stop either before or during a period of violence. A lone wolf terrorist will not have the network of communications that are sometimes able to be infiltrated by law enforcement agents. There is no terrorist organisation to infiltrate. And lone wolves are dangerous. In a number of cases, lone wolf terrorists have killed and injured more people over the duration of their engagement in terrorism than terrorist organisations. Pursuing the lone wolf terrorist is a very challenging task for law enforcement and security agencies and

[1] Douglas and Olshaker (1996, pp.155-156).

both the Central Intelligence Agency (CIA) and the Federal Bureau of Investigation (FBI) have documented their concerns:

> ...I am particularly concerned about loosely affiliated terrorists and lone offenders, which are inherently difficult to interdict given the anonymity of individuals that maintain limited or no links to established terrorist groups but act out of sympathy with a larger cause. We should not forget the Oklahoma City bombing in 1995, for example, which was carried out by individuals unaffiliated with a larger group — Robert S. Mueller III, Director, FBI[2]

> ...The Department also supports making permanent section 6001(a) of the Intelligence Reform and Terrorism Prevention Act of 2004. This provision, which has come to be known as the "lone wolf" provision, allows the government to gain court approval for FISA surveillance of a non-United States person when there is probable cause to believe that he or she is engaged in or preparing to engage in international terrorism, whether or not he or she is known to be affiliated with a larger terrorist group. While this provision is currently scheduled to sunset at the end of this year, unfortunately, the threat to the United States posed by known or apparent lone wolf terrorists will not similarly cease on December 31, 2005. Therefore, the Department strongly endorses the enactment of section 102 of the Committee's draft legislation, which would remove the sunset on the lone wolf provision — Valerie Caproni, General Counsel, FBI[3]

As these quotes indicate, the FBI has been concerned about lone wolf terrorism for a long time. In 2011 these concerns were reiterated by both the President of the United States, Barack Obama, and the U.S. Homeland Security Director Janet Napolitano. Both the President and the Homeland Security Director named lone wolf terrorism as the greatest threat that the United States must guard against. Janet Napolitano was quoted as saying, "There's been a lot of evolution over the past three years. The thing that's most noticeable to me is the growth of the lone wolf."[4]

Although recent attacks have served to reinforce this perception of lone wolf terrorism, it should not be overlooked that lone offenders have been a threat to society for many decades. Whether we classify them as lone wolf terrorists, serial murderers or 'spree shooters', individual violent offenders have inflicted a large amount of human tragedy within the United States and in other places around the world long before the actions of Anders Behring Breivik re-emphasised the deadly nature of the threat. Political grievances or similar motivations and religious extremism are often given headline attention in popular coverage of terrorism and in academic research. However, violent offenders who fall into the category of being lone wolf terrorists have not always been motivated by anything other than anger, hatred and a desire to do violence. As such, lone wolf terrorists can emerge from almost anywhere within the fabric of a society and there is no archetypal set of motivations or behaviours that we can really look for when trying to pre-empt him. For this reason, the broader debates that dominate terrorism studies, which are guided by overarching paradigms, are not well-suited to the provision of operationally relevant advice to law enforcement agencies.

[2] Mueller (2003).
[3] Caproni (2005).
[4] Associated Press (2011).

While it could be reasonably expected that terrorism studies[5] may assist in the effort, pursuing the lone wolf terrorist requires more from terrorism studies, including the economic analysis of terrorism, than it has traditionally been able to provide. Although researchers have provided many important insights from a variety of different perspectives into the nature and causes of terrorism and, to a more limited extent, lone wolf terrorism, much of the work is too broad to be applicable in a particular case and sometimes the results are too ambiguous to be useful within a particular investigation. An important example concerns psychology and the psychological investigations of terrorists. Although many potential psychological motivations for terrorist behaviour have been posited, there is no single psychological profile that fits an archetype terrorist (see Victoroff 2005). Terrorists come from all sorts of socio-economic-familial backgrounds and those cases that have been studied closely reveal no consistent evidence of psychological illness indicative of insanity, broadly speaking (see Rasch 1979). And so we are left with a lot of information about potential motivations, political and socio-economic, but no real framework has emerged from 'terrorism studies' that might be used as an 'inference generator' to develop a profile for use in an actual investigation in pursuit of a particular UNSUB.

When our attention is turned towards the investigative process aimed at pre-empting or pursuing a particular individual rather than the broader themes of terrorism and its motivations, what we ask of terrorism studies changes entirely. This does not mean that what we have learned about terrorism and terrorist behaviour when we have studied it from the viewpoints of economics, political science, international relations and psychology becomes irrelevant. What it does mean is that we arrange our accumulated knowledge within frameworks that yield inferences regarding particular cases. It requires frameworks that facilitate analysis that is directly operationally relevant to the investigative process in a particular case. If we observe a characteristic of a particular terrorist attack such as the attack method that the terrorist has chosen, what does this fact tell us, given our knowledge of terrorism and terrorist behaviour, about the actual person or persons responsible for the act of terrorism? Where will the lone wolf terrorist be found? Is he close to his targets or far away? When and where will the lone wolf strike next? What attack methods will the lone wolf use? How many fatalities and injuries can we expect the lone wolf to inflict? Will he strike again? Providing analysis that assists law enforcement and security agencies directly engaged in the pre-emption or pursuit of the lone wolf terrorist represents the new horizon for the economic analysis of terrorism. It is a new horizon where the 'investigative economist', not just the investigative psychologist or offender profiler, contributes behavioural investigative advice to law enforcement.

THE LONE WOLF TERRORIST AND ECONOMICS

Economics deals with opportunities and choices and, in particular, it sets down the logic of choice or decision-making. The world is an uncertain and risky place. There are no rules of choice and people will decide and act or, conversely, suffer from crippling indecision or decide and act and then change their minds. It is only that things get done and plans get

[5] Terrorism studies encompass political science, international relations, critical studies, economics and parts of psychology.

fulfilled at all that leads us to wonder about the logic of choice. If nothing ever got done and no plans were ever fulfilled, we would have little indication that there was any such thing as the logic of choice but despite all of the uncertainty, people make decisions and act and things get done. Economics provides many different models of this process. Like all models, they abstract from reality to varying degrees. Some models are more popular than others. Some are expressed in words and others are expressed in mathematics. They all try to explain how people choose from the available opportunities and, by and large, they all start from the premise or axiom that people act purposively to achieve some end or other. From that point on, however, the models of choice that are contained within the economics literature are quite varied and many of them have been attributed, by economists themselves, with properties that are not true or accurate strictly speaking but more caricatures of the underlying theory of choice (see Becker 1968). The most well-known of the caricatures is the model of 'rational choice'. Economics, so far as it pertains to decision-making, is widely held to be synonymous with rational choice.

This is okay if we are clear about what rational choice means. On this point, the economists have been their own worst enemy and it is certainly the case now that rational choice means, in the minds of many, something along the lines of 'perfectly calculated' decision-making. This seems to be the case when you read an economist's analysis of terrorist behaviour and it is clear from any reading of a psychologist's review of terrorism studies that economics and rational choice analysis are one and the same and the latter depicts the terrorist as divining all of his opportunities, assigning the odds, using a mathematical function to compute the satisfaction or utility that he expects to derive from each, ranking each opportunity on the basis of its expected utility and choosing the opportunity that sits highest on the ranking. This will be the opportunity that maximises expected utility in the mathematical sense. It is hard to believe that this actually happens. The terrorist makes mistakes. The terrorist probably does not consider all of his options and he may judge poorly those that he does consider. Terrorists fail. They get caught. They suffer from crippling indecision and do not act. They misjudge their chances of success. However, it is the case that the terrorist has some end in mind and chooses a way to achieve that end and acts accordingly. The terrorist does act purposively. He does survey some opportunities and he does make a choice and he does act and terrorist plans do get fulfilled and terrorism does happen. This makes us wonder about the underlying logic or decision-making process that leads to perpetrated acts of terrorism, some of which display skilful planning in the same manner that the serial killer successfully accumulates victims whilst eluding the grasp of law enforcement.

Rationality in the sense of purposeful action directed at using the available means to achieve a desired, though perverse, end is exhibited by terrorists but this does not mean that it is a simple or straightforward matter to use the existing economic models of choice to analyse terrorism. Economics can defend itself against the argument that terrorist choice is depraved and illogical and therefore unanalysable. For one thing, most terrorists are not insane. Like serial killers, they may very well be 'sociopathic' or 'psychopathic' but this is reflected in their perverse ends or objectives and not in illogical decision-making when it comes to achieving those ends. There is a difference between this type of behaviour and deranged psychotic behaviour (Douglas and Olshaker 1996). A stronger argument that is invited by the translation of economic models of choice into the terrorism context is the argument that the very ends or objectives that terrorists have, such as overturning a government, are inherently illogical and decision-making processes that would put means into action to achieve such ends are also inherently illogical (Crenshaw 2000; Victoroff 2005). This argument relies upon a particular view of terrorism that is outdated and, one might argue, never held any relevance to lone wolf terrorism.

The reason why governments, law enforcement agencies and civilians get concerned about terrorism is because terrorism causes injuries and fatalities. List any of the 'traditional' goals of terrorism. It does not matter how unlikely or implausible any of them are when one considers that those to whom such goals are attached actually set out in any particular act of terrorism to inflict injuries and fatalities. On the day that the act of terrorism is undertaken, the objective is the act of terrorism and that objective involves inflicting some amount of human tragedy. A serial killer may ostensibly hold the unlikely or implausible objective to eradicate a particular type of person from society but the implausibility of this objective, even if it is sincerely held, does not automatically render his actions illogical in any particular instance of murder because within that instance his actions are purposeful and his means are directed purposively towards the perpetration of that act of murder. Instead of attaching lofty and somewhat implausible goals to terrorism we should recognise that the objective of terrorism, at least within the context of any particular attack, is to inflict injuries and fatalities. Given that some terrorists have stated a desire to kill as many people as possible and given that the types of attacks that terrorists have undertaken could not have been designed with anything other in mind, we might even argue that the overarching and not just attack-specific objective of terrorism is the infliction of human tragedy. This objective of terrorism is far from unlikely or implausible and the purposeful direction of means towards the achievement of this objective may be approached from the viewpoint of the logic of choice.

The task remains for the economist to link the logic of choice with the objective of inflicting human tragedy in a manner that equates 'optimal choice' and 'most deadly choice'. If this is accomplished, another criticism of economic analysis can be dispensed with. This criticism is that terrorists do not choose rationally. Even if it is accepted that the terrorist's objective is to inflict injuries and fatalities, he still may choose imperfectly, randomly, haphazardly and, in short, in a manner that renders economic analysis beside the point. This, in fact, may be true. However, if the terrorist's rational choice is also the choice that will inflict the highest expected number of injuries and fatalities, would the critic of rational choice advise us to abandon any analysis of the terrorist's most devastating opportunities on the grounds that the terrorist is too irrational to choose them? I do not think so. What is needed then is as complete an understanding as possible of the terrorist's most dangerous potential choices and an analysis that does not assume that we can rely on the terrorist to make mistakes when choosing which attack method he will use to inflict an amount of human tragedy. Obviously, if we are interested in the terrorist's opportunities to inflict injuries and fatalities, the place to start is with the small number of attack methods that are available for him to choose from. These attack methods reflect the lone wolf terrorist's opportunities to inflict human tragedy.

The lone wolf terrorist has opportunities. These are attack methods, each with a number of injuries and fatalities that can be expected to result. The lone wolf can choose from among the attack methods. Our view is that it is the soundest course of action to start with the idea that the lone wolf terrorist chooses rationally in the sense that he chooses the attack method that delivers the highest expected amount of human tragedy at the level of risk that he feels comfortable with. The risk that he faces in undertaking an act of terrorism is the possibility that the amount of human tragedy he actually inflicts is greater or less than the terrorist expected. These 'expected payoff-risk pairs' represent the lone wolf's opportunities. These opportunities are not limitless or without bound. Indeed, we shall be able to delineate the lone wolf's opportunity set quite concisely. It is from this delineated set of opportunities that the lone wolf must make his choices. He will try to choose the attack method or combination of attack methods that yields the highest amount of human tragedy for a given level of risk. This is his optimal choice. He might make a mistake and he might fail to choose the optimal attack method combination but by working on the basis that he tries to choose optimally from his set of opportunities we shall be prepared for the most dangerous outcome. This is a much more effective and practical use of the 'rational choice' approach than that which has traditionally been found within economic analyses of terrorism.

Pre-Empting the Lone Wolf Terrorist

Even if we say that the lone wolf's opportunities are the attack methods from which he can choose or, more precisely, the combinations of expected payoffs and risks that emerge from the available attack methods, it still seems that the lone wolf's opportunities appear to be limitless and without bound. This is not necessarily the case and it depends on how the problem is approached. When a terrorist plans to use a particular attack method, it is entirely possible that he has formed some idea about the amount of human tragedy he will inflict with it and the chances that he will fall short or exceed his expectation. This expectation may easily be formed on the basis of a familiarity with terrorism developed from publicly available sources, especially news reports covering successful and unsuccessful terrorist attacks (see, for example, Rohner and Frey 2007). It is this historical record which, when collected in complete and detailed form, that also provides the foundations for an analysis of the terrorist's opportunities and choices. Not only does the record of terrorism incidences allow us to be quite precise in setting down an expected number of fatalities for a particular terrorist attack method it is also characterised by a 'statistical structure' that allows us to construct a very interesting and, in its way, complete picture of the lone wolf's opportunities which shows the shape of the trade-off between expected fatalities and risk (or variability) that he confronts. When we draw it we see a positively sloping line or curve in expected payoff-risk space. This tells us that the more risk or variability the lone wolf is willing to bear the more fatalities he can expect to inflict. The other thing that we see when we draw the set of opportunities confronting the lone wolf is that the trade-off between expected fatalities and risk is 'bowed inwards'. It is concave. This tells us that the lone wolf's expected fatalities are higher, perhaps much higher, than what we would be led to believe if we thought the true picture of the opportunity set was a straight line rather than a concave curve.

What is interesting about this is that it is a complete opportunity set if the opportunities we are interested in (or view as most important) are the lone wolf terrorist's opportunities to inflict human tragedy by using particular attack methods. Despite the seeming complexity of the problem, we can have a picture of everything from which the lone wolf can choose and we can have a picture of his best choices if we define the context precisely in terms of the terrorist's ends or objectives and the means that he can use to achieve those objectives. This is the first part of economics' dual focus on opportunities and choices. If choice is to be analysed, we must define some collection of opportunities from which the choices will be made. It is relatively easy for the optimal or rational choice or choices to be determined. The rational choice approach, as we have just discussed, is left open to criticism if the rational choice is relevant only as a pure benchmark against which to assess actual choices. We undermine this criticism by giving the optimal or rational choice meaning within the practical and operational terrorism context. The lone wolf who chooses optimally or rationally from the set of opportunities that we have defined will choose the attack method or combination of attack methods that maximises the fatalities that can be expected to result at a particular level of risk. If he chooses optimally, we are prepared for it. If he chooses more and more optimally over time or tries to choose optimally, then we know where his choices will lead. If he chooses sub-optimally, then he chooses in a manner that was less dangerous than the choice we had prepared for. Rational choice is given real operational meaning.

The actual choices that the lone wolf makes from the set of attack method opportunities available to him depend on his appetite for risk. The decision-making process is one that requires the weighing up of risk and reward. It is worthwhile highlighting again the fact that all of the relevant information about risk and reward is contained in the large number of media reports and other publicly available information about successful and unsuccessful terrorist attacks. It is entirely likely that any person with an interest in terrorism would be able to estimate just how many people may be expected to injured or killed from a particular type of attack. And it is entirely likely that the same person would be able to estimate a range, plus and minus, from that expected value. Weighing these two things, expected outcomes and the variability of those outcomes from the expectation, and comparing across a relatively small number of attack methods is not a difficult computational task. It would be a mistake to think that the risks and rewards of different terrorist attack methods could not be determined and assessed by a potential lone wolf terrorist because it requires too much computation. This is far from being the case. When we say that the lone wolf weighs up the risks and rewards of the different attack methods, we are not imagining a task which requires extraordinary computational ability or information beyond that which is reflected in the daily news. It will be clear enough to the lone wolf terrorist which attack methods will be more or less suitable given his expectations regarding payoffs and his expectations regarding the chances that the outcomes of his attacks may be more or less deadly than he anticipated. His actual choice will depend on his appetite or preference for risk.

Risk preference in economics refers to the amount of extra expected payoff the lone wolf needs in order to bear an extra amount of risk. When risk increases, the lone wolf requires additional expected payoff. If this is the case the lone wolf is described by what economists call ‘risk aversion’. A lone wolf is very risk averse if he requires a very large increase in expected payoffs for bearing an additional amount of risk. A lone wolf is not very risk averse if he only requires a small increase in expected payoffs for bearing an additional amount of risk. We could also say that this lone wolf is more risk seeking but we must be careful with our use of terminology. Just because a lone wolf terrorist is engaged in risky activities like terrorism does not mean that he is ‘risk seeking’. ‘Risk aversion’ means that some increase in expected payoffs is required whenever there is an increase in the risk that must be borne. ‘Risk seeking’ means that the lone wolf deploys only the riskiest attack method and gives up expected payoffs in order to take on more risk. Since we do not usually see this type of behaviour from lone wolves, it is safest to start from the position that the lone wolf is risk averse. If he is not very risk averse he might engage in very risky activities if he is compensated appropriately with additional expected payoffs. He does not give up expected payoff to take on more risk. He takes on more risk in order to obtain higher expected payoffs.

In general, it is possible to divide the population of lone wolf terrorists into two or three categories based on their risk preferences: (1) highly risk averse; (2) moderately risk averse; (3) more risk seeking. This categorisation is possible because particular attack methods dominate the lone wolf's optimal choices over wide ranges of the set of opportunities. As we shall see, each one of these 'types' of lone wolves is more likely to be predisposed to choose a particular type of attack method. A highly risk averse lone wolf is more likely to choose 'assassination' as his attack method choice. This attack method has a low expected payoff but the payoffs exhibit very low variability. A moderately risk averse lone wolf terrorist is more likely to choose armed attacks and bombings. A more risk seeking lone wolf terrorist (i.e. a lone wolf who is not very risk averse at all) will choose hostage-taking or unconventional attacks. These attack methods have high expected payoffs but the payoffs exhibit very high variability. There is a much greater chance of an outcome that diverges considerably from that which was expected. Through this sort of analysis and reasoning, we can identify those attack methods that are more likely to be chosen. We could, if the data were available, do the same thing for other types of opportunities that are relevant to the lone wolf terrorist. These could include target choice and fatalities or attack method choice and media coverage. In each case, insight into the lone wolf's opportunities and choices can be obtained by thinking about his opportunities in terms of a trade-off between risk and reward. In this context, the lone wolf's risk preference emerges as a most important consideration which, in conjunction with the available opportunities, leads us directly to a set of inferences about the types of attack methods that are likely to be chosen.

Without understanding the technical meaning of the terms it is hard for some people to accept that individuals engaged in activities such as terrorism may be risk averse rather than risk seeking. It also leads people down the dangerous path of attributing a particular type of risk preference to a particular type of individual. They conclude that terrorists or criminals are risk seeking. This behavioural prescription undermines one of the main advantages of economic analysis. This advantage is the non-reliance on personality traits to explain choices. Personality trait-based models of behaviour have long been recognised to be fundamentally weak. Psychologists have known about this for a long time and the economists who developed the first economic models of criminal behaviour never fell into the trap of assigning particular personality traits to particular individuals. When individuals make decisions under conditions of risk and uncertainty, they reveal a type of risk preference. Usually, risk aversion is the risk preference that is revealed and what we see empirically is the revelation of some level of risk aversion. This revealed risk preference is not a personality trait associated with particular types of individuals. However, once the individual has revealed his risk preference by making an observable choice, we are able to explore the implications of this revelation for his present and future choices. Revealed risk preference becomes the basis for a 'profile' of the lone wolf terrorist.

THE PROFILE

We began our introduction with an example of an offender profile constructed by investigative psychologists or profilers working for the FBI. The profiler constructs the profile of the offender by drawing inferences about the type of person he might be from the evidence that is left at the crime scene. Although the investigative psychology literature is beset by debates and disagreements, the practice of profiling usually relies on looking at various aspects of the crime and crime scene and classifying the offender as either 'organised' or 'disorganised'. Organised and disorganised 'types' of offender are assumed to display particular organised or disorganised types of behaviour in their non-criminal lives. An offender whose crime scene displays features of organisation is assumed to display particular features of organisation in his other activities and vice versa for a disorganised crime scene. Of course, this is a personality trait-based model of offender behaviour and this is a part of the disagreement that characterises the investigative psychology literature. Fortunately, our approach to developing a profile of the lone wolf does not have this problem. Our approach involves drawing inferences about the lone wolf on the basis of the risk preference he reveals in his choice of attack methods and attack method combinations.

Inherent within the organised/disorganised typology that still holds a place of prominence in investigative psychology is an assumption of 'consistency' on the part of the offender. A disorganised offender always commits disorganised crimes and a disorganised offender always has a disorganised life away from the crime scene. These sorts of assumptions weaken the inference generating foundations of the organised/disorganised typology and render it, at best, a special case applicable only to those offenders who do actually display this sort of consistency. Interestingly, risk preference in economics has an inherent flexibility in this regard that completely contrasts with the consistency assumption of the organised/disorganised typology. Not only does risk preference shape the amount of risk that the lone wolf terrorist tolerates but it also shapes the amount of risk he tolerates over time as his victims accumulate. Risk preference itself may be increasing, decreasing or constant over time as the lone wolf accumulates victims. A lone wolf terrorist with increasing risk aversion will engage in less risky attacks as his victims accumulate. The opposite is true for a lone wolf terrorist with decreasing risk aversion while the riskiness of the attacks of the lone wolf with constant risk aversion will show no tendency to move up or down as victims accumulate over time. Risk preference is an important shaper of choice but it is flexible and can encompass choice dynamics that may be very relevant to the lone wolf's choices from attack to attack or during the time period spanned by a single attack such as a prolonged shooting spree. Our lone wolf need not display the same risk preference and, therefore, the same types of choices over time. In fact, it is probably the case that he will not.

Our picture of the lone wolf terrorist is one who chooses attack methods from a set of attack method opportunities. The defining characteristic of the opportunities available to the lone wolf terrorist is the number of injuries and fatalities that are expected to result from the use of a particular attack method and the variability or risk of the actual outcomes from the outcomes that were expected. His choice is shaped by his risk preference. Because the set of attack method opportunities are dominated over particular ranges of risk by certain attack methods, it is possible to categorise lone wolf terrorists into three overarching risk preference categories and identify the attack method choices that are most likely to characterise each risk preference category. These sorts of conclusions are relevant to the task of pre-empting, difficult as that remains, the lone wolf terrorist before he strikes. After he strikes, law enforcement begins the investigative process that aims to identify, find and apprehend the lone wolf. It is during this phase of the investigative process that a profile of the lone wolf may be useful. A profile developed on the basis of our analytical framework is one that links the lone wolf's attack method choice with his risk preference. A lone wolf who undertakes a particular type of attack reveals something about his risk preferences. If we can identify the lone wolf's risk preference, we can make further inferences about him including inferences about how his risk preference may be expected to change over time and what that means for the amount human tragedy we can expect him to inflict if he is not apprehended before he strikes again.

We know from our analysis what sorts of attack methods and combinations of attack methods are more risky and what sorts of attack methods and combinations are less risky. We know which attack methods and attack method combinations will be chosen by a lone wolf with a particular type of risk preference. Once the lone wolf strikes, he reveals his preference for risk by his choice of attack method or attack method of combination. Once the lone wolf strikes, we can classify him as being either a 'highly risk averse type' or 'more risk seeking type' or somewhere in between. This is the economic analogue of the organised/disorganised typology. Within the economic theory that describes criminal and terrorist behaviour, risk preference has various implications for the behaviour that we can expect the criminal or terrorist to exhibit. Working through these implications allows us to draw inferences about the lone wolf on the basis of his terrorist activity. These inferences constitute a profile constructed from the view point of economic science.

What the Profile Can Say

Investigative psychologists and offender profilers have been accorded a great deal of prominence in popular culture. The profiler is an essential and popular character in certain types of television programs and has been for three decades. The example with which we opened the chapter is a 'classical' example of an offender profile that explains why offender profiling has proven to be so fascinating to scholars, law enforcement and the general—television watching and detective fiction reading—public. The profile says a lot about the offender and it is remarkable to think that a profiler could be equipped with such insights as to be able to step into the mind of the offender and draw all sorts of inferences about him simply from an observation of crime scene. These include everything from intelligence and type of employment to whether the offender knew his victims to the type of vehicle the offender could be expected to drive. It is not the case that these sorts of inferences can be drawn from any framework that emerges from an economic analysis of choice. Indeed, it is probably the case that these sorts of inferences are not able to be legitimately drawn from any psychological framework. Much of the debate within the investigative psychology discipline centres on what is a conflicting view of the importance of the profiler's special skills relative to the theoretical frameworks of psychology. Inferences that lie beyond the scope of psychological theory must be due to either the special skills of the profiler or speculation (if no such special skill can be identified). It is these sorts of debates that we wish to avoid in building a profile on the basis of an economic model of choice.

A profile constructed on the basis of economic theory is neither a personality trait-based profile nor a profile that requires some sort of consistency in the behaviour of the lone wolf. The organised/disorganised typology assumes that the organised offender will continue to be organised over time. Our economic approach allows for a more sophisticated profile of the lone wolf that includes a facility for risk preference and attack method choice to change over time as the lone wolf terrorist accumulates victims. An economic approach should yield a profile that has something to say about whether the lone wolf will likely be a specialist in terrorist violence or whether he will engage in both terrorism and other non-violent forms of expression. It should be able to say whether the lone wolf terrorist will be found close to his targets or far away. It should be able to say whether the lone wolf will likely escalate his terrorist activity or fade away in response to law enforcement or attention from the popular press. It should also be able to say whether the lone wolf will escalate his terrorist activity or fade away as his success or failure to generate injuries and fatalities accumulates. These are some of the very valuable insights that may be drawn from an economic profile of the lone wolf. The contributions that the investigative economist is able to make to an investigation into the lone wolf terrorist may be a valuable complement to current profiling methodologies.

Each of the inferences that may be drawn from a profile based on an economic model of choice under risk emerges from the logic of the risk-reward trade-off inherent within the lone wolf's set of opportunities. If a lone wolf is highly risk averse then he is less likely to specialise in terrorism and he is more likely to spend his time doing other things. This is because the more resources, including time, the terrorist allocates to terrorism the higher his exposure to risk. This is especially the case if, following the traditional approach in economics, we view legitimate employment as risk free in the sense that the actual outcome (the pay check) rarely diverges from that which was expected on any given day. If he is highly risk averse he is likely to be found far away from his targets and his targets might be dispersed rather than concentrated in a particular location. This is because following an attack we expect the risk-reward trade-off to change in a manner that is disadvantageous to the lone wolf. A repeat attack at the same location may yield fewer expected fatalities with a higher amount of variability. He will need to seek out more appropriate targets and to do so he must shift from place to place. One of the other more interesting aspects of a profile based upon an economic model of choice under risk is the inference that the lone wolf's engagement in terrorist activity may increase or decrease as his victims accumulate. It is usually assumed that most people exhibit decreasing risk aversion. This would lead us to suspect that the lone wolf can be expected to increase his engagement in terrorist activity and, importantly, engage in riskier attacks as he accumulates victims. We would not expect the lone wolf to fade away after a successful attack. In fact, we would expect him to increase the intensity of his attacks. This is because, in weighing up the risks and rewards of a new attack, the number of victims that he has already accumulated shape the way in which he views the variability of the outcomes of his planned attack.

New Horizons

Terrorism studies, including the contributions made to it by economic science, have produced a number of significant insights and a large volume of collected facts that inform our knowledge of the terrorism context. Most of this work, even that which focuses on the behaviour of individual terrorists, has been aimed at producing broad security policy guidance rather than advice relevant to the investigative processes unfolding within the context of a particular individual case. Broader policy guidance will always be an important part of what economics and the other contributing disciplines to terrorism studies can provide for governments and security agencies but logical extension of the theoretical frameworks that constitute the economic analysis of terrorism leads to a promising new horizon. This new horizon for the economic analysis of terrorism places it alongside the emerging discipline of investigative psychology in attempting to provide operational or investigative advice to law enforcement and security agents for use in actual cases. This is far removed from the academic analysis of the broad trends in transnational terrorism or the academic debate concerning the definitions that are used in terrorism studies. It involves placing economics and its analytical frameworks for the study of terrorism at the disposal of law enforcement and security agents involved in actual cases of pursuing individual terrorists and preventing terrorist attacks.

The extension of economic analysis along these lines may be particularly useful and perhaps even necessary if economists are to provide any substantial contribution towards not only understanding the threat of lone wolf terrorism but assisting with the pre-emption and pursuit of individual lone wolf terrorists. With the traditional analysis of terrorism we can attempt to *understand* the lone wolf. These analytical frameworks must be extended if we are to *pre-empt and pursue* the lone wolf. The lone wolf terrorist operates alone. He does not operate within a command structure. He chooses his own attack methods and targets. He undertakes his own planning. He does not have extensive network connections and communications networks. Until he strikes, law enforcement may have no idea that the lone wolf exists. After a pattern of attacks emerges and the terrorist actions are attributed to a single individual, the challenge of identifying and pursuing the lone wolf terrorist is as challenging as the hunt for a serial killer. Providing advice to law enforcement during this investigative phase is a new horizon for the economic analysis of terrorism. In pursuit of the lone wolf, law enforcement may utilise a variety of tools and methods. Economic analysis is among them.

Concluding Remarks

This is a book about lone wolf terrorism and the ways in which economic science may contribute to the investigative processes that are designed to pre-empt and pursue the lone wolf terrorist. Economics is about opportunities and choices. Cutting through the detail to provide a stark picture of the opportunities available to the potential lone wolf terrorist is the first phase of an economic analysis of lone wolf terrorism. In this book we aim to do this in a manner that is computable rather than abstract. We do not imagine that the lone wolf terrorist has a certain abstract set of opportunities from which he will choose. On the contrary, given what we know about the attack methods that terrorists have chosen to undertake their attacks with, we can develop a clear picture of lone wolf's opportunities. These opportunities to inflict human tragedy are the available attack methods each characterised by an expected number of injuries and fatalities and a variability or risk that reflects the extent to which the actual outcomes of a terrorist attack using a particular attack method will vary from those outcomes that were expected. The opportunity set is characterised by a trade-off between risk and reward. A higher reward can only be obtained by bearing more risk. Importantly, the trade-off is concave and the rewards are higher at each level of risk than could be expected if the trade-off was linear. It is these sorts of details that emerge from the sort of economic analysis that we wish to undertake.

Like other parts of economics, we start with the assumption that the lone wolf terrorist does or tries to choose rationally or optimally from the set of opportunities. However, we highlight the fact that this need not be the case. What we also highlight is that our analytical framework equates the lone wolf's most dangerous opportunities with his optimal or rational choices. If the lone wolf chooses optimally, he inflicts the most human tragedy at the level of risk that he has chosen to bear. If he chooses less than optimally or makes a mistake, he inflicts less human tragedy than that which we prepared for. Under this setup, rational choice has a relevant meaning that would be unwise to ignore. We should not ignore the lone wolf terrorist's optimal or most deadly set of opportunities on the grounds that he is irrational and will choose sub-optimally. Overcoming the criticism pertaining to the irrelevance of rational choice, even as a pure benchmark against which actual choice can be assessed, is a step forward for the economic analysis of terrorism. The manner in which we have overcome this criticism also represents a step forward for terrorism studies. A long held and ingrained belief concerning the reality of some of terrorism's more implausible goals has clouded the analysis of terrorism from all perspectives. Even if the stated goals of terrorism have some grounding in reality, the immediate objective of terrorism is to inflict human tragedy using attack methods none of which have an expected inflicted fatality count of zero. The words and deeds of terrorists confirm this. The lone wolf terrorist is an efficient killer and it would be unhelpful to assume that some unlikely political objective shapes his actions during the planning and execution of an attack more than considerations about the attack itself, the attack method to be used and the number of victims that are expected to result. It seems very strange that scholars within the terrorism studies domain had not simply worked on the assumption that the terrorist's goal is to inflict harm. It may be true that some terrorists mean no harm to civilians but it is the ones that do, including all lone wolves, that it must be our prime concern to stop.

No overarching or archetypal profile of the lone wolf terrorist or any terrorist for that matter has emerged from socio-economic-psychological analysis of terrorism and individual terrorists. Terrorists come from all different backgrounds with nothing in particular in common. Under such circumstances, broader theoretical frameworks are unlikely to be particularly useful in particular cases. What is required are analytical frameworks that provide operationally relevant results and which can be applied to particular cases. In its orthodox construction, economic analysis would not fulfil these criteria. A full expected utility analysis with a strong rational choice requirement provides, at best, a benchmark against which to compare the optimality of actual choices. A full expected utility analysis across all attack methods and outcomes would require too much of the lone wolf terrorist in terms of computational ability and, in fact, it would not even be possible for the analyst to determine a preference ordering over attack methods without a series of probability estimates for each possible outcome. Obviously, this becomes a very complex task unless the perspective is narrowed so much as to become an insignificant part of the terrorism context. Most important, though, it seems doubtful that law enforcement and security agencies would find a full expected utility analysis to be a useful investigative tool.

Terrorism involves decision-making under risk. A terrorist who engages in a violent action using an attack method such as bombing, assassination, armed attack or arson must expect to inflict some amount of human tragedy. None of the attack methods have a zero expected fatality count. It is also the case that a terrorist who engages in a violent action with one of the available attack methods must accept the possibility that the actual outcomes of his attacks may diverge from that which was expected. This is the risk. The trade-off then is one between reward and variability. A higher payoff only comes with a higher risk. A sufficient knowledge of the rewards and the risks associated with different attack methods is obtainable from publicly available new reports that cover successful and unsuccessful terrorist attacks. Indeed, even the analyst only requires the dataset of attacks and the fatalities generated by them. There is no additional knowledge or explicit probability estimation requirement. Although the analyst will undertake a precise computation, it is not as far removed from an informal (but informed) weighing up of risk and reward as a full expected utility analysis that involves multiple outcomes and their associated probability outcomes. Higher expected payoffs can be obtained only by bearing additional variability. The attack methods that are available and whose outcomes in use are reflected in media reports have quite distinct risk-reward payoffs and the lone wolf terrorist's assessment of risk and reward may be expected to be at least approximately correct even if it is formed on the basis of focused but informal analysis.

The pre-emption and pursuit of the lone wolf terrorist must be a multidisciplinary effort. What is most important is that the strengths of the different disciplines that have contributed to terrorism studies are harnessed in the direction of operationally relevant conclusions that are relevant to particular individual cases. Psychology, through the development of investigative psychology, has shown itself to be capable of playing a role within the investigative process and it has come to be valued by law enforcement agencies. An economic model of choice consciously developed with the aim of providing information about a terrorist's actual set of opportunities and combined with an optimal or rational choice requirement that is defined in a manner that makes it operationally relevant is also capable of contributing something to the investigative process in particular cases. In the first instance, providing a lens through which important aspects of the attack method opportunities of the lone wolf can be viewed more starkly helps to diminish a portion of the perceived and actual complexity of the problem confronting law enforcement agencies. The opportunity set is concave, it yields higher expected payoffs at each level of risk when attack methods are combined and there is a positive relationship between risk and reward that forms the foundation for a fundamental aspect of the lone wolf's choices, the weighing up of risk and reward.

When the lone wolf's opportunities are presented starkly as a risk-reward trade-off, other features become more clearly defined. Over particular ranges of the risk-reward trade-off certain attack methods dominate others. It becomes clear, for example, that assassination is an attack method that exhibits very little variability while bombing exhibits a moderate level of risk. The choices of a lone wolf who must choose from the set of opportunities so defined will be shaped by his assessment of risk and reward and his appetite or disliking for risk. Because certain attack methods dominate others over particular risk ranges, our stark picture of the lone wolf's opportunities is also a stark picture of the choices that will be made by lone wolves with a particular type of risk preference. Lone wolves with a strong appetite for risk will venture down the path of hostage-taking or unconventional attacks while those with a strong distaste for risk will venture down the path of assassination or a combination of assassination and bombing. This is interesting but more interesting still is the way in which this framework emerges as an 'inference generator' for the provision of investigative advice. Once a lone wolf strikes, he reveals a risk preference by the nature of his attack and this revealed risk preference is the opening that is needed for the drawing out of more operationally relevant inferences about the lone wolf who has struck and who law enforcement now pursue.

In this book, our focus will be on an economic model of choice that is capable of yielding computable results without the assumption of superhuman computing capacity. We want to show how one, though not necessarily the only, picture of the lone wolf's opportunities can be starkly depicted as a trade-off between risk and reward. The lone wolf's choices from this set of opportunities depend on his assessment of risk and reward and his appetite for risk but his choices do not depend on flawless rationality. If he does choose optimally or if he chooses more optimally over time then he chooses most (or more) dangerously but his choices are not more devastating than we have prepared for. We do not ignore the optimal choice on the grounds that the lone wolf would never choose it, not least because we have taken steps to equate the optimal choice with the most deadly choice of attack method. Where orthodox economic analysis would stop here we instead invert the analysis and ask our frameworks to allow us to draw inferences about actual lone wolf terrorists who have struck and who remain at large. These inferences flow from the revealed preferences of the lone wolf. We have linked attack methods and risk. When an attack method is chosen, risk preference is revealed and risk preference is linked in turn with other characteristics. It is in this manner that we wish to start economic analysis down the path of providing operationally relevant advice within the context of lone wolf terrorism. This is a more pragmatic approach to economic science than tradition would dictate but, in the end, it would seem that a useful insight which contributes to the investigative processes aimed at pre-empting such an insidious threat could hardly be discarded because the frameworks of economic science were made to yield it by more pragmatic methods than would traditionally have been the case.

Chapter 2

THE (TRADITIONAL) ECONOMIC ANALYSIS OF TERRORISM

> A new breed of hijackers, known as parajackers, appeared in late 1971. A parajacker demanded both ransom money and a parachute to escape from the seized aircraft. The first such individual, the alias 'D.B. Cooper,' parachuted en route to Reno with $200,000. Neither Cooper nor the ransom money has ever been found. This was followed by seventeen more attempts in which ransom demands averaged over $300,000. None were successful. Five offenders were apprehended after their jumps, three were shot and killed, another was shot and captured, and eight more were captured. Of the eleven sentenced to prison (three others were committed to mental institutions) the average sentence was forty-three years. This was indeed a risky activity. One success in eighteen tries with severe penalties for failure ——Landes 1978, p.4.

The label 'defence economics' is in many respects an outdated label. The use of economic tools and techniques and models to study phenomena that emerge in the sphere of human peace and conflict is now too broad to be encompassed by this label and, what is more, many of tools and techniques are commonly used by a range of social and political scientists and economists alike. Partitioning the work of economists into a separate area is to highlight the differences rather than the commonalities that characterises a lot of the work undertaken within 'peace and conflict studies' and, when the subject matter is terrorism, 'terrorism studies'. We shall prefer, therefore, to use the name 'terrorism studies' to refer to the broader social-political science area of investigation within which the contributions that are made by economists may be classified as the 'economic analysis of terrorism'. The distinguishing features of the economic analysis of terrorism have traditionally been its 'rational choice' approach, individual preferences, the application of expected utility models of choice under risk and uncertainty and the 'representative agent' framework where a single theoretically constructed individual 'stands in' for the multiplicity of real-world individuals or groups within the theoretical model. In many respects, the representative agent construction is the defining characteristic of much economic analysis of terrorism[1].

While rational choice was once the defining characteristic of the economists' contributions to the study of peace and conflict, game theory has become a commonly

[1] However, an argument could be made that the defining characteristic of the economics of terrorism is its focus on individual or group preferences as distinguished from environmental and social factors and social 'norms' (see Eide 1994, p.10).

deployed theoretical-analytical tool within the political and social sciences. Game theory, of course, is based on the axiomatic treatment of rational choice developed by von Neumann and Morgenstern (1944). Another point that can be made in this regard is that much of what is published as 'defence economics' is not something that is uniquely 'economic' but is rather an application of some of the tools, perhaps originating in economic science, that are now widely used within a broad sweep of social sciences or, still more common, an analysis of something relating to the economic system, such as the relationship between poverty and terrorism. Such studies are for the most part more properly classified as social scientific contributions to terrorism studies. While economic categories may be a prominent part of these sorts of studies and while the tools that are used might have grown out of 'econometrics' they do not necessarily constitute an economic analysis as such. This includes most of the studies that examine the economic impact of terrorism, on gross domestic product for example, those that examine the relationship between various social factors such as education and poverty and terrorism and those that analyse trends and patterns in the time series of terrorism incidences and so on and so forth. In short, those studies which examine socio-economic and statistical aggregates using tools which are by now commonly used across the social sciences.

Analysis that develops and investigates the implications of microeconomic theory directed towards the explanation of a particular type of human behaviour is economic analysis. When the work that economists do in studying terrorism is separated from the work that constitutes economic analysis as such we find a relatively small number of contributions that attempt to explain aspects of terrorist behaviour within expected utility-representative agent theoretical frameworks. In this book we lay the foundation stones for an extension of this type of economic analysis so that it may provide investigative advice that assists law enforcement in the pre-emption, the profiling and pursuit of lone wolf terrorists. This means adding to the tools and methods that law enforcement and security agencies currently deploy in their pursuit of terrorists—including investigative psychology and offender profiling. To do this, the traditional economic frameworks will need to be extended. In order to approach this task in an orderly fashion, it is necessary to first present an overview of the traditional economic analysis of terrorism and terrorist behaviour. We shall focus on the essential building blocks that apply in general and form the foundation for the majority of analytical work in this field and leave aside the details of particular cases that have been dealt with in the terrorism studies literature. The economic analysis of terrorism and the economics of criminal behaviour out of which it emerged generate several empirically supported predictions built on a logically coherent theoretical structure. Furthermore, a number of the problems that have beset investigative psychology, especially the controversy concerning the personality trait-based organised/disorganised typology, have been avoided or mitigated within the economics literature.

The Traditional Approach to the Economic Analysis of Terrorism

Although it has its critics and although many of the shortcomings those critics have identified are real, it is the case that expected utility (EU) theory is a powerful and flexible tool that may be used to analyse behaviour. Although the mathematics can become very complicated and somewhat unrealistic much can be accomplished without high levels of abstract formalism. Building on the foundations established during the later part of the 19th century and expanded by von Neumann and Morgenstern (NM) (1944), the application of expected utility theory to an ever-widening array of human behaviours occupied economists during the 1950s and beyond. Many times the applications were surprising and quite novel because no-one expected that behaviours that appeared to lie far away from traditional 'economic' behaviours could be analysed within an orthodox economic theoretical framework. It took a new generation of economists to break with tradition and extend economic theory in new directions. As Becker (1968, p.170) noted, the neglect of 'crime' by economists may have been due to the attitude that criminal activity is 'too immoral' to deserve systematic analysis by economists. Once this attitude was overcome the application of economic analysis to different types of human behaviour proceeded at pace. In hindsight no-one should have been surprised that this application was possible. After all, expected utility theory is a theory of choice and should capture at least some elements of any conceivable choice scenario[2].

Economic imperialism, as it might be called, refers to the encroachment by economic theorists on the subject matter of other disciplines. In its most aggressive manifestations, economic imperialism seems to want to sweep away everything that had stood as accepted knowledge before and replace it with the far-reaching, pure and rigorous economic theoretical model. It is no doubt true that many economic theorists have been bold to say the least in declaring the superiority of a newly created rigorous economic theory over existing theoretical frameworks in a particular field of study. There has been understandable resistance to these sorts of efforts and economic science has itself been treated as an object of scorn or ridicule in turn. With unrealistic-seeming mathematics, misplaced notions of equilibrium and a wagon load of apparently ridiculous assumptions it is little wonder. While some of the scorn may have been earned and deserved, claiming the theoretical high ground is unproductive and retards progress. Crime and terrorism is, along with other social phenomena, complex and its full explanation can only be approached by a multidisciplinary effort aimed at uncovering pieces of the underlying puzzle. Economic models, of which expected utility theory is a most prominent (and dominant) example, cannot completely explain such phenomena but, the truth is, neither can any theory. Economics does not explain everything. However, it is wrong to say that it explains nothing. Like every other reasoned logical structure, it explains at least something.

Mounting a defence for expected utility theory and economic analysis is not on our list of things to do. We will point out deficiencies in the critics' arguments when necessary and we will state some of the strengths of the expected utility approach forcefully. However, it is the case that much of our view of the ways in which economic analysis can be applied to terrorism and much of the new ground that we shall break is not in complete accordance with the orthodoxy, either of economic theory in general and especially not the received orthodoxy that prevails within the economic analysis of terrorism. In a moment, we shall turn our attention to the 'economics of crime' which contains the origins of the economic analysis of terrorism. The economic models that have been developed to explain crime, criminal

[2] EU theory is widely misunderstood. There is no requirement or assumption of self-interest and rationality does not mean perfect or error-free decision making. The latter Becker (1968) describes as a caricature of economic theory.

behaviour and the effects of deterrence measures such as heavier prison sentences have been subjected to immense scrutiny. If one reads Eide's (1994) discussion, one can see why. There appears to be more assumptions at every turn and, of course, rationality looms large. Many of the assumptions, it must be remembered, are needed to make the mathematics work and to the traditional mathematical-logical reasoning intact. For most of the time since 1950, it has been essential for economic theorists to conform to the mathematical orthodoxy. If we only want to make the economics work and if we are willing to be pragmatic rather than tied to a particular mode of reasoning, we can mitigate much of the more objectionable theoretical moves made within orthodox economic theory.

Rationality is purposeful, not perfect, behaviour which involves the use of (scarce) means to achieve given ends. We can look at it as choosing the best available way to achieve a given end. Of course, people do not always choose in the best way and so objections to this line of reasoning emerge. But it is best to keep in mind that people do choose, they do choose from among different ways of doing something and they do achieve ends that they had in mind. This happens every minute of every day. Things get done. Along the way, plans get sidetracked, people change their minds and mistakes are made. Economic theory provides some frameworks within which this behaviour can be examined and explained. When expressed in mathematical form, additional assumptions are necessary because we are trying to make two things work: economic logic and mathematical consistency. The mathematical approach has come to dominate economic theory but we should not let its strictures prevent us from using economic theory more pragmatically. Unfortunately, some economists are unwilling to allow any of the mathematic-deductive 'rules' be broken, even if the result is approximately the same and easier to arrive at. The philosophy and methodology of orthodox economics must be kept in mind when assessing orthodox work. It does not explain everything but it does explain something. What is more, it may explain even more if it is freed from its own constraints. Economic theory should be a generator of thoughts and insights some of which can only be reached by proceeding to the limits of the application of economic logic. These ideas can be placed in the hands of law enforcement to consider in light of their experience. A mixture of experience, theory, logic and argument is likely to produce more relevant economic analysis even if certain mathematical-axiomatic rules, though not *economic reason*, are accorded less importance in the process.

BECKER'S MODEL OF CRIME

As we have said, expected utility theory is the most prominent and most dominant of the models of choice under risk that is to be found in the economics literature. During the middle part of the 20th century, expected utility theory was the battering ram that sat at the head of the advancing imperialism of economic theory. Its application to diverse areas of human behaviour and endeavour, though unwelcomed by some resident disciplines, yielded some extremely innovative insights. Among the most interesting and important applications of expected utility theory during this time was Becker's (1968) application of the theory to crime and Ehrlich's (1973) important contributions in developing this application and extending it such that it incorporated a number of aspects of the choice to engage in criminal behaviour. It is in these contributions to the economics of crime and criminal behaviour that the origins of the economic analysis of terrorism can be found. The economic analysis of crime and criminal behaviour involves writing down an expected utility function that includes the factors that contribute positively and negatively to the criminal's behaviour or the subset of behaviour that is under analysis. The expected utility function is the basic building block for this type of economic analysis. For example, when Becker (1968) wanted to describe the criminal's behaviour as part of his broader theoretical analysis of the social costs of crime and the optimal public and private policies to combat illicit behaviour, he started with the following:

$$EU_j = p_j U_j(Y_j - f_j) + (1 - p_j)U_j(Y_j)$$

This function describes the utility or satisfaction that a criminal obtains from engaging in criminal behaviour. Y_j is the criminal's payoff from an offense (both in money terms and 'psychic' terms). Contrary to some opinion, this type of theoretical framework does not deal solely with monetary payoffs. It can easily incorporate non-monetary payoffs such as the thrill of engaging in a criminal activity. The criminal's satisfaction or utility from an offense depends positively on this payoff. The criminal, however, does not obtain any payoff with certainty. The world is a risky place. There is a chance that the criminal will be apprehended and punished. If that happens, society will impose a punishment that Becker (1968) captures in the term f_j, the monetary equivalent of the criminal's punishment if he or she is caught. The probability of the two outcomes is given by p_j and $(1 - p_j)$.

In making his or her choice to engage in criminal activity, the potential offender makes an assessment of the likelihood of being apprehended. This would appear to involve assigning a high degree of rationality or computational ability to the individual. However, 'weighing up the odds' is something that most people do to some degree every day and this does not have to be perfect or error-free. People make mistakes. The key idea in these analytical models, sometimes neglected by their architects, is simply that the criminal undertakes his or her actions with some end or objective in mind. The objectives are ranked in order of preference and the individual tries to arrange his or her resources or means in such a way as to achieve the best-ranked objective. In Becker's function, the potential offender is deciding between an offense and some other alternative that Becker leaves unnamed or implied. If the odds of being captured are thought to be too high or the payoff for the offense is too low given the risk that needs to be taken, the potential offender may simply decide to forget about it. Maybe he or she will commit some other offense or not engage in criminal behaviour at all. Maybe he or she will miscalculate, engage in an activity that was more risky than thought and get caught.

The expected utility approach formalises this sort of 'weighing up' and allows the economist to say something about the likely impact on the criminal's choices of changes in various relevant factors. The potential offender weighs the odds of the possible payoffs: (1) a payoff of Y_j with a probability of $(1 - p_j)$; and (2) a payoff of $(Y_j - f_j)$ with a probability of p_j. The utility that can be expected from engaging in the offense is the sum of the probability-weighted utilities for each of the possible outcomes. The potential offender compares this expected utility against the expected utility that is associated with alternative activities[3] and either makes the choice to commit the offense or not. This is a very powerful way of capturing some of the important aspects of choice under risk and uncertainty. What is more, once these aspects are embedded in a formal model or function, the economist should be able to say something about how changes in the terms contained in the function may be expected to affect the individual's choices.

The first step in making some statement about the ways in which different circumstances may alter the individual's choice is to carefully note the ways in which the various terms in the function affect expected utility. In Becker's function, the payoff Y_j adds to the potential offender's expected utility while the payoff f_j subtracts from the potential offender's expected utility. If p_j or f_j increases or if Y_j decreases, the potential offender's expected utility declines and vice versa. An increase in the payoffs associated with criminal offenses is likely to be associated with an increase in participation in those offenses. The bigger the payoff, the more attractive the offense becomes. Conversely, the greater the chance of being caught and the greater the punishment that is imposed, the less attractive the offense becomes. If the government imposes a bigger penalty on the offense and at the same time increases the probability of being caught by increasing the numbers of police officers working to prevent the offense, there should be a two-fold negative effect on expected utility. This may push the offense down the order in the potential offender's preference ranking and result in less offenses of that type being undertaken.

Ehrlich's Important Contribution

Because Becker, at least in his 1968 paper, is interested in addressing the question of optimal allocation of resources to crime prevention and law enforcement and the optimal amount of punishment that should be accorded to particular offenses, he leaves many important aspects of the offender's choices either implicit in his analysis or does not incorporate them at all. This was addressed by Ehrlich (1973) who made a number of important steps towards a complete expected utility analysis of crime and criminal behaviour. Ehrlich accomplished this by explicitly incorporating alternative, legitimate activities, which the potential offender considers as alternatives to criminal offenses. Ehrlich's model is what Eide (1994) calls a 'portfolio' model because criminal and legitimate activities are combined in different proportions. Rather than a choice to offend or not offend, Ehrlich's analysis allows the potential offender to combine legitimate activities with illegitimate activities. Further along these lines, Ehrlich is able to formally encompass occupational choices and opportunities within the analysis. This provides a much richer choice context that provides many important conclusions related to the matter of participation in illegitimate activities. It also lays the foundation for further expansion of the analysis into terrorist behaviour.

In Becker's analysis the potential offender weighs up the payoffs and the risks and determines whether the expected utility of an offense makes it worthwhile when compared to other, presumably legal, activities. Ehrlich's analysis recognises that the decision to engage in illegal activities is not a decision that requires completely forsaking the 'straight and narrow'

[3] Left implicit and unnamed by Becker.

and vice versa. Rather, the straight and narrow can be strayed from temporarily or at certain times and some individuals may even straddle the path by simultaneously combining legitimate activities such as a regular job with illegitimate activities. It all depends on how the individual decides to spend his or her time once all the options and their risks and rewards have been considered. Based on the expected utility that the individual attributes to each choice—remembering that this attribution may be erroneous and any choice may later turn out to be a mistake—the individual ranks the choices in order of preference. The choices, rather than being single mutually exclusive legitimate or illegitimate activities may be combinations of both. The individual chooses the activities (or combinations of activities) with the highest expected utility and allocates his or her scarce resources, including time, to the pursuit of that expected utility.

In many ways, Ehrlich's analysis is an analysis of this time allocation between legal and illegitimate activities. The idea is, once again, to capture the choice scenario within an individual's expected utility function. Here the individual chooses his or her participation (the amount of time spent) in two types of activities: illegal activity i and legal activity l. The illegal activity is risky while the legal activity is not. This means that while the legal activity gives a certain payoff for the amount of time that is allocated to it, the payoffs to the illegal activity are uncertain and depend on whether the offender happens to get apprehended or not. The payoffs to the legal activity are given by the function $W_l(t_l)$ and the payoffs to the illegal activity are given by the function $W_i(t_i)$. In each case, t is the amount of time that is spent on the activity. As in Becker's analysis, the probability that the offender is apprehended, a, is given by p_i and the probability that the offender beats the law enforcement efforts, b, and gets away is given by $(1-p_i)$. If the offender is apprehended his payoffs are diminished by $F_i(t_i)$.

To simplify the analysis, Ehrlich assumes that there are only two possible states of the world, a and b, and a single time period during which the offender aims for the highest expected utility. Although this sounds restrictive, there may be little difference between the behaviour implied by a single period analysis and behaviour implied by a multi-period analysis. Ehrlich cites Fama (1970) in this regard but the matter of 'time periods' or 'time horizons' comes up time and again in economics. Incorporating more time periods into an analysis makes for a richer mathematical framework but probably adds little to our understanding of the individual's decisions. Proceeding with the assumption that there are only two states of the world—apprehended, a, and not apprehended, b—Ehrlich denotes the payoff that occurs in each state of the world as X_a and X_b[4]. The payoffs, either X_a or X_b, and the time not spent on either illegal or legal activities, t_c, enter into the individual's expected utility function that the individual uses to rank his or her preferences for activities:

$$EU(X_s, t_c) = (1-p_i)U(X_b, t_c) + p_i U(X_a, t_c)$$

[4] The payoffs are formally defined as: $X_b = W' + W_i(t_i) + W_l(t_l)$ $X_a = W' + W_i(t_i) - F_i(t_i) + W_l(t_l)$ In each case, W denotes net returns (monetary and 'psychic') to each type of activity.

Like everyone, the offender makes his or her choices under constraints. Time is limited. Therefore, it can be said in this case that the offender attempts to maximise expected utility—choose the activities or combinations of activities which, from the offender's point of view and information, have the highest expected utility—subject to the constraint that the time spent on illegal, legal and other activities cannot exceed the total amount of time available and the time allocated to each activity must be either zero or some positive amount:

$$t_0 = t_i + t_l + t_c$$

$$t_i \geq 0; t_l \geq; t_c \geq 0$$

As we saw with Becker's analysis, changes to the magnitude of the expected payoffs and changes in the probability of getting caught and the magnitude of punishment if apprehended are important shapers of the offender's choice to engage in illegal activities. These results also hold in Ehrlich's analysis. However, Ehrlich's analysis allows us to say something about the amount of time the offender will allocate to illegal activities and legal activities. Ehrlich assumes that the legal activity is risk free and the illegal activity is risky. If illegal activities are risky while legal activities are risk free, we should find that individuals who specialise to a greater degree in illegitimate activity are less risk averse than those who do not specialise in illegitimate activity. This is not a personality trait-based assumption but rather a general logical extension of what we know about behaviour under conditions of risk and uncertainty. If an individual is observed to specialise in risky activity and minimise participation in the safer activity, it may be inferred that that individual reveals a low level of risk aversion. Because illegal activities are risky, individuals who we observe allocating substantial amounts of time to illegal activities may be inferred to be less risk averse (more risk seeking) and individuals who spend less time in illegal activities may be inferred to be more risk averse (less risk seeking). This is a revealed preference and not an assumption that criminals are of the risk seeking type.

Attitudes towards risk play an important role in determining how much of an effect the imposition of larger punishments or higher probabilities of apprehension will have on the individual's decision to engage in the illegal activities. If the individual is risk averse, the effect of an increase in the punishment associated with an offense will be more than proportional in its effect on deterring the individual from committing the offense. Conversely, if the individual prefers risk, the effect of an increase in the punishment associated with an offense will be less than proportional in its deterrent effects. In fact, as Ehrlich points out, an increase in the riskiness of the offense may attract risk preferring individuals. Of course, much of this analysis holds true for the legal activities and the 'other' activities to which the individual may devote some of his or her time. If the opportunities and payoffs to legal activities are enhanced, there is less incentive for the individual to engage in illegitimate activities. If the opportunities for allocating time to 'other' activities are decreased, there is likely to be an increase in participation in both illegal and legal activities. After all, the individual must completely allocate his time to something.

INCENTIVES AND THE ADVANTAGES OF ECONOMIC ANALYSIS

Incentives play a major role in the economic analysis of behaviour, including criminal behaviour. Analysis that is based on the ways in which individuals respond to incentives is at a considerable advantage over analysis that attempts to encompass many individual and unique motivations for behaviour (or personality traits). As Ehrlich (1973, p.522) suggests, rather than resorting to analysis based on unique personal characteristics and social conditions in order to explain criminal behaviour, one need only recognise that potential offenders, like everyone else, respond to incentives. This is the case even if potential offenders and actual offenders are actually characterised by systematic differences *vis-a-vis* law abiding citizens. Although there is a multiplicity of individual and unique circumstances ascribing to every individual, all individuals respond to incentives. With respect to criminal activity, these incentives may be the payoffs to crime, the possibility of getting caught, the punishment that will be administered and the opportunities and rewards associated with legal activities. The ways in which individuals respond to these incentives within an expected utility framework permits conclusions to be reached without becoming mired in the multiplicity of individual circumstances. With a characteristic boldness, Becker (1968, p.170) suggests that we, "... dispense with special theories of anomie, psychological inadequacies or inheritance of special traits and simply extend the economist's usual analysis of choice."

TERRORISM AND TERRORIST BEHAVIOUR: FOUNDATIONS

Like the behaviour of criminals, the behaviour of terrorists was also thought to lie outside of economic analysis. Indeed, many political scientists and international relations scholars probably still hold this view[5]. Terrorists have objectives and they must use their scarce resources to meet their objectives. The ranking of objectives and the ways in which resources are allocated towards the achievement of objectives are precisely the sorts of behaviours that economic analysis explains. The terrorist has an objective. This could be the furtherance of some political cause. It could be publicity. It could be to cause death and injury to civilians. There are a number of ways that the objective could be achieved. There are legitimate methods such as pamphlets and rallies. There are illegitimate methods such as bombing, assassination, hostage-taking and armed attacks. Because of resource or geographical constraints, some other methods such as 9/11 style unconventional attacks may not be possible for the particular terrorist, though he or she may very much like to engage in them. The resource constrained preference ordering may look something like this:

[5] Crenshaw (2000) suggests that the ostensible goal of terrorism may be so unlikely to be achieved by the chosen course of action as to cast doubt on any 'rational' theory of terrorist behaviour. Of course, what Crenshaw means by 'rational' is probably different to what the economist means. More importantly, if the terrorist aims to inflict human tragedy then as Phillips (2009) has shown, economic analysis is very well suited to the analysis of terrorism.

Bombing Attack, Target A
Armed Attack, Target A
Bombing Attack, Target B
Hostage Taking
Assassination
Legitimate Methods
Bombing Attack, Target C
Bombing Attack, Target D

The terrorist pursuing his or her objective will choose the best ranked alternative means of attaining that objective. In this case, the bombing of Target A will be chosen. The expected utility analysis that underlies the formal treatment of choice under risk and uncertainty makes some general assumptions about the ways in which these preference orderings or rankings are formed. These are the famous von Neumann and Morgenstern (1944) axioms:

1. Completeness (or Comparability). Given two alternatives, A and B, the terroristic agent or group must be able to state: (1) A is preferred to B, $(A \succ B)$; *or* (2) B is preferred to A, $(B \succ A)$; *or* (3) the agent or group is indifferent between A and B.
2. Transitivity. Given three alternatives, A, B and C and if the terroristic agent or group prefers A to B and B to C, the agent or group prefers A to C: $(A \succ B)$ and $(B \succ C)$ implies $(A \succ C)$.
3. Non-satiation. More of any good—political influence, fatalities caused, resources, supporters, media coverage—is preferred to less.
4. Convexity. The rate at which the terroristic agent is willing to give up some good in exchange for another while remaining indifferent after the exchange is decreasing.
5. Certainty Equivalent. For every gamble there is an amount of political influence (or some such good) such that the terroristic group is indifferent between the gamble and the certainty equivalent.

Economic analysis concentrates on explaining terrorists' behaviour as terrorists: choice of targets, attack methods, combinations of attack methods, recruitment, negotiation strategy and so on[6]. The fundamental idea is means and ends, resources and objectives. Terrorists have different objectives and different ways of achieving those objectives. Economists are interested in determining the terrorist's opportunities and determining how the terrorist will choose from the available opportunities. If, for example, the terrorist's opportunities are contained in the preference ordering above, then the economist wants to know how the opportunities have been ordered and, if possible, the order that emerges from this decision-making process. Knowing the order will tell the economist which opportunity is more likely to be taken[7].

Building on the foundations set down by Becker and Ehrlich, the early contributions to the economic analysis of terrorism set about constructing expected utility analysis that captured particular elements of terrorists' decisions and choices. The response of terrorists to

[6] This does not mean that important 'psychological' aspects of behaviour that may relevant for explaining terrorist behaviour are ignored or that economic analysis is not capable of including them. Recent work on identity and terrorism shows that this is far from the case (see Phillips and Pohl 2011).

[7] The answer is the one that the terrorist has ranked above all of the others.

incentives, both positive and negative, played an important role in the analysis (as it continues to do today). It was during this time that one of the key building blocks of the economic analysis of terrorism was presented in the literature. The analysis of incentives and the ways in which governments and law enforcement could manipulate incentives in order to reduce instances of terrorist behaviour produced the theoretical prediction that 'negative incentives' such as increased security, increased chances of apprehension and larger prison sentences should be expected to reduce participation in terrorist actions. A theoretically rigorous explanation of the role of incentives in deterring terrorists from undertaking terrorist activities represented an important step forward. The 'deterrence prediction' was found to be well supported by empirical evidence. Interestingly, however, at this time the economists involved did not really view themselves as defence economists and the analysis of terrorism did not exist as an independent field of study within economic science. Indeed, Landes (1978, p.26) viewed his work as a contribution to the 'economics of deterrence'.

Landes' (1978) paper is among the foundational papers in the economic analysis of terrorism, although the hijackers whose behaviour he analysed had quite different objectives than those responsible for the 9/11 terrorist attacks. Indeed, for the most part, the objective of Landes' hijackers was 'transportation to Cuba' and, later, financial payoffs in the form of ransoms (Landes 1978). During the 1960s and 1970s, in pursuit of these objectives, hijacking of aircraft in United States reached extremely high levels. There were 19 hijackings between 1961 and 1967. This was followed by a very sharp increase between 1968 and 1972 when there were 124 hijackings (Landes 1978) and a very sharp decline after 1972 to just 56 hijackings in the years between 1972 and 1978. Landes seeks to explain, using economic analysis, this pattern of hijackings and especially the sharp decline after 1972. He does so by setting up a by-now familiar function:

$$EU = (1 - P_a)U(W_j) + P_a P_c U(W_i - S) + P_a(1 - P_c)U(W_j - C)$$

Here the hijacker's expected utility depends upon the probability of apprehension in country i, P_u, the probability (given apprehension) of being convicted and sentenced to prison, P_c, the hijacker's wealth, W_i and W_j, in each of two countries, i and j, the monetary equivalent of the sentence, S, in country i and the monetary costs, C, associated with apprehension but no sentence (example, costs of defence). Many of these elements are familiar to us in light of Becker's and Ehrlich's work. Landes' model demonstrates the power and flexibility of the EU analytical framework. By carefully choosing arguments for the function that are salient to the particular behaviour being analysed, Landes was able to develop a function for a specific type of offender on the foundations provided by Becker and Ehrlich.

If the model is correct, we should expect to find that the 'negative incentives' were offset by the positive payoffs associated with hijacking in the years 1968 to 1972 while the opposite should be the case for the years 1961 to 1968 and post-1972. The changes to the incentives structure, which are reflected in the choices of the individual, appear to point in this direction. Both the probability of apprehension and the severity of the penalties imposed increased. The positive payoffs associated with free transportation to Cuba were diminished by a treaty between the U.S. and Cuba that allowed for extradition and punishment of hijackers. Landes

(1978) lists a number of important changes to the incentives structures that characterised hijacking during this time period:

- Until 1968, the percentage of hijackers who were apprehended was just 15 percent.
- By 1972, the percentage of hijackers who were apprehended had risen to 60 percent and after 1973 to 100 percent.
- Before 1971, sentences were low and variable. After 1972, sentences averaged 30 years in prison.
- Before 1971, no offenders were killed during a hijacking. After 1971, 10 percent of hijackers were killed during hijacking attempts.
- After 1970, weapons screening was undertaken on persons fitting a 'hijacker's profile' and large numbers of air marshals began riding 'shotgun' on certain flights.
- After 1973, all carry-on luggage was electronically screened for weapons. All hijackers were apprehended following this security enhancement.
- After 1973, Cuba and the U.S. entered into a treaty to extradite and punish hijackers.
- When ransom became the primary objective of hijackers (rather than passage to Cuba), a further 'risk factor' came into play. The preferred method of hijacking was to obtain ransom money and depart the aircraft by parachute. In addition to the risks of being captured or shot, the 'parajacker' faced a strong possibility of death during the jump after modifications to aircrafts prevented rear doors from being opened during a flight. A jump from the forward doors increases the likelihood of being struck by the plane.

Within the parameters of the EU model constructed by Landes, we see that there was likely an increase in P_a, P_c and S after the late 1960s and early 1970s. Furthermore, the positive payoffs of a successful hijacking were likely decreased, particularly by the treaty between the U.S. and Cuba in 1973. One might think that this sort of higher level piece of information would not be relevant to individual hijackers and, possibly, they would not even know about it or take it into account. However, this is similar to the notion that terrorists would not really be able to estimate the risk-reward trade-off for a particular terrorist activity. Information has a habit of diffusing. Therefore, it would be very much mistaken to overlook the ways in which terrorists may be able to get some idea about the 'odds'. The same is true for Landes' hijackers. As Landes suggests, information about the adverse treatment in Cuba of apprehended hijackers became available in the U.S. and, to the extent that potential hijackers took it into account, it would enable them to reach some negative conclusions about the risk-reward structure characterising their potential hijacking actions. This would add to the unfavourable imbalance that appeared to emerge between risk and reward to hijacking during the late 1960s and 1970s.

We should not be surprised if a rational individual re-ranked hijacking to a lower position in his or her preference ranking in light of the unfavourable innovations in the incentives structures that characterised hijacking after 1972. The predictions of the economic model are that increases in P_a, P_c and S and decreases in W reduce the expected utility of a planned hijacking and vice versa. A lower chance of apprehension, a lower probability of conviction and a lower expected sentence should be associated with an increase in the expected utility of hijacking as too should increases in the payoffs, *W*. This apparently characterised hijacking during those periods of time when incidences of hijacking increased dramatically while the opposite is true for periods of time when incidences of hijacking were low or decreasing. Higher expected utility means that hijacking compares more favourably—though not necessarily favourably enough to place it at the top of every offender's list—when compared to other ways of achieving a particular objective such as obtaining passage to Cuba while a lower expected utility places it at a comparably less favourable position vis-à-vis alternatives. Fitting hijacking into a rigorous model of choice and providing both sound theoretical foundations and empirical support for 'deterrence' in this case represented an important step. The path was open for further contributions, especially the economic analysis of transnational terrorism.

TRANSNATIONAL TERRORISM AND THE EMERGENCE OF THE 'ECONOMICS OF TERRORISM'

Throughout the 1970s, transnational terrorism was a growing problem. In 1968, according to the RAND Corporation's MIPT Database, there were 98 incidences of transnational terrorism. There were more than 200 incidences each year after 1974, including 327 in 1976. With the foundations for an economic analysis of terrorist behaviour in place, the time had come for the economic analysis of terrorism to emerge as a distinct field of study. If terrorism is defined as the "premeditated, threatened actual use of force or violence to attain a political goal through fear, coercion or intimidation," (Sandler, Tschirhart and Cauley 1983, p.37), then transnational terrorism is terrorism that involves terrorists, governments or citizens from two or more countries. The 9/11 terrorist attacks are an example of transnational terrorism but many of the instances of terrorism reported to have occurred in Iraq or Afghanistan during the 2000s are not. The dataset for transnational terrorism will therefore be a subset of the complete terrorism dataset. Transnational terrorism has been the primary focus of economists in the West because of its relevance to Western governments and citizens at home and abroad.

The problem of transnational terrorism had attracted some attention from political scientists during the 1970s. In the early 1980s, economists began to apply the Becker-Ehrlich analysis to the problem. Sandler, Tschirhart and Cauley (1983) were the first to develop a more or less complete theoretical framework for hostage-taking situations and other instances of transnational terrorism, such as kidnapping and hijacking, where the terrorists issued demands and entered into bargaining or negotiation with the government. The taking of hostages, kidnapping or hijacking is a means towards an end. Like the other types of models that we have discussed, Sandler et al. set up a function for a terrorist (or group of terrorists) that captures the essential features of the situation being analysed. In this case, the negotiation process is the focus of the analysis. Important features will therefore be the payoffs to terrorist demands that are met by the government and the probability that the government will indeed meet the terrorists' demands:

$$U = U(L, D, \Pi; C^*)$$

The terrorist has an objective. This may, perhaps, be the promotion of a particular cause. There are two ways that this objective may be achieved. The first is by legal methods, such as lobbying or producing and distributing pamphlets. These activities have a payoff L. The second is by illegal or terroristic methods that involves taking hostages and making demands, D, of the government. The outcome of this risky activity is uncertain. The probability that the demands are met is Π and the most recent concession granted by the government is C^*. The terrorist's expected utility depends upon the payoffs available from legal activities, the payoffs available from terrorist activities and the probability distribution that governs these payoffs. An increase in L will increase the attractiveness of legal activities vis-à-vis terrorist activities. An increase in D will increase the attractiveness of terrorist activities (as will an increase in the probability of success). In most of the important respects, we can see that Sandler et al.'s model is very similar in principle to those developed by Becker, Ehrlich and Landes. The differences lie not just in the application of expected utility analysis to negotiation scenarios but also in the extension of the model beyond a choice situation to incorporate strategic elements of bargaining with a government that is also trying to maximise its expected utility. In Sandler et al.'s model, the government has an expected utility function:

$$G = G(C, \Omega, a_2; D^*)$$

The government's expected utility depends upon its concessions policy, C, the probability of re-election Ω, the amenities of office, a_2, and the demands of the terrorists, D^*. With these two expected utility functions in place, the economic analysis proceeds to the examination of various 'comparative statics'. This means that, holding all other variables constant, the logical outcomes of changes in one of the parameters are explored. The interaction between the terrorists and the government in a hostage-taking negotiation scenario yields a number of important comparative statics results within the Sandler et al. (1983) theoretical framework:

- Sandler et al. derive the standard 'deterrence effect' that we saw emerge from the Becker, Ehrlich and Landes analyses. If the government can increase the 'price' of a terrorist activity, the terrorist's demands will decline. The price may be increased by increasing sentences, increasing the likelihood of capture or increasing the difficulty in reaching a particular target. Sandler et al. (1983) suggest as an example that an increase in the effectiveness of a commando force (a counter-terrorism unit, for example) would decrease terrorist activities.
- Another result, the 'substitution effect', flows next. If the government increases the price of a particular type of terrorist activity, terrorists may be diverted into other types of terrorist actions. For example, an increase in security at embassies may lead to a decrease in armed attacks or bombings of embassies but an increase in assassination attempts on embassy staff and officials outside of the embassy compounds (Sandler and Enders 2004). Deterring terrorists from some particular type of attack may cause an increase in another type of terrorist activity.
- A third result is the 'resources effect'. An increase in terrorists' resources will increase terrorists' demands. Unambiguously and without an unfavourable substitution effect, the government can decrease terrorist activity by reducing

terrorists' resources. If terrorists' resources are increased by cooperation between terrorist groups or by increases in state or non-state sponsorship, terrorist activities will increase.

- Several 'risk effects' also flow from the analysis. Most importantly, if the government increases the 'risk' associated with the terrorist's demands by increasing the variance that characterises its concessions, terrorists may change their demands and their involvement in terrorism. The exact nature of the changes depends on whether terrorists are more averse to risk or less averse to risk (more risk seeking). If terrorists are averse to risk, the government may reduce terrorism by increasing the variance of its granted concessions. However, if the terrorists seek risk, this government action will increase terrorism.

The Sandler et al. (1983) analysis is quite far-reaching and sets down many of the foundations for the economic analysis of terrorism. Although the results are richer than those contained in our summary sketch, it is clear that the economic analysis of terrorism and expected utility analysis in particular can generate important results. Some of these results appear to be straightforward. However, placing them within a economic-mathematical framework allowed them not only to be confirmed theoretically but also built a solid foundation of logical and proved results upon which further extensions and analytical developments can be based. Over the next three decades, the economics of terrorism literature gradually accumulated. Along with game theoretical analysis, many contributions utilised expected utility theory to shed light on various aspects of the behaviour of terrorists and terrorist groups. In addition, expected utility theory has formed the foundation for empirical economic analysis of the terrorism time series data. Much of this work is traceable to the foundations laid by Becker, Ehrlich, Landes and Sandler.

An important feature that each of these analytical contributions share is that they construct models of choice in which the directions of changes in the opportunity variables, such as probability of being caught, allows the prediction of the direction of changes in the choice variable. This tends to push the preference ordering process into the background of the analysis. The potential offender is making a choice between some criminal or terrorist action and the 'not offend' alternative. Within the Sandler et al. (1983) model, this choice process is extended to include a choice of 'magnitude' or 'intensity' of offence, especially as it relates to the demands that the terrorist group makes of the government during a negotiation scenario. However, these economic analyses do not usually attempt to make a complete list of the criminal's or terrorist's opportunities and find his optimal choice or set of choices even within a particular part of the terrorism or criminal context. As a result, the main conclusion that is able to be extracted from this type of analysis is of the type that certain variables, usually deterrence or incentive variables, affect the potential offender's choice in a particular direction. Increases in deterrence variables reduce expected utility and tend to push the offender's choices away from that particular offense while increases in incentives increase expected utility and pull the offender's choices towards a particular offense (and vice versa). This is useful for separating out the effects of particular variables on the directions of offender choice and may yield surprising results that run counter to 'conventional wisdom' but the operational relevance of these types of models to law enforcement and the investigative process as applied within a particular case is somewhat weak.

A Note on the Use of Monetary Equivalents

We have mentioned in passing a very peculiar analytical device that is used both in the economic analysis of crime and the economic analysis of terrorism. This is the 'monetary equivalent'. Economics as a science of choice emerged first as a science of wealth and choices involving wealth are still where a large proportion of economists direct their analytic efforts. When I tell someone that I am interested in 'defence economics', their first thought is usually that I am interested in defence budgets and spending. One of the more prominent criticisms of economics that I have heard is that it monetises all of its decision-variables and can only deal with decisions involving money. Economics is, for better or worse, inextricably linked in many people's thoughts with monetised decisions. Despite the fact that much of the now 'classical' economics literature dealing with choice explicitly identifies both monetary and 'psychic' payoffs and returns as the key analytical variables, many economists have continued to construct models of choice where 'psychic' payoffs are monetised. An example from the economics of terrorism literature is Enders and Sandler (2002) who use 'monetary equivalent' gains and losses from terrorist activity as the main decision variable in their model of terrorist behaviour. They do so even though the gains and losses from terrorist activity are obviously not monetary in nature, except in special circumstances. In applying this analytical technique and monetising the non-monetary—including psychic payoffs and such things media coverage, release of political prisoners and so on—payoffs to terrorism, they are following a tradition that characterised much of economic analysis of crime.

Eide (1994, p.66) briefly discusses the reasons for the use of monetary equivalents in expected utility analysis. While the payoffs, positive or negative, that an individual receives as a result of a particular choice need not be monetary in nature and may just as easily be something like the 'thrill' obtained from engaging in an illicit action, the mathematics is much less clear in its conclusions when non-monetary payoffs replace their monetary equivalent reflections in the analytical models. For one thing, unless the analysis is purely theoretical psychic factors such as 'thrills' or, perhaps, 'regrets', are not easily measured and so economists who wish to undertake some sort of empirical analysis of crime or terrorism restrict their variables to those that are either measurable or able to be represented in monetary terms (such as the costs of legal defence and lost wages due to imprisonment, for example, rather than on the presumably negative psychic payoffs associated with trial and incarceration such as shame, regret, heavy conscience and so on). Furthermore, as Eide (1994) points out, the introduction of non-monetised 'attributes' to illegal activity into an orthodox model such as that presented by Becker, Ehrlich or Landes may yield ambiguous results making it unclear whether changes in the 'opportunity' variables will increase or decrease illicit behaviour.

The fact that monetary equivalents may be necessary to derive a model that yields unambiguous results is a significant restriction on the scope of economic analysis and one that certainly stands as an obstacle to be overcome on the way towards an economic analysis that can provide operationally relevant results. However, it is not necessarily the case that we need to develop a model that incorporates all relevant psychic payoffs to terrorism. What we need is a model that does not aim at identifying the relationships between terrorist choice and a list of relevant variables. We will always find it difficult when a payoff cannot be measured but we should be able to find a way to analyse terrorist choice as it pertains to any measurable payoff variable. A prime example is media coverage. In some parts of the terrorism studies literature it is accepted that the media coverage that terrorists receive following a terrorist action is a critically important payoff and, possibly, the only payoff the terrorist cares about. We can measure media coverage in minutes, lines or column inches. Rather than constructing a model where media coverage sits alongside a 'time allocation to terrorism' decision variable, we can avoid potential analytical problems that may increase the ambiguity of the results and express the terrorist's utility directly in terms of the amount of media coverage and its variability around an average[8]. If different attack methods can be linked to different amounts of average media coverage, a preference ordering over attack methods in terms of the media coverage they are expected to generate is within our grasp. Because the terrorist makes decisions based on publicly available knowledge (the amount of coverage received by different types of attacks) the opportunities and choices are much more concrete, there is no need for monetary equivalents and law enforcement can see more clearly how a relevant variable is expected to influence terrorist choice not in terms of amount of time allocated to terrorism but the type of attack method chosen (or some other equally operationally relevant consideration).

CONCLUDING REMARKS

If I could choose one article that a newcomer to the economic analysis of terrorism should read it is Landes (1978). It does not tell us everything there is to know about the economic method or expected utility analysis but it is one of the most clearly developed analyses and one that can be used as the foundation for further explanation and understanding of the orthodox economic method. It should be noted that economic analysis is not exactly the easiest thing in the world to understand. The way in which it is presented and its language are sometimes obscure. This leads some people, usually economists themselves, to see more within the mathematical-analytical frameworks than what is really there and leads others to see less. Part of the problem certainly stems from the a-historical approach to economic education which fails to separate out all of the strands of thought in manner that leads to a clear understanding of the origins and scope of the economic method and the importance of language, even to highly mathematical pieces of analysis. So we find certain pieces of the superstructure held up as being unassailable because, within the narrow frame of reference in which that piece of the superstructure has developed in the analyst's mind, it *is* unassailable. In the bigger scheme of things, it is not. Learning the difference is not something that is acquired easily, within a short period of study or with study focused on only particular parts of economic theory and history.

Landes (1978) sets out to explain the rise and fall of hijacking incidences in the United States in the 1960s and 1970s. The number of hijacking incidents that were recorded is striking. One of the more interesting figures quoted by Landes is the probability that a particular aircraft would be hijacked on any given day. This was small because the number of flights is so large. The probability for 1969 was 0.000007. However, the probability was 300 times greater than an individual being murdered on a given day. This probability for 1969 was 0.0000002. The rise and fall of hijacking incidences can be explained without reference to

[8] I thank Gabriela Pohl for this insight.

formal economics. If one has the facts, reason and logic will provide a plausible explanation along the lines that desperate individuals seeking money or passage out of the United States to Cuba struck upon hijacking as a feasible means. One might even surmise that some sort of trend or fad was started by the early adopters of the hijacking method that was followed in greater numbers. This might have worked in conjunction with an exacerbation of the socio-economic-political circumstances that give rise to such behaviour. When authorities increased the penalties and enhanced the security at airports and on planes, hijackers were effectively stopped before they had a chance to board and divert an airplane.

The economic model seems to add little to this 'commonsense' explanation or reasoning. This has been a criticism directed towards Becker and his work applying rational choice to all sorts of day-to-day situations (such as marriage and the decision to have children)[9]. When the economic model is applied, with all its mathematical rigour, do we not end up with a set of conclusions that were either accessible without the model and, therefore, a meaningless but exact agreement between the economic model and the empirical observation? Who would not have expected metal detectors and air marshals to be associated with a decline in terrorism? Economic analysis explains *why* we see a decline in *attempted* hijackings and not simply an increase in the number of hijackers being *apprehended*. That is, the analysis explains the decision-making and choices of potential hijackers—those contemplating the various means available to achieve an objective of obtaining monetary payoff or passage to Cuba—and predicts changes to the results of those decision-making processes when the decision-maker is confronted with changed circumstances. When there are changes to the payoffs, potential hijackers reorder their preferences away from hijacking and do not even attempt it. The security measures that were implemented at airports and on planes and the extradition treaties with Cuba diminish the expected payoffs to hijacking. Offenders are more likely to be apprehended or otherwise fail and avoid hijacking. The decline in hijackings is due to this behaviour, which is explained by the economic analysis, rather than an increased level of 'interceptions' of offenders at airports or onboard airplanes.

The development of a list of relevant context or 'opportunity' variables and an analytical framework within which the relationship between those variables and the terrorist's choices or preferences may be determined is a meaningful contribution to the study of terrorism. Sometimes, the discipline of having to work out the mathematics as well as the economics highlights a flaw in conventional wisdom. Always, the main contribution of orthodox economic analysis is a reasoned exposition of the likely relationship between particular variables and terrorist choices. A good example of the types of explanation that emerge from such analysis is the explanations that economists have furnished regarding why policy initiatives such as deterrence may have been or may be effective and how terrorists might react to such policy initiatives. An increase in security at embassies may lead to a decrease in armed attacks or bombings of embassies but an increase in assassination attempts on embassy staff and officials outside of the embassy compounds (Sandler and Enders 2004). The important thing that the economic model explains is not so much the terrorist's (obvious) response to enhanced security but the fact that there is a response at all and how this might play out in subsequent periods. Terrorists do not simply continue to attack the embassy as if nothing has changed and meet with increased resistance and defeat and they do not simply give up their terroristic ambitions now that a prime target has been defended. They choose a

[9] See Blaug (1992, especially p.223).

different target or another type of attack method and so it goes on. The dynamics of the choices in relation to opportunities is something that emerges from a careful application of the orthodox economic method to the analysis of terrorism.

It is clear, however, that such orthodox results are unlikely to be particularly relevant to law enforcement agencies engaged in a particular investigative process. This does not mean that the orthodox model or a variant of it or an excrescence from it could not be made to yield operationally relevant advice. It must be remembered that while the economic analysis of terrorism has produced broader policy advice based on the types of analytical conclusions that we have discussed, economic analysis in many respects always serves more than one master. Conforming to the orthodoxy is of considerable importance and this involves conforming to particular mathematical-theoretical-methodological-philosophical frameworks. Always, the work of economists is a contribution to economic science first and a contribution to understanding whatever particular phenomenon that is the subject of analysis second. The latter not being acceptable unless shaped in a manner demanded by the former. It is not that rigorous orthodox economic models cannot be made operationally relevant to law enforcement (or to professionals in any other context) but developing such models is challenging for a number of different reasons. Where compromises have to be made, it has usually been the case that the orthodox position would remain steadfast. The introduction of greater flexibility in this regard, particularly with regards to the use and interpretation of mathematical analysis, is what we mean by a pragmatic approach that better allows for practical understanding to not only shape the models but to shape and assess the interpretations that are extracted from them. It is a combination of computation and intuition analogous to the use of a computer to assist a champion chess-player. The intuition must be permissible even if, perhaps just for the moment, it cannot all be expressed mathematically.

It should be clear that opportunities and choices represent the foundations of economic analysis. Economic analysis does not require that individuals are self interested or that they are only interested in money. It does not require or imply that individuals are perfect calculators of the odds. It does not require or imply that individuals do not make mistakes. If individuals have an objective and choose among scarce means in order to achieve those objectives, the logical theoretical framework of choice can be applied to examine those choices. Terrorists have an objective and allocate scarce resources towards the achievement of that objective. Expected utility theory is applied to analyse those choices and to examine the possible effects of changes to the context in which the choices are made. Some of the analytical results are straightforward and obvious *a priori*. Others are surprising and contradict 'conventional wisdom'. If a terrorist has the preference ordering contained in the table presented earlier in this chapter, a bombing attack on Target A is the best ranked alternative to achieving a particular objective. If the government increases security at Target A, the terrorist may de deterred from making this choice. This is the 'deterrence effect'. If the terrorist is deterred from bombing Target A, he or she may choose an assassination attempt instead. This is the 'substitution effect'. If the government can strike at the terrorist's scarce resources, some or all of the terrorist's alternatives may become unattainable. This is the 'resources effect'. If the risk-reward trade-offs that characterise the alternatives change, the order of alternatives in the terrorist's preference ranking may change. These are 'risk-reward effects'. Together, these effects represent logical foundations on which further analysis can be based. It is building upon these foundations that shall take us towards the provision of operationally relevant advice in pursuit of the lone wolf terrorist.

Chapter 3

THE RISK-REWARD TRADE-OFF AND THE STATISTICAL STRUCTURE OF THE TERRORISM CONTEXT

"[Joseph Paul Franklin] gunned down the civil rights leader Vernon Jordan outside a Marriott in Fort Wayne, Indiana, tearing a hole in Jordan's back the size of a fist. In the same period in the late seventies, ... Franklin says that he robbed several banks, bombed a synagogue in Tennessee, killed two black men jogging with white women in Utah, shot a black man and a white woman coming out of a Pizza Hut in a suburb of Chattanooga, Tennessee, and on and on a violent spree that may have spanned ten states and claimed close to twenty lives, and, following Franklin's arrest in 1980, earned him six consecutive life sentences."[1]

The lone wolf terrorist must take risks in order to generate a payoff. This is the same as saying that the all of the potential payoffs that are available to the lone wolf are variable and may vary from what he expects before carrying out the attack. If the lone wolf terrorist was interested in generating 'minutes of cable news coverage', terrorist actions directed towards such a goal are risky in the sense that their outcomes are variable. While some news coverage might be expected from a terrorist attack—and coverage seems to be correlated with the number of people that injured or killed—the actual amount of coverage might be more or less than expected. Expected utility analysis incorporates this quite explicitly and changes in the risk-reward trade-off can be analysed within the Becker, Ehrlich, Landes and Sandler models. In other parts of economics, especially financial economics, the expected utility analysis of decision-making under risk and uncertainty has advanced to a very considerable extent and these models may provide us with the types of analytical tools that we are after. That an analysis of risk and reward can be undertaken at all is due to the statistical structure that characterises the terrorism context and, in particular, the outcomes of particular attack methods. Although the data that is generated by the activities of terrorists and terrorist groups appears to be quite haphazard, there is an underlying statistical structure to the risks and payoffs available to terrorist activities that provides the modicum of order necessary to construct a theoretical economic framework. Understanding this structure and its implications

[1] Gladwell (1997).

for terrorist choice provides an important next step in understanding the ways in which the lone wolf terrorist may approach his decisions in the presence of risk.

MEASURING RISK AND REWARD

Logical results such as 'deterrence', 'substitution' and 'risk-reward' effects allow conclusions to be reached about the choices of terrorists and the impact on those choices of particular changes in the opportunities available. We can say, for example, that an increase in the risk associated with a particular type of terrorist attack method will deter terrorists from using that attack method (other things being equal). If the logic of choice can be accompanied by computable results that provide numerical answers to questions such as, how risky are bombing attacks compared to assassinations? Or, what combination of bombing attacks and hostage taking yields the highest payoff for a particular level of risk? Or, after how many attacks or how many fatalities will a lone wolf terrorist discontinue his involvement in terrorist attacks? Then we have the first steps towards a much more operationally relevant economic analysis of terrorism. In order to construct such a theoretical economic framework for lone wolf terrorism it is necessary to have quantitative or numerical measurements for risk and reward.

For a lone wolf terrorist contemplating a terrorist activity, he may be interested in two important factors: (1) the expected payoff from the activity and (2) the risk involved in the activity. For the moment, we leave aside the question concerning the payoff that the terrorist desires, whether media coverage, political voice or human tragedy. Whatever payoff we choose, whether minutes of media coverage or number of injuries and fatalities, the expected payoff from the activity might be estimated in a number of different ways. The simplest option and the one that is most realistic is simply the arithmetic mean or average payoff from similar activities in the past. If the actual outcome of the terrorist activity can vary from that which was expected, the terrorist activity is risky. The magnitude of this risk can be measured by some statistical measure of dispersion such as standard deviation or variance. Such a measure captures the idea that divergences of the actual outcomes from the expected outcomes constitute an important part of the nature of risky choices. The higher the standard deviation or variance of a terrorist activity's payoffs, the higher the possibility that the actual outcome will diverge from that which was expected. On average, for example, the lone wolf may expect a bombing attack to kill two people and injure fifteen. The actual outcome of a particular attack may be quite different. The bomb may fail to detonate and there may be no injuries or fatalities. Alternatively, the bomb may detonate prematurely and result in more injuries and fatalities than the lone wolf had expected.

For numerical or computable results to be generated rather than purely logical conclusions about risk and reward it is necessary to base the analysis upon some series of payoffs to terrorist activity. As we have already discussed in passing, there are at least several options. For some types of terrorist activity it may be the case that monetary payoffs are the most relevant. For example, in kidnapping scenarios the terrorists' demands for ransom monies may be considered. Almost $70 million dollars in ransoms were paid during the 1970s alone (Sandler et al. 1983). The series of ransoms paid over time could constitute the basis for a statistical analysis. Unfortunately, this would only be applicable to particular types of terrorist activity and not really applicable at all to lone wolf terrorism given the types of attacks that lone wolf terrorists have tended to engage in. Another possibility is the press coverage generated by the terrorist activity. This is an important payoff and a proxy for an intangible good such as political influence. The amount of press coverage generated by particular terrorist activities is measurable and could constitute the basis for a statistical analysis. This would encompass a larger array of terrorist activities. Another possibility is iconoclastic, particularly for those who believe that terrorism involves the pursuit of noble political objectives and that murder is an unfortunate by-product of this pursuit. Phillips (2009) bases his analysis on the assumption that the terrorists' objective is to cause human tragedy that is measured by the number of fatalities and injuries. This encompasses all violent terrorist attacks and since many recent acts of terrorism have been accompanied by statements from their perpetrators confirming that the objective was to kill as many people as possible it seems all the more appropriate.

Terrorists sometimes justify or explain their actions by reference to some political objective or grievance. Definitions that rely on encompassing these 'political motives' distract from the terrorist's underlying objective: to inflict some amount of human tragedy. Overlooking this fact means that much of the terrorism studies literature is unprepared and ill equipped when it comes to explaining the acts of those terrorists, including Bin Laden, who have stated very clearly that their objective is to inflict as much human tragedy as possible. Even if it is not expressed in words, this statement is expressed in deed whenever an act of terrorism is committed deliberately in a place where many people gather such as a market, a baggage carousel at an airport or at peak hour on the subway. Even if, by some definitions of terrorism, this objective is obscured or denied, it is terrorists who set out to kill—to do murder—for whatever reason, who constitute the most significant threat and who must be compromised by effective analysis and law enforcement actions. It would be a gross miscalculation to undertake analysis that ignored or resisted the treatment of the most devastating outcome of terrorism as being, also, its most devastating objective.

It seems quite obvious that the infliction of injuries and fatalities can be treated quite plausibly as the 'end of terrorism' in the vast majority of cases. Even if some other end such as political expression or media coverage sits deep within the terrorist's motivations it need not even be the case, though it quite clearly is, that there is a positive correlation between injuries and fatalities and media coverage. All that needs to be realised is that none of the terrorist attack methods has an expected fatality count of zero and anyone who embarks upon an arson, assassination or bombing attack (or a hijacking, hostage-taking or kidnapping) must expect to inflict some amount of human tragedy (though this may be greater than planned). All of this can be realised without the admissions by the terrorists themselves who by word and deed aim to inflict as many injuries and fatalities as they can within the context of the particular attack method they have chosen[2]. If this seems obvious, it is true to say that it is a view that meets some resistance within the terrorism studies literature. In fact, the infliction of injury and fatality is not usually listed as a terrorist objective. It must, however, be the objective of terrorists who engage in violent attacks using attack methods that are expected to inflict a positive number of injuries and fatalities. Overlooking the possibility that the direct outcomes of terrorism are in fact its objectives has led to much discussion that is beside the

[2] For example, the terrorist who engages in an assassination attack may expect to inflict a single fatality while the terrorist who engages in an armed assault may expect to inflict many more.

point. Not only that, refusing to accept anything other than some political-social-religious-economic goal as the objective of terrorism robs terrorism studies of its ability to see that terrorists who aim to inflict injuries and fatalities are our most dangerous threat. It cannot see what it does not look for. This leads to further analytical weaknesses including a failure to consider that terrorists may copy and try to outdo their predecessors in terms of the devastation caused by their attacks[3]. Surely, terrorism that inflicts injury and fatality is the terrorism that concerns us most. To analyse this effectively, we must accept that terrorist attack methods are deployed with an expectation of injury and fatality. This expectation, the choice of attack method, sits well within the grasp of economic analysis. In fact, it is more within our grasp than the 'political influence' that has been traditionally assumed to sit at the heart of terrorism.

INJURIES AND FATALITIES AND TERRORISM

Transnational terrorists have been responsible for many fatalities and injuries over the past four decades. For each type of terrorist attack method, data is available that shows how many fatalities and injuries have been caused and how many we can expect, on average, each attack method to inflict in future attacks. This data series provides a foundation for statistical analysis. The data, available from the RAND-MIPT database, permit the computation of the expected risk and payoffs to particular acts of transnational terrorism when payoffs are measured in terms of injuries and fatalities. For the most part, the attack methods that have produced the highest number of fatalities and injuries are also the riskiest, though at any given point in time there may be attack methods that may provide payoffs that are more than commensurate with the risks involved. In equilibrium the risk-reward ratio[4] would be the same for every attack method. In reality we never reach this equilibrium point so there will always be some attack methods with different risk-reward ratios than others. The actions of both terrorists and law enforcement will influence the risk-reward ratio that prevails for any given attack method at a particular point in time.

The risk-reward ratio is a good way to picture the trade-offs that might be facing the lone wolf terrorist and the dynamic interplay between the terrorist's choice of attack method and the risk-reward ratios revealed in historical data. When the risk-reward ratio is high for a particular attack method, that attack method provides a higher expected payoff at each given level of risk vis-à-vis other attack methods. It might be expected that the lone wolf terrorist will engage in that attack method. By doing so, he presumably attracts the attention of law enforcement and the risk associated with that attack method increases. The lone wolf terrorist may then find that another attack method presents a better opportunity. This can be depicted by a simple diagram as shown in Figure 3.1.

[3] There are some exceptions, including Caruso and Schneider (2013) and Caruso and Locatelli (2008).

[4] This is calculated as the average or expected payoff divided by the standard deviation. A high (low) risk-reward ratio means that the relationship between risk and reward is 'steep' ('flat'): at each level of risk, a higher (lower) payoff is available but, conversely, at each level of payoff, a higher (lower) level of risk must be borne.

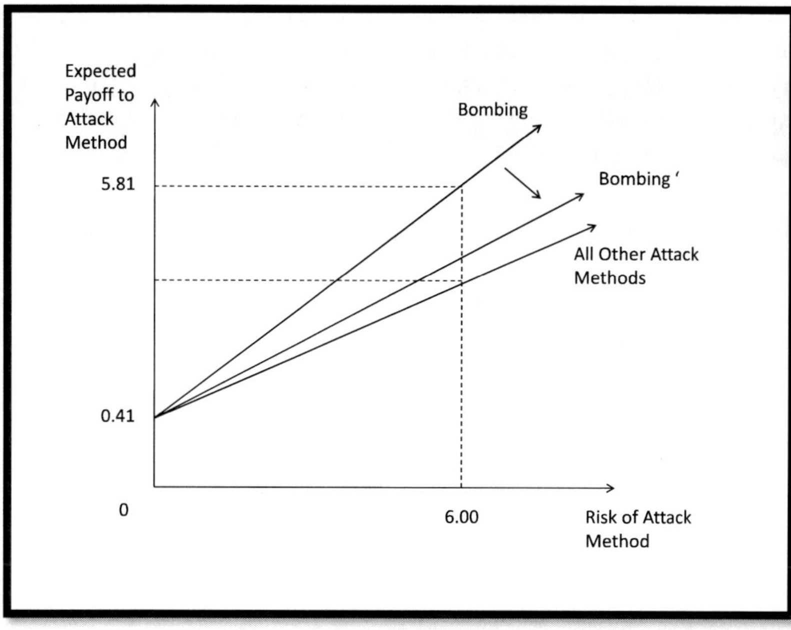

Figure 3.1 Attack Methods: Payoffs, Risks and Substitution

In Figure 3.1, the lone wolf can obtain 0.41 fatalities with zero risk (see Phillips 2010). If he is willing to bear more risk he can obtain a higher expected payoff. Assume for argument's sake that all other attack methods have the same risk-reward ratio while bombing has a higher risk-reward ratio. The lone wolf may be attracted to the utilisation of bombing because he can obtain a higher expected payoff at each level of risk than if he deployed any other attack method. By engaging in bombing he attracts the attention of law enforcement and security agencies who take steps to counter the deployment of bombing attacks. These steps may include greater security at particular targets or the implementation of enhanced bomb detection technology at particular locations. We could then expect the risk-reward ratio of bombing to drift back towards the ratio that is common for all attacks. The situation is dynamic. By focussing on preventing bombing, law enforcement may cause an increase in the risk-reward ratio associated with arson or armed attacks. Or the terrorist may switch his attention to developing some innovation in bombing that offsets law enforcement efforts and keeps the risk-reward ratio for bombing relatively high. All of these things are entirely plausible and do happen in reality. This risk-reward picture is just a very good way of depicting and thinking about these things.

In reality, the RAND-MIPT data shows that for the most part the attack methods that would usually be thought of as being risky, especially hostage taking and unconventional attacks such as the 9/11 attacks, are characterised by higher standard deviation of payoffs. Assassinations (where the targets may be single individuals) and kidnappings are lower risk activities. The variability of the outcomes of each of the RAND-MIPT attack method categories is shown in Table 3.1. An expected payoff of 1.54 fatalities and injuries per assassination attack per year and a standard deviation of 0.71 implies that the terrorist can expect 1.54 fatalities and injuries to be the outcome of an assassination attack but will generate either 0.80 fatalities and injuries or 2.25 fatalities and injuries on 68 percent of occasions (if the payoffs are assumed to be normally distributed). If the target is a single individual, the statistical structure implied by the mean and standard deviation of the payoffs generated by assassination as an attack method is one that is most likely to be characterised by a failure to kill or injure the target on the one hand or to produce collateral fatalities and injuries on the other. Conclusions of this nature may be reached for the other attack methods.

Table 3.1. Average Outcomes and Variability: RAND-MIPT Attack Method Categories

Attack Type	Average Fatalities and Injuries Per Attack Per Year	Standard Deviation
Armed Attacks	5.32	15.00
Arson	0.72	1.85
Assassination	1.54	0.71
Hostage	11.46	38.18
Bombing	5.88	6.09
Hijacking	3.91	10.82
Kidnapping	0.46	0.35
Other	1.14	3.02
Unconventional	7.48	42.94
Unknown	1.11	4.04

The measure of risk that has been chosen, variance or standard deviation, encompasses the multiplicity of circumstances that may generate an outcome for a terrorist attack that diverges from that which was expected. This includes the risk of failure, the risk of apprehension and the risk of generating more or less fatalities and injuries than expected. The measure of risk, standard deviation, encompasses those circumstances that result in an outcome that is different to what was expected. An attack method, such as hostage taking, is very risky because the terrorist must seize hostages, control a specified space, manage negotiations with law enforcement and attempt to execute an escape plan in the event of failure. At many points there is a chance that the actual outcomes will diverge from what was expected. It is not surprising that the series of fatalities and injuries generated by hostage taking exhibits high standard deviation (risk). Similar comments could be made about bombing and armed attacks. The chances of divergence of actual outcomes from expected outcomes are high because devices must be planted or delivered, targets may not be guaranteed to occupy the attack space at the attack time and the weapons and materials deployed are volatile in nature. A measure of dispersion, such as standard deviation, of actual outcomes from expected outcomes encompasses these types of possibilities and indicates more about the risk of a terrorist attack than what might at first be expected.

Mean-Variance Expected Utility Analysis

Together with what is called 'full' expected utility analysis, it is possible to construct a utility function for a terrorist on the basis of the mean and variance of the fatalities and injuries expected to be generated by a terrorist attack. Whereas the Becker, Ehrlich and Sandler functions contained arguments or terms in the functions to encompass particular aspects of terrorism—such as the probability of getting caught, the length of the prison sentence that would be imposed and the magnitude of the concession granted by the government—an expected utility function for the terrorist can be constructed on the basis of the two moments of the distribution of fatalities and injuries generated by terrorist attacks. That is, the mean or average of this distribution and the standard deviation. This means that we can analyse the lone wolf terrorist's decisions about the type of attack method to use as if the basis for those decisions was the mean and standard deviation of the fatalities and injuries that the attack is expected to generate. Just as terrorism researchers, government agencies and law enforcement have some idea about the human tragedy that could be expected to result from the deployment of a particular type of terrorist attack method so we must presume that the lone wolf terrorist understands enough from publicly available information about the outcomes of terrorism such as is found in news reports to form an expectation about the likely impact of a particular attack and the variability that might characterise its outcomes[5]. From this analytical viewpoint, the lone wolf terrorist will rank alternatives on the basis of risk and reward and choose the best ranked alternative given his or her attitudes towards risk. The result is an expected utility analysis that is expressed numerically and constructed on the basis of computable rather than strictly theoretical results.

That we are not asking the lone wolf terrorist to be a perfect calculating machine is a point that we must continue to stress because of the tendency of orthodox economic analysis to either imply this or be interpreted as having implied this. The choice process that we are depicting is one where the lone wolf terrorist obtains some idea about the rewards and risks associated with particular types of terrorist attacks from observing information that is made public. A person who is planning a terrorist attack may look for such information with an intensity that is higher than a 'normal' person. We could expect him to know, more or less, how many fatalities have been inflicted by some recent lone wolf terrorist attacks (and terrorist group attacks) and we could expect him to have some idea about the number of fatalities that have been inflicted by the attacks of more prominent or notable predecessor lone wolf terrorists. If he has been paying particularly close attention, he might know exactly how much human tragedy has been inflicted by different lone wolf terrorists using a small number of different attack methods. He will also have some idea that the payoffs are variable. Some lone wolf terrorist attacks that have used the same attack method have inflicted far more fatalities than others. In choosing from among a small number of attack method opportunities the lone wolf trades off expected payoff against expected variability. This is not a computation so much as a weighing up of perceptions regarding what he knows about the possible number of fatalities that may be inflicted. An assassination may inflict a small number of fatalities but the outcomes are less variable. An armed assault may inflict a higher number of fatalities but there is a greater chance that the number will be more or less than expected. A higher payoff versus less certainty about what the outcome may be. A mean-variance expected utility analysis formalises this process using as complete a set of statistical data as is available. Although the lone wolf's actual choices may be imperfect by comparison, it will be very useful for law enforcement to know the most dangerous attack method choices at each level of risk and be able to picture the lone wolf terrorist as attempting to choose the most dangerous attack method on the basis of risk and reward. If lone wolf terrorist ranks his

[5] It must be remembered that he might not and need not do this perfectly but he can, on the basis of publicly available information, form some expectation of risk and reward.

preferences for attack methods on the basis of reward and risk, the generic mean-variance expected utility function for the lone wolf terrorist is:

$$EU = U\left(E_R, \sigma_R^2\right)$$

In this case the expected payoffs, *R*, are the fatalities and injuries that can be expected to be generated by an attack method. The risk of an attack method—the possibility that the actual outcome will diverge from that which was expected—is given by the variance. This utility function says that the lone wolf's utility depends on the risk and reward expected from an attack. An increase in the number of injuries and fatalities that the lone wolf terrorist expects from an attack method will increase the expected utility of that attack method. An increase in the risk or the variability of the outcomes that the lone wolf can expect to result from the attack method will decrease the expected utility of that attack method. In analytical work, the historical mean and variance (or standard deviation) is used as proxies for the unobservable expected values of the returns series. This is desirable in any case because we expect the lone wolf to form his expectations based on the publicly available historical information about terrorism incidences. The maximisation of this expected utility function results in the choice of the most dangerous attack method at the level of risk that the lone wolf terrorist is willing to bear. The advantage of this approach is that the optimal choice is the most dangerous or deadly one. The usual criticism of the rational choice or optimisation approach that is built into this type of economic analysis cannot be applied without implying that we should not be prepared for or interested in the lone wolf's most dangerous or deadly choice because he is not rational and would not choose it. The lone wolf might make a mistake but we will not rely on the lone wolf erring in his choices.

One of the strongest advantages of the mean-variance risk-reward approach to analysing risky choice is that it uses data that are available to the lone wolf terrorist to determine the lone wolf's preference ordering. Unlike the Landes model for example where the probability of apprehension and other important aspects of the opportunity set are computed by the analyst, the mean-variance approach simply uses the list of fatalities (or whatever payoff we are interested in) inflicted by the different terrorist attack methods over time. Risk or variability is embedded in the 'ups and downs' that characterise the list of fatalities. As we said before, the lone wolf terrorist may not use the RAND-MIPT or GTD data but it is very plausible to expect that the lone wolf terrorist will have a good idea about what the historical distribution of injuries and fatalities associated with particular attack methods looks like. A lot of information about the outcomes of particular terrorist attacks is reported in the press or is otherwise publicly available. Information about the outcomes of both successful and unsuccessful terrorist attacks is available in sufficient quantity to act as signals about the potential risk and reward involved. The terrorist does not need to start from a completely blank slate or a position of complete uncertainty about what outcomes may be expected and how the actual outcomes may diverge from these expected outcomes. If the lone wolf terrorist has a good idea about what to expect *on average* then an analysis that is based on just two moments (mean and variance) of the distribution of fatalities and injuries generated by terrorist attacks is likely to produce a set of choices that approximate those that would be arrived at by a full but practically incomputable analysis involving ranking of preferences on all relevant criteria.

The difference between what we call a 'full' expected utility analysis and a 'mean-variance' expected utility analysis is of the utmost importance if we wish to provide operationally relevant advice. Landes presents a full expected utility analysis. His payoffs series include, as we discussed previously, the positive payoffs from a successful operation and the costs or negative payoffs of an unsuccessful operation. Each payoff is monetised and the hijacker is depicted as weighing up his wealth 'if successful' versus his wealth 'if unsuccessful'. The weighing up involves a weighting. In the tradition of orthodox expected utility analysis, each payoff is weighted by its probability of occurrence. We call this a full expected utility analysis because every possible outcome (within the context of the model) is considered along with its probability of occurrence. Although Landes considers just two opportunities (hijack or not hijack) with three possible outcomes (successful, unsuccessful and convicted, unsuccessful and not convicted), a more encompassing analysis of the terrorist's opportunities would depict the decision-maker as determining the outcome, usually as a wealth equivalent, of each opportunity, weighting each outcome by its probability of occurrence, ranking each opportunity on the basis of its expected utility and choosing the best ranked outcome.

In all of this, the payoffs series are, so to speak, one step removed. This will be the case whenever wealth equivalents are used but even where the payoffs might be plausibly measured in monetary terms, such as the ransoms obtained from a hijacking or the costs of a legal defence, the payoffs series by no means sits in the public domain. If we wish to move beyond purely theoretical work and undertake an empirical analysis like Landes, then the payoffs series must be estimated and, based on the historical record, the probabilities that would be used to weight the outcomes must be extracted. That this might just be 'the long way round' should be quite clear but the economic analysis of terrorism had no feasible analytical alternative. Mean-variance expected utility analysis was introduced into the literature only in 2009. The advantage of this analytical method is not only its relative simplicity, including as it does only the average payoff and risk as relevant aspects of the opportunity set, but its computable results based on a payoffs series that is immediate rather than one step removed and sitting more conspicuously within the public domain. Rather than have the decision maker determine the outcome of each opportunity, the opportunities are presented as outcomes. That is, they are presented as 'pairs' of reward and risk. There is no explicit probability weighting but a direct ordering or ranking of opportunities on the basis of risk and reward. A higher reward is trade off against a higher variability (less certainty) of the outcomes. For payoffs series such as the fatalities inflicted by different types of terrorist attacks or the amount of media coverage associated with a particular number of fatalities, the payoffs are there in the public domain to be observed by the potential terrorist and used by the analyst to determine preference orderings directly and without recourse to further analytical manoeuvres such as the estimation of the probabilities of each outcome.

As a final example, consider a terrorist who is choosing from among the ten or so attack methods that are commonly reported in the terrorism databases such as RAND-MIPT and GTD. The payoff that he seeks is some amount of human tragedy. A full expected utility analysis could be used to find the terrorist's ranking of different attack method opportunities when the relevant payoffs series is the fatalities expected to be inflicted. Traditionally, the positive utility deriving from the payoffs series would be contrasted with a negative utility generating aspect of the opportunities which is usually something like 'failure' or 'apprehension and punishment'. These aspects, however, have no obvious measurement unit and resort is nearly always had to monetary equivalents at this point. For each aspect of each opportunity both a payoff and a probability is required. Each opportunity becomes transformed into a weighted payoff that is the sum of the probability weighted positive and negative payoffs. Of course, probabilities can only be obtained by assuming that the outcomes conform to some probability distribution and this might be fraught with considerable difficulties when the payoffs series is synthetic, as a monetised payoffs series is bound to be, rather than directly observable. Not only does more appear to be required of the terrorist whose decision making is being represented but it would seem doubtful that law enforcement could easily be convinced of the operational relevance of a ranking of attack methods obtained from such a procedure.

By contrast the choice process embedded within the mean-variance approach is much more amenable to visualisation. As before, the terrorist is choosing from the small number of attack methods to which all of the terrorist incidences recorded over the past four decades have been attributed. The payoffs series is the fatalities expected to be inflicted by each attack method. This expectation is formed simply on the basis of the historical average and, as we have said before, could be estimated from news reports and so forth. Unlike the orthodox approach, our negative utility generating aspect of the opportunities is risk or variability. The outcome of any given attack may vary from the average or expected outcome. Risk or variability encompasses all of those things that lead inflicted fatalities to diverge from the number that was expected. A bomb may explode too early or too late or not at all. An assassination target may be accompanied or surrounded by more people than expected. A law enforcement intervention may stop a shooting spree after an unexpectedly short amount of time. Like the average number of fatalities that can be expected from a particular attack method, the variability of those payoffs may also be estimated on the basis of news reports and other publicly available information about successful and unsuccessful terrorist attacks. There is no need for monetary equivalents or explicit estimates of probabilities for each outcome. Each attack method is simply represented as a risk-payoff 'pair' and, as such, to choose from among or rank three different attack methods, the lone wolf terrorist would only need to form an expectation of six things: the payoff and variability of each of the three attack methods. He then trades off higher expected fatalities against lower uncertainty.

One might wonder how 'fatalities' are transformed into expected utilities. This transformation is traditionally undertaken by the expedient of an expected utility function. What is particularly interesting about this type of preference ordering is that no particular expected utility function is required. A utility maximising terrorist can simply be depicted as arranging his opportunities, his attack methods, on the basis of risk and reward. If we think back to the previous chapter and the roots of expected utility analysis a question that emerges at this point is how the mean-variance expected utility analysis relates to the famous von Neumann and Morgenstern axioms. In economic analysis, conforming to these axioms has been accorded considerable importance and any deviation is frowned upon. What this means is that any preference ordering, like a ranking of alternative attack method opportunities, should conform to the axioms in order to allay the concerns of the orthodox economist. A preference ordering formed on the basis of risk and reward (variance and average payoff) will be consistent with the axioms if the payoffs series is normally distributed *or*[6] if the function that is used to assign expected utility to each opportunity is a quadratic function. The first of

[6] It is important to note that this is an 'or' not an 'and'.

these conditions might be violated and the second condition, quadratic utility, involves the possibility that the decision-maker may become satiated or fully satisfied after receiving a particular payoff and not seek more within the same period. For economists applying such an analytical device to financial decisions involving monetary payoffs the idea that a person could become satiated was unthinkable and more is always preferred to less. Considerable debate ensued.

The results of two decades of research vindicate both the mean-variance utility analysis and quadratic utility. Mean-variance expected utility analysis will produce a preference ordering over opportunities that closely approximates a full expected utility analysis even if payoffs are not normally distributed and utility is not quadratic. Those who would seize upon the early criticisms of mean-variance utility analysis and use them in modern debates regarding applications of the technique in different settings run considerable risk of revealing a less than thorough engagement with the literature. If we do wish to assign to the terrorist a quadratic expected utility function and thereby guarantee that the preference ordering formed on the basis of risk and reward conforms to the Neumann and Morgenstern axioms, the main criticism that we shall face is that of introducing 'satiation' into the analytical framework. It is unclear to me whether critics of the quadratic utility function understand that 'satiation' is the primary concern that the financial economists hold about this particular representation of expected utility or whether they have just divined from a cursory review of the literature that the quadratic utility function is 'flawed' and should be avoided. Two important points must be made. First, the quadratic utility function approximates a broader class of expected utility function and the analytical results obtained from an analysis based on an assumption of quadratic utility will not be radically different from a more 'appropriate' analytical foundation. Second, is it not feasible that satiation is a property of the terrorist's decision making that we should understand rather than discard simply because the financial economists are averse to the prospect of analysing decisions where no amount is ever 'enough'?

We shall have more to say about these matters later. What must be understood at the moment is that mean-variance analysis depicts the terrorist as making a trade-off between risk and reward when choosing from among different attack method opportunities. This involves making a choice on the basis of a series of payoffs that are completely observable in their 'raw' form and do not need to be extracted or synthetically constructed by analytical methods. By using the mean-variance analytical framework we can work with a data series that is equally available to both the lone wolf terrorist and the analyst who seeks to analyse his opportunities and choices. A mean-variance expected utility maximising lone wolf terrorist will rank terrorist attack methods on the basis of these two moments of the distribution and choose the best ranked alternative. It is important to note that the alternative attack methods are ranked on the basis of expected utility and not simply on the basis of expected value (or the mean payoff). That is, the lone wolf terrorist will not simply choose the attack method with the highest mean number of injuries and fatalities. Rather, the expected utility for attack methods is 'computed' on the expected payoffs and risks associated with the attacks. Depending on the lone wolf terrorist's attitudes towards risk, he or she may prefer an attack method with a lower mean payoff and lower risk to an attack method with a higher mean payoff and higher risk. Economic analysis uses the expected utility function to represent this weighting of payoffs and risk. Although we need not necessarily assume any particular form of function to represent the lone wolf's choice process, a quadratic function will guarantee that the preference ordering of attack methods that is derived on the basis of the two moments of the distribution of fatalities and injuries generated by attacks is consistent with the von Neumann and Morgenstern axioms that were listed earlier.

NOTES ON SPECIFYING A FUNCTIONAL FORM FOR THE EXPECTED UTILITY FUNCTION

Although it need not be done explicitly, payoffs are transformed or turned into expected utility by way of an expected utility function. There are four commonly used expected utility functions in economic theory. These are the quadratic, power, exponential and logarithmic expected utility functions. Of course, an expected utility function is a mathematical object and as such each type of expected utility function has different mathematical properties that make a function more or less applicable in a particular scenario. We must not forget that within the orthodox economic literature certain analytical steps are taken for mathematical reasons and not solely on grounds of economic logic. At times, it has proven useful to depict an individual as having a logarithmic expected utility function. This is one of the more straightforward functions and simply depicts the utility derived from a particular payoff as being the natural logarithm of that payoff. Weighting the utility obtained from a particular payoff by the probability of the payoff's occurrence gives the expected utility (rather than the expected value) of the particular opportunity under consideration. A simple example using the hypothetical data in Table 3.2 will suffice to show how this process works.

Table 3.2. Attack Method Choice and Logarithmic Utility: An Example

Terrorist Attack Type A		Terrorist Attack Type B	
Fatalities	**Probability**	**Fatalities**	**Probability**
12	0.07	15	0.10
6	0.08	2	0.12
1	.85	0	0.78

Assume, for example, that a terrorist group is characterised by a logarithmic utility function where utility is derived from the number of fatalities F generated by a particular terrorist attack.

$$U(F) = \ln(F)$$

For the data contained in the table, the utility of 12 fatalities is equal to $\ln(F) = 2.48$, the utility of 6 fatalities is 1.79, the utility of 15 fatalities is 2.70, the utility of 2 fatalities is 0.69 and the utility of one or zero fatalities is zero. The NM expected utility is computed for attack types A and B as follows:

$$E(U)_A = 2.48(0.07) + 1.79(0.09) + 0(0.85) = 0.33$$

$$E(U)_B = 2.70(0.10) + 0.69(0.12) + 0(0.78) = 0.35$$

The terrorist group is assumed to maximise expected utility. Therefore, the group would choose attack type B. This type of analysis may be quite useful when probabilities may be assigned to the fatalities (or whatever the object of analysis may be) associated with particular attack methods deployed by terrorist groups. For various specifications of terrorist groups' utility functions it is possible to determine the attack methods (or combinations of attack methods) that generate the highest utility.

If we want to use a mean-variance analysis we effectively state that the terrorist's expected utility is a function of the risk and reward associated with a particular attack method. We say this formally by writing down a generic or non-specific utility function of the following form:

$$EU = U\left(E_R, \sigma_R^2\right)$$

This utility function is not specific. It is not a quadratic, power, exponential or logarithmic function. As we have said, we do not need to specify a particular functional form for this function but if we did choose to make such a specification we would choose the quadratic functional form. The functional form expresses the way in which the lone wolf will assess and weigh the risk and payoffs associated with particular attack methods. Each of the possible functional forms for the expected utility function describes a different 'weighting scheme' and each has advantages and disadvantages. The reason why the quadratic functional form is chosen when dealing with mean-variance analysis is that this particular functional form ensures that the preference rankings of attack methods exactly conform to the von Neumann and Morgenstern axioms: consistency, transitivity, completeness and so on. If the lone wolf terrorist is choosing on the basis of risk and reward and if his choices can be described by a quadratic form of utility function his choices will conform to these axioms. Because these axioms underlie the mathematical structure of important parts of orthodox economics, especially game theory, orthodox economics views this conformation favourably.

If we express the generic non-specific expected utility function that relates utility to risk and reward as a specific quadratic functional form then the specified expected utility function for our generic mean-variance expected utility function is:

$$U(R) = c + aR - d\sigma_R^2$$

Like the Becker, Ehrlich, Landes and Sandler functions, this function depicts a terrorist obtaining utility from some factors. In this case, the two relevant factors are reward and risk, measured by the injuries and fatalities expected to be generated by a terrorist attack and the standard deviation of those injuries and fatalities. Because additional reward is 'good' and adds to the lone wolf's utility R enters positively into the function. Because additional risk is 'bad' and detracts from the lone wolf's utility, σ_R^2 enters negatively into the function[7]. This function says that the lone wolf ranks his attack methods and makes choices on the basis of risk σ_R^2 and reward R. He will not just rank the attack method with the highest expected injuries and fatalities as the best attack method. He will consider the risks involved. The result is a preference ranking for attack methods that depends on how the lone wolf feels about the risk-reward ratio of each attack method. If we wanted to, we could compute expected utility for each attack method and construct a ranking of attack methods using only the historical averages and variability of each attack method as inputs. The mean-variance approach not only simplifies the analysis but also allows computable results to be generated rather than purely theoretical results. Because we can see what the two moments of the distribution of injuries and fatalities generated by terrorist attack methods are, we can analyse terrorists' choices as if they were made on the basis of this distribution and reach computable numerical conclusions about those choices. This takes us a considerable step closer to providing operationally relevant results.

Risk Preference

There is an added dimension to this analytical setup that deepens the analysis and the results that we can obtain. This added dimension is our consideration of the lone wolf terrorist's appetite for risk. There will not just be one single possible ranking of the attack methods given the historical averages and variability but rather a number of rankings that emerge depending on how risk averse or how risk seeking the lone wolf terrorist happens to be. Risk preference is incorporated into the utility analysis by the expedient of a risk aversion coefficient. If the lone wolf happens, for a given payoff, to prefer a smaller variance of payoffs (reward) to a larger variance, then $d > 0$ and vice versa. It is easy to see that the lone wolf's preferences for risk, captured by the parameter d in the quadratic form of the function, are of critical importance. The lone wolf's preferences for risk play a significant role in shaping his choice of attack methods. Depending on the value of d, the lone wolf will rank riskier activities relatively higher (if d is smaller or negative) or lower (if d is larger). Economic science delineates three types of attitudes toward risk or risk preference: (1) risk averse; (2) risk seeking; (3) risk neutral. For the most part, economists have correctly assumed that individuals are risk averse to some degree. The available empirical evidence is very strong, including the simple facts that people buy insurance and do not allocate all of their retirement savings to the riskiest possible assets. When it comes to terrorist behaviour, however, it is likely that some people will assume that, because terrorism is a risky activity, only risk seeking individuals will be involved in it. According to this point of view, terrorists could not possibly be risk averse. Such a conclusion is understandable on the basis of the lay definitions of these terms but quite mistaken when one considers both the economic definitions of risk aversion and risk seeking behaviour and the inappropriateness of drawing personality trait-based conclusions.

The technical economic meaning of risk aversion and risk seeking behaviour refers to the rejection or acceptance of a 'fair gamble'. A fair gamble is a risky choice where the expected

[7] We can deal with a situation where risk is good. This will be discussed when risk preferences are considered.

payoff is equal to the cost of playing. If the lottery promises a 50-50 chance of \$100 or \$0.00 and the cost of playing is \$50, the lottery is a fair bet[8]. A risk averse individual will reject a fair gamble. A risk seeking individual will accept a fair gamble. Risk neutral individuals are indifferent to either accepting or not accepting. This definition is augmented somewhat in modern financial economics and the distance between the economic definition and the lay definition is extended. When individuals are making choices on the basis of risk and reward, a risk averse individual will bear risk but will require a reward commensurate with the risk being borne. It is not the case that risk aversion implies that individuals will not bear risk. Risk averse individuals may bear a great deal of risk if they feel as though the expected payoffs are sufficient reward for doing so. Because of this, it is probably a very sound approach to treat the lone wolf terrorist as being risk averse to some degree. If the lone wolf terrorist does not require very much additional return to compensate for an increase in risk, it can be said that he is less risk averse (more risk seeking). If the lone wolf terrorist does require a substantial increase in expected returns to compensate for an increase in risk, it can be said that he is more risk averse (less risk seeking). This avoids the rather extreme conclusion that comes with assuming that the lone wolf is risk seeking and prefers more risk to less.

Risk seeking behaviour has implications that we do not often see manifested in reality. Risk seeking implies that individuals making decisions on the basis of risk and reward will give up payoffs in order to take on more risk. In the context of terrorism, whatever good is assumed to be the terrorist's payoff—the level of human tragedy, press coverage, political influence—is given up by the risk seeking terrorist in order to pursue more risk. That is, the terrorist trades payoff for risk rather than risk for payoff. It is difficult to find an empirical example that is in accordance with such behaviour. Another implication or way of looking at risk seeking behaviour is that risk seeking behaviour implies that the risk seeking individual will move to the point of maximum risk and maximum payoff (see Tobin 1958). From the choice of possible terrorist attack methods, a risk seeking terrorist would choose the riskiest attack method with the highest expected payoff. If all terrorists are risk seekers then we should expect to see no instances of the less risky and lower payoff terrorist activities. This is, of course, far from being the case.

Rather than rule out risk seeking behaviour or risk averse behaviour for that matter, it will be wiser to keep these economic definitions and implications at the forefront of our minds whenever risk preference enters into the analysis. We should also not overlook the importance of relative differences in risk aversion. In Ehrlich's (1973) model of crime and criminal behaviour, risk preference affects the relative amount of time spent in risky criminal activities and less risky (or zero risk) legal activities. In Ehrlich's model, the risk seeking criminal will spend more time engaged in criminal activities than his risk averse counterpart. However, this is also true of the less risk averse individual vis-à-vis the more risk averse individual. If we agree that it is sensible, by and large, to work on the basis that terrorists require some increase in payoff for an increase in risk, then we can distinguish between more risk seeking (less risk averse) individuals and less risk seeking (more risk averse) individuals rather than draw a dividing line between risk averse and risk seeking terrorists and inadvertently introducing a terrorist who prefers to give up payoff in order to pursue more risk. If we wish to explicitly deal with such a type of terrorist, we can draw the dividing line at that time in the full

[8] Because $0.50(\$100) + 0.50(\$0.00) = \$50.00$.

knowledge of the implications of the economic definitions of risk aversion and risk seeking behaviour towards risk.

CONCLUDING REMARKS

Each attack method that may be chosen by the lone wolf terrorist has an expected payoff (mean or average) and risk (standard deviation or variance). In making choices, the lone wolf terrorist faces the prospect of trading off reward against risk. If he is less risk averse he will choose more risky attack methods with higher expected payoffs. If he is more risk averse he will choose less risky attack methods with lower expected payoffs. Changes in the risk-reward ratio for the different attack methods may lead to the lone wolf avoiding an attack method that has become more risky without a commensurate increase in expected payoffs, perhaps after law enforcement has devoted more attention towards it, or it may lead to the lone wolf being attracted to an attack method that has become less risky while the rewards available stay the same or increase. The analysis of attack methods available to the lone wolf through the lens of risk and reward provides a clear picture of choices facing the lone wolf whilst encompassing all of the results of traditional economic analysis. Indeed, we may go so far as to construct an expected utility analysis on the basis of the two moments of the distribution of the payoffs to terrorist attack methods: mean and variance.

In all of the expected utility representations of terrorist behaviour of various sorts, the economic agents involved face risk. The trade-off between risk and reward enters into these analyses with different levels of clarity and the results that are generated are usually logical-theoretical in nature. By explicitly incorporating the risk-reward trade-off into the analysis, the lone wolf terrorist's choices under risk and uncertainty can be examined with reference to numerical or computable measurements of risk and reward. Terrorism causes injuries and fatalities. Terrorists have through their actions and their deeds given clear enough indication that this most tragic outcome of terrorism is in fact its objective. Whether it is a sub-objective to something like political influence or publicity, which is certainly correlated with the amount of human tragedy an attack inflicts[9], does not change the fact that violent terrorists set out to do murder. The injuries and fatalities generated by particular attack methods provide the basis for a mean-variance analysis of terrorist behaviour. The lone wolf terrorist makes his choices from a preference ordering formed on the basis of two moments of the distribution: the mean expected injuries and fatalities and the standard deviation of actual outcomes from those that are expected. Because the properties of the distribution are observable not only to the lone wolf terrorist but to the economist, we have a window through which we can look deep into the choices of the lone wolf terrorist.

[9] See Nelson and Scott (1992).

Chapter 4

THE ATTACK METHODS

> New Haven, Connecticut. In the second incident of its kind this week, a mail bomb exploded Thursday and severely injured a noted scientist. David Gelernter, an associate professor of computer science at Yale University, was in a critical condition Thursday evening with severe injuries to his right hand, right eye and chest after opening a parcel in his fifth-floor office on the Yale campus. Law enforcement agencies were investigating to see if there was a possible link to a mail bomb that exploded Tuesday at the San Francisco home of Dr Charles Epstein, a prominent geneticist at the University of California San Francisco[1].

The lone wolf terrorist engages in attacks that have the potential to cause human tragedy and, it must be noted well, are *expected* to cause human tragedy. If terrorist actions never caused human tragedy, terrorism would not be a particularly insidious problem, it would not have attracted the attention of so many different researchers and it would not be absorbing any substantial amount of law enforcement resources. But there are *no* attack methods that have zero expected injuries and fatalities and anyone who uses one of the attack methods that have been used in terrorist attacks in the past must expect to inflict some amount of human tragedy. The lone wolf terrorist forms these expectations and engages in terrorism independently and outside of the command structure of a terrorist group or organisation. Although he might have some type of political or ideological motivation, the lone wolf terrorist's operational objective that we wish to interrupt, pre-empt and prevent is the objective to inflict injuries and fatalities by engaging in violent acts of terrorism. If law enforcement is unsuccessful in the pre-emption of this operational objective, the next task is to contribute to law enforcement's efforts to pursue and apprehend the lone wolf terrorist who has perpetrated acts of violence and who remains at large. Whether motivated by politics or ideology or narcissistic rage or desire to do murder, the lone wolf terrorist's utilisation of attack methods to inflict a level of human tragedy is the operational objective that we wish to encompass within our analytical framework.

Obviously the lone wolf terrorist's choice of attack method is of the utmost importance and is a choice that shapes the terrorism context. The choice of attack method contains within it the expectation of an amount of human tragedy and the trade-off between the size of this inflicted tragedy and its variability. It also contains within it the potential outcomes that, if

---

[1] Shogren (1993). Excerpt from the Los Angeles Times, June 1993, discussing one of Theodore Kaczynski's attacks.

realised, will be additions to the historical record of terrorism. The study of attack method choice also has the additional advantage of avoiding the need to delve into the multiplicity of motivations that have been attributed to or claimed by terrorists. Since the 9/11 terrorist attacks, it is probably true to say that many people in the general public would attach a high degree of significance to religious extremism as a motivation of terrorist behaviour and view religious fundamentalists as the most significant terrorist threat. If this were true, the analysis of terrorism would be much easier. If all or most terrorist attacks were motivated by religious extremism and if all religious extremism were of a particular type then it would be easier to focus our attention and resources and it would be easier to build an archetype behavioural model of the terrorist. The same would be true if all terrorists displayed a particular form of psychosis or psychiatric disorder. Unfortunately, apart from being predominantly male, lone wolf terrorists do not have much in common. According to the Webster Commission (2012), only 7 percent of terrorist attacks in the United States have been motivated by Islamic fundamentalism. A study of the record of lone wolf terrorism during the 20th century and the first part of the 21st reveals a multitude of different alleged motivations including racism and anti-abortion activism. The historical record also reveals that lone wolf terrorists have chosen, like terrorist groups, to engage predominantly in armed attacks, bombings and assassinations. Where the motivations of lone wolf terrorists are numerous, the attack methods from which they can choose to inflict the human tragedy and the attack methods that they have chosen when they have set out to inflict it are much more neatly delineated.

If we want to study the attack method choices of the lone wolf terrorist using the tools of economic analysis then we must define the lone wolf terrorist's opportunities and choices. The first step in this particular task is to identify the types of attack methods from which the lone wolf may choose. Although there may seem to be an endless list of potential attack method opportunities, the attack methods that are available to the lone wolf may be assigned to a very small number of categories and the opportunities to inflict human tragedy (as measured by the average fatalities and the variability of those fatalities) are constrained by the attack method categories. Identifying these attack method categories is the first step in delineating the lone wolf's opportunities and choices. Each of these attack method categories is characterised by an average number of injuries and fatalities which might be expected to be inflicted each time they are used. Each attack method category is also associated with a particular level of standard deviation or risk or variability. When deployed in a particular instance, the injuries and fatalities that are generated may diverge from the average to some degree. This divergence of actual from expected outcomes is more prominent for some categories of attack methods than others. In choosing attack methods from his set of opportunities, the lone wolf terrorist assesses the risk and reward and ranks his preferences for the attack method categories. He will choose the attack method category that promises the highest level of reward for the level of risk that he wishes to bear.

CATEGORIES OF ATTACK METHODS

Although there may be specific technical differences[2] between the materials and devices deployed in any given attack, the attack methods that have been deployed historically may be categorised under several headings. One such categorisation is the categorisation scheme used by the RAND Corporation in constructing its RAND-MIPT transnational terrorism database. In recording incidences of transnational terrorism over the past four decades, RAND-MIPT has only found it necessary to utilise ten attack method categories or labels. All incidences of terror can be encompassed by these ten categories. For the time being, incidences like 9/11 are recorded under the category 'unconventional' attacks. If, however, 'hijacked-plane-targeted-crashes' became a commonly used attack method, it might separate from 'unconventional' and become a new attack method category. Given that researchers have observed a long time series of many thousands of terrorist incidences and still only found it necessary to make use of ten attack method categories we may venture to say that evolution and innovation within the attack methods developed and utilised by terrorists proceed slowly and may be more or less complete. However, we will not be so bold as to suggest that terroristic innovation has ceased because there is no doubt much thought being put into new more deadly ways to deploy the existing attack methods and, perhaps, the development of new and as yet untried attack methods. Our reason for being interested in the attack methods that have been used by transnational terrorists is two-fold. On the one hand, we wish to note the similarities in the choices of both transnational terrorist groups and lone wolf terrorists. On the other hand and more importantly, there have been many more incidences of transnational terrorism than of lone wolf terrorism. The average fatalities and the variability of the outcomes that characterise each attack method are better observed from the transnational terrorism data. What is more, it is analytically sound to use 'out-of-sample' data rather than estimate the lone wolf's expected payoffs and risks on the basis of the lone wolf terrorist incident data. Table 4.1 shows the incidences of terrorism and the fatalities and injuries that resulted from the deployment of each type of attack method.

Table 4.1. RAND-MIPT Attack Method Categories and Human Tragedy: 1968 to 2007

Attack Type	Total Number of Incidences 1968 to 2007	Total Fatalities and Injuries 1968 to 2007
Armed Attacks	7114	26310
Arson	1019	709
Assassination	2357	4282
Hostage	210	3123
Bombing	17856	120550
Hijacking	229	858
Kidnapping	2164	1641
Other	168	578
Unconventional	56	5444
Unknown	404	836

[2] For example, differences in ammunition or explosives components.

It is probably not surprising to learn that among transnational terrorist incidences, the most commonly used attack method is bombing. Between 1968 and 2007, there were 17,856 transnational terrorist incidences involving the utilisation of bombing. The second most commonly utilised attack method is armed attacks. There were 7,114 incidences of armed attacks during the period. Unconventional attacks such as the 9/11 terrorist attacks were the least commonly used attack method. RAND-MIPT records only 56 unconventional attacks for the entire period. This indicates that for the most part terrorists deploy tried, tested and more common attack methods. These are also the attack methods for which terrorists may have a greater knowledge of the distribution of injuries and fatalities. Bombing attacks generated the highest number of fatalities and injuries. During the period 1968 to 2007, there were 120,550 fatalities and injuries from transnational terroristic bombing attacks. Armed attacks resulted in 26,310 fatalities and injuries between 1968 and 2007. Unconventional attacks resulted in 5,444 fatalities and injuries.

ATTACK METHODS AND HUMAN TRAGEDY

The statistics presented in Table 4.1 reveal that all of the attack method categories have been responsible for generating considerable levels of human tragedy when deployed by transnational terrorists over the period 1968 to 2007. The 'headline' figures do not tell the whole story. While bombing and armed attacks have generated almost 90 percent of the injuries and fatalities associated with transnational terrorist attacks, this comes in a context characterised by the predominance of incidences of these two most common attack methods. It is important, therefore, to investigate the ratio of the number of fatalities and injuries to the number of incidences of each attack method. When this calculation is performed it is revealed that unconventional attack methods have generated the highest level of human tragedy proportionally with the number of incidences of unconventional attacks that have been observed. Just 56 attacks resulted in more than 5000 injuries and fatalities. Most interestingly, hostage taking ranks second. Just 210 incidences of transnational hostage taking have generated more than 3000 injuries and fatalities. This is shown in Table 4.2.

Table 4.2. Injuries and Fatalities Per Incident 1968 to 2007

Attack Type	Ratio of Total Injuries and Fatalities to Total Number of Incidences
Armed Attacks	3.69
Arson	0.69
Assassination	1.81
Hostage	14.87
Bombing	6.75
Hijacking	3.74
Kidnapping	0.75
Other	3.44
Unconventional	97.21
Unknown	2.06

When I first started analysing terrorist choice in a context where the immediate payoff or positive-utility-generating aspect of terrorism is the fatalities and injuries inflicted by an attack, a query that was raised concerned the place of hostage taking incidences in such an analytical framework. It seems to me that the perception of terrorism studies researchers is such that they view hostage taking and hijacking as not directed towards the infliction of injuries and fatalities and, perhaps, not usually associated with high levels of human tragedy. These attack methods are not viewed as being overtly violent in the same sense as a bombing attack or armed attack are viewed as violent. On the surface, this particular opinion is easy to understand. However, it is quite plainly the case that these attack methods do generate considerable levels of human tragedy. Whether he has deliberately planned it or not, a terrorist who engages in hostage taking or hijacking *must expect* injuries and fatalities to be the result. Likewise, of course, law enforcement and security agencies must be aware that attack methods that might not be immediately perceived as being associated with high levels of human tragedy may, in the end, generate high levels of injuries and fatalities relative to the number of times such attack methods are deployed. Viewed from this standpoint, hostage taking ranks well above the more overtly violent attack methods of bombing and armed attacks.

What is most interesting from an investigative and law enforcement point of view is that despite the stated objectives or demands of a lone wolf terrorist (or a terrorist group), if the lone wolf terrorist has as an underlying objective the infliction of some level of human tragedy we must be aware that this might not necessarily be achieved solely by the deployment of the more overtly violent attack methods. Furthermore, although on the surface of things a hostage taking incident may appear to be designed to extract concessions from the government rather than inflict fatalities and injuries, hostage taking is in fact a relatively potent generator of human tragedy. Hostage taking cannot be set apart from bombing and armed attacks and the other more overtly violent attack methods. Given this, a lone wolf terrorist may engage in hostage taking precisely because he knows that even if his demands are not met by the government, he will have a chance to inflict a relatively high level of human tragedy and collect the payoffs for doing so. These payoffs may be the injuries and fatalities themselves or payoffs that are a function of these such as media coverage. If this is the case, the political objectives become quite subsidiary to the infliction of injuries and fatalities despite what it may look like on the surface of things. We should, however, not be too side-tracked by such discussions. Historically, lone wolf terrorists have engaged predominantly in armed attacks, bombings and assassinations. In short, attack methods the intended outcomes of which are quite clear.

Another query concerned the attack method 'assassination'. Obviously, the objective of assassination is to inflict human tragedy so in this respect 'assassination' did not raise any concerns in relation to any assumption that the terrorist who deployed it aimed to inflict at least one fatality. Rather, the query concerned the inequality of fatalities. The murder of an 'important person' yields a higher 'payoff' than the murder of an ordinary person, or so the argument went. What is missing from the argument and what took me a long time to figure out, is the unit of measurement of the payoff that is being considered. We are considering, first and foremost, a terrorist who wishes to inflict human tragedy. Human tragedy is his payoff. If he chooses assassination he expects to inflict one or a small number of fatalities whilst bearing a smaller amount of variability or risk. In making the argument that unequal targets (i.e. an important or well-known person versus an ordinary person) result in unequal payoffs we have subtly and perhaps unconsciously changed the unit of measurement of the payoff from human tragedy to some other payoff such as media attention, for example. Since we know that more media attention would indeed flow from the assassination of an important person the admittance of this payoff into the analysis is understandable. Indeed, one reason for focussing on the amount of human tragedy as a payoff is its positive relationship with media attention. If we switch between human tragedy as the payoff and human tragedy as the proxy for the real or underlying payoff, we must be conscious of doing so. A terrorist who embarks upon an assassination attempt expects to inflict a particular amount of human tragedy and bears a particular risk in doing so. The outcomes of assassination are less variable than those of other attack methods but the expected fatalities are much lower. Herein lays the trade-off. A small, but possibly significant, amount of human tragedy obtained with less probability of divergence of actual outcomes from those that were expected versus a larger, and possibly just as significant, amount of human tragedy with more probability of divergence of actual from the expected outcomes. The lone wolf terrorist weighs the risks and rewards and deploys his attack method choice. Once he commences his attack, all that matters to him is the human tragedy that is inflicted and the degree to which it diverges from that which was expected.

In thinking about assassination more carefully, it also becomes clear that it might not always be directed towards 'important' targets. When we make the argument that the payoffs from different fatalities are unequal we are imagining the assassination of a celebrity or leading government figure versus the killing or an ordinary civilian. This is the extreme example and therefore the most irrelevant consideration both analytically and from the viewpoint of the terrorist. Assassination has usually been directed towards targets that are viewed as important by a terrorist or terrorist group rather than targets that have some broader celebrity appeal. This might apply, for example, to the targeted parcel bombings that formed a part of the Unabomber's long campaign of terrorism whose victims included university professors or the several instances of lone wolf terrorism involving the murder or attempted murder of abortion clinic staff. If assassination were only directed towards the upper echelon of celebrity or government officialdom assassination would not be as prominent a part of the historical record of transnational terrorism. Assassination has been responsible for approximately two fatalities per incident and more than 4,000 fatalities and injuries between 1968 and 2007. It is almost certainly the case that these attacks were not all directed towards well-known individuals. Assassination is an attack method that is designed, by definition, to inflict human tragedy. Most formally, assassination is a targeted attack method where the objective is to inflict fatalities subject to the constraint that those fatalities include particular individuals or a single individual. There are no years within the period 1968 to 2007 where the deployment of assassination as an attack method failed to inflict either fatalities or injuries. This may be compared to arson attacks where some years between 1968 and 2007 have been characterised by multiple arson attacks that did not result in any injuries or fatalities. The targeted nature of assassination must not cloud the investigator's assessment of this attack method. A lone wolf terrorist who deploys assassination as an attack method may be targeting a particular level of human tragedy[3] but his goal, nonetheless, is to inflict it.

[3] This level may be one individual.

LONE WOLVES IN AMERICA

The biographies of the lone wolf terrorists are written most clearly in the violence which they have perpetrated and the methods they used to do so. In the end, this is the only biography that matters. The terrorist is defined by the outcomes of his attacks. Researchers have searched for patterns in the psychological-socio-economic backgrounds of terrorists only to find that there are no common threads that run through the lives of every terrorist. There is no archetypal profile. Proceeding backwards from the terrorist event brings decreasing clarity as the terrorist attack itself becomes blended with real or fabricated motivations or justifications and the terrorist's expectation of human tragedy becomes lost within the broader narrative of the circumstances leading up to the attack. Because the motivations, real or alleged or fabricated, of terrorists show no substantive patterns the biographical narrative of the terrorist contributes to a perception of terrorism as a multifaceted (which it is) and intractable (which it is not) problem. Among all of the biographical details of the terrorist that we may list the one that is most easily overlooked but which is at the fore during the time leading up to an attack is his expectation of the outcomes of the attack. This expectation depends to a considerable degree not on a multiplicity of biographical circumstances but on the attack method that has been chosen. The attack method choice shapes the expectations of terrorism. It shapes the outcomes of terrorism. It shapes the degree of divergence between the expectations of terrorism and its outcomes. Where other things are unclear or show no substantive patterns, the biographies written in the violence of the attacks and the methods that were used to perpetrate them are characterised by a statistical structure of risk and reward derived from the history of terrorist incidences that shapes the outcomes of any given attack and which, in turn, is shaped by each attack.

If we look closely at the historical record of American lone wolf terrorism we find a long list of perpetrators and an even longer list of victims stretching back more than five decades. The Instituut voor Veiligheids en Crisismanagement has compiled a chronology of terrorist attacks undertaken by suspected or confirmed lone wolf terrorists. This chronology sticks closely to the definition of lone wolf terrorism and does not include the attacks undertaken by any terrorists suspected of working with an accomplice or a terrorist organisation. For example, the Oklahoma City bombing has primarily been attributed to Timothy McVeigh and he might sometimes be identified as a lone wolf terrorist. He was, however, assisted by at least three accomplices and cannot be defined as a lone wolf terrorist. In the United States, at least 32 lone wolves were active during the period 1940 to 2012. Some have made an indelible impact on the American memory. Others have faded away. The majority—28 out of the 32—of lone wolves inflicted some level of human tragedy. The deadliest was Joseph Paul Franklin. Among the most well-known or infamous is certainly Theodore Kaczynski. Not all of the lone wolf terrorists that have been active in the United States have been American born or American citizens. Between 1940 and 2007, the lone wolves were responsible for 87 fatalities and 322 injuries in the United States. This is considerably more human tragedy than some terrorist groups have managed to inflict. These lone wolf terrorists are listed in Table 4.3. The list is based on that provided by Instituut voor Veiligheids en Crisismanagement (2007). Adjustments have been made to the fatalities and injuries data on the basis of further investigation of news reports and other archival information. Further delineation has been made to the 'attack type' to clearly indicate the level of time-concentration evident in an attack or attacks. It should be noted that reports about events differ and in some cases the facts remain unclear even after extensive review of the publicly available material. As such, fatality and injury counts differ somewhat across different reports. Most of the time, however, the facts are in broad agreement.

Table 4.3. Lone Wolf Terrorism in the United States

Lone Wolf Terrorist	**Attack Method and Time-Concentration**	**Time Period**	**Total Injuries & Fatalities**
George Metesky	Bombing, Serial	1940s to 1960s	15
Byron De La Beckwith	Assassination, Unique	1960s	1
Sirhan Sirhan	Archetype Assassination, Unique	1960s	6
Mark Essex	Armed Attack, Spree	1970s	22
Neal Long	Armed Attack, Serial	1970s	17
Muharem Kurbegovich	Bombing, Serial	1970s	38
Theodore Kaczynski	Bombing, Serial	1970s to 1990s	26
Joseph Paul Franklin	Armed Attack, Serial	1970s	23
Joseph Christopher	Armed Attack, Serial	1980s	12
Frank Spisak Jr. (serial shooting)	Armed Attack, Serial	1980s	5
Walter Leroy Moody Jr.	Bombing, Serial	1980s	2
Mir Aimal Kansi	Armed Attack, Spree	1990s	5
Michael Griffin	Armed Attack, Abortion Clinic Shooting, Unique	1990s	1
Rachelle Shannon	Armed Attack, Abortion Clinic Shooting, Unique	1990s	1
Colin Ferguson	Armed Attack, Spree	1990s	25
Rashid Baz	Armed Attack, Spree	1990s	3
Paul J. Hill	Armed Attack, Abortion Clinic Shooting, Unique	1990s	3
John Salvi	Armed Attack, Abortion Clinic Shooting, Unique	1990s	7
Larry Shoemake	Armed Attack, Spree	1990s	12
Eric Rudolph	Bombing, Serial	1990s	153
Ali Hasan Abu Kamal	Armed Attack, Spree	1990s	8
James C. Kopp	Armed Attack, Abortion Clinic Shooting, Unique	1990s	1
Buford Furrow	Armed Attack, Spree	1990s	6
Ronald Taylor	Armed Attack, Spree	2000s	5
Richard Bauhammers	Armed Attack, Spree	2000s	6
Hesham Mohamed Ali Hadayet	Armed Attack, Spree	2000s	6
Mohammed Reza Taheri-azar	Other, Unique	2000s	9
Naveed Afzal Haq	Armed Attack, Spree	2000s	6
Nidal Malik Hasan	Armed Attack, Spree	2009	56

While the biographies of the lone wolves show no substantive patterns that may be used to construct an archetypal profile of the lone wolf terrorist the lone wolf terrorists may, nonetheless, be categorised according to the biographies of their violent acts and the attack methods they used to perpetrate them. The dominant attack methods deployed by the lone wolves active in the United States have been 'bombing' and 'armed attacks'. Eight of the lone wolves engaged in bombing attacks or purported to have an explosive device. Twenty-two of the lone wolves engaged in armed attacks. These armed attacks were predominantly either targeted shootings somewhat analogous to assassination or shooting sprees. One of the lone wolves engaged in an archetype assassination. This was the assassination of Robert F. Kennedy by Sirhan Sirhan. One of the lone wolves engaged in what must be classified as an 'other' or 'miscellaneous' attack. In 2006, Mohammed Reza Taheri-azar drove a vehicle into a crowd of students at the University of North Carolina injuring 9 people. Despite a small number of exceptions, when we examine the historical record of attack methods utilised by the lone wolf terrorists engaged in terrorism in the United States we find that the most common attack methods among the lone wolf terrorists are also the most common attack methods among the transnational terrorists: bombing and armed attacks. Most lone wolves tend to specialise in one of these two methods. Some lone wolves have combined them.

Lone wolf terrorists have predominantly used 'armed attack' and 'bombing'. These attack method categories encompass attacks that mainly involve the use of firearms (i.e. shootings) and explosive devices. In choosing these two attack method categories, lone wolf terrorists have chosen similarly to transnational terrorist groups. In order to develop more detailed biographies of the violence perpetrated by lone wolf terrorists it might be useful to develop some sub-categories for 'armed attacks' and 'bombings'. Like the RAND-MIPT categories themselves, any sub-categories that we develop will evolve as lone wolf terrorists deploy different variants within these categories or as more information emerges about the crimes of the lone wolf terrorists[4]. Because we will use the payoffs and risks associated with the RAND-MIPT attack method categories 'armed attacks' and 'bombing' as the basis for our analysis of the expected payoffs and risks that confront the lone wolf terrorist our main concern is to further define the 'time concentration' of the lone wolf's attacks. The lone wolf terrorist's attacks may be 'unique' in the sense of being 'single and non-recurring', 'serial' or 'spree'. Both bombings and armed attacks can be unique, serial or spree in nature. Unique, serial or spree bombings and unique, serial or spree armed attacks (usually shootings) encompass a large portion the actions of our list of lone wolf terrorists. A further categorisation based on the 'targeted' or 'non-targeted' nature of the attacks might be useful but the attack methods do tend to meld when such a categorisation is applied. For example, a targeted armed attack or a targeted mail bombing resemble assassination and the expected fatalities and variability of outcomes may be more similar to assassination than to either armed attacks or bombings. Another problem involves defining 'targeted'. In one sense, a shooting spree might be untargeted in the sense that it does not concentrate on particular individuals but it might be targeted in the sense that individuals at that particular location are the targets. When the target location is significant, such as a place of worship, the boundaries between targeted and non-targeted are blurred.

---

[4] It is the case for some of the lone wolf terrorists on our list that the full extent and details of their crimes is still not clear.

With an attack method categorisation of 'armed attack' and 'bombing' and a definition of time concentration of unique, serial and spree we can encompass the actions of most of the lone wolf terrorists on our list. The other RAND-MIPT categories (and our time concentration definition) encompass the remainder. Let us now delve deeper into the biographies of the attacks and attack methods beginning with a subcategory of bombing: serial bombings. We start with George Metesky (The Mad Bomber). In photographs, the bespectacled Metesky appears as the quintessential 1950s gentleman in his brown suit, dark tie and felt hat. As his nom de plume suggests, his attack method of choice was bombing. Middle-aged when his terrorist activities began, he was finally apprehended after an intermittent bombing campaign that lasted more than 17 years, involved more than 30 bombing devices and inflicted 15 injuries, some serious[5]. Although Metesky's stated grievances were directed towards his ex-employer, Consolidated Edison, Metesky would place bombs in public places around New York City and his victims were civilians with no connections to Con Ed. At one stage police described the actions as 'publicity seeking'[6]. The bombs were usually carefully hidden from view such as within upholstered seats at movie theatres which Metesky had slashed open in order to plant his devices. A smiling 55 year-old Metesky appears in black and white photographs following his arrest. Metesky was deemed unfit to stand trial and spent more than a decade in a psychiatric hospital. Interestingly, Metesky was released at age of 70 and lived the remainder of his life without any further engagement in the activities that brought him such notoriety. Metesky did invoke considerable terror during his campaign but his actions were relatively benign when set alongside those of lone wolf terrorist bombers who would emerge in subsequent decades, especially Theodore Kaczynski (The Unabomber).

When FBI agents apprehended Kaczynski at his remote Montana cabin in early 1996, Kaczynski looked every bit a bedraggled woodsman, bearded and dishevelled from leading a solitary existence on the edge of a vast wilderness for two decades. But he was also a one-time assistant professor of mathematics at Berkeley's prestigious department of mathematics and the author of a manifesto that railed against industrial society and, most significantly, the man responsible for more than twenty injuries and three fatalities inflicted during a long bombing campaign that had earned him the name, The Unabomber[7]. This name was given to him by the FBI as an abbreviation of 'University and Airline Bomber', a name that reflects Kaczynski's choice of targets. His bombing campaign began in 1978 and his method delivery was predominantly by mail. Fatalities were inflicted in 1985, 1994 and 1995. The three people killed by these parcel bombs were a computer store owner in California, an advertising executive in New Jersey and a timber industry lobbyist in California. Among the injured, some seriously, were several university professors or other university staff. Kaczynski's most deadly attack could have been the bombing of an American Airlines flight out of Chicago in November 1979. The bomb did not explode but passengers were treated for smoke inhalation. Apart from the attempted airline bombing, Kaczynski's attacks were targeted parcel bombings designed to inflict injury or death upon the parcel's recipient. As a serial bomber whose campaign ebbed and flowed over two decades, Kaczynski's actions represent a primary example of lone wolf serial bombing.

---

5 New York Times, January 23 1957.

6 New York Times, May 7 1953.

7 Details can be found in Gibbs and Allis (1996), Lacayo and Cole (1996), Dubner (1999), Spaaji (2010) and Phillips and Pohl (2012).

In many ways, Kaczynski's actions were those of an individual who was more averse to risk. Each parcel bomb had a low expected fatality or injury count but also a very low variability. The average number of injuries per attack was 0.823 but the standard deviation of the injuries and fatalities inflicted by Kaczynski had a standard deviation of only 0.392. Only three times did Kaczynski's devices fail to inflict physical injury or death. Although Kaczynski is probably the most well-known of the lone wolf terrorist bombers that were active during the 1970s, 1980s and 1990s, there were several others who also inflicted a considerable amount of human tragedy and invoked a degree of terror with equal cunning. Muharem Kurbegovich began his campaign of lone wolf terrorism with a series of arson attacks in late 1973[8]. This was followed by threats of chemical or nerve gas attacks. Kurbegovich communicated his threats of terroristic violence to the press by leaving cassette tapes at the Los Angeles Times and by placing telephone calls to radio stations and newspaper editors. His threats of gas attacks were never realised. However, his use of conventional bombing inflicted multiple casualties. In August 1974, a bomb planted in a locker at Los Angeles International Airport exploded. Three people were killed and many others were injured. A second large explosive was found a few days later in a locker at a Los Angeles bus depot. Just as Kaczynski had placed the initials F.C. for 'Freedom Club' in his bombing devices presumably to give the impression that a group was behind the attacks rather than a lone individual, Kurbegovich claimed to be the chief military officer of 'Aliens of America'. He earned the name 'Alphabet Bomber' because of his threat to plant bombs at locations spelling out the name of his fictional terrorist group. The first bomb was placed at an airport; the second in a locker and so on it would go (see Dickey 2003). Kurbegovich became a suspect when bomb components were linked to him. Kurbegovich was arrested following a period of surveillance by police before further devices could be planted.

It is easy to see how Kurbegovich's actions may be considered to be more risk seeking. He actively communicated with the press. He left cassette tapes in public locations, called newspaper editors and radio stations. Both his arsons and his bombings involved his presence at the scene of the attack. His single effective bombing attack killed three people and seriously injured several others. From the list of lone wolf terrorists, the actions of Walter Leroy Moody and Eric Rudolph also place them in the category of lone wolf terrorist bombers. Moody, like Kaczynski, mailed his bombs to his targets. Like Kaczynski's, Moody's bombs proved to be efficient at inflicting human tragedy. Two bombs were sent and two fatalities resulted. Moody's attacks occurred in late 1989 but he had been convicted in the early 1970s for several years for possessing a bombing device. It was the link between the engineering of the earlier and the later bombing devices that brought the authorities to Moody[9]. A quick arrest was not forthcoming in the Eric Rudolph case. In his mid-thirties when his offences were perpetrated, Rudolph is the youngest of the lone wolf bombers. In photographs, Rudolph appears in public, under police guard, wearing an orange prison-issue jumpsuit and bullet proof vest. He stares intently into the distance. The concentration line between his eyes clearly creased, his brow furrowed, his short-cropped hair and moustache betray nothing of his five years on the run in the mountains of North Carolina. He is the man responsible for the Olympic Park bombing in Atlanta in 1996 and several subsequent bombings of nightclubs and abortion clinics. His attacks inflicted two fatalities (one at the

---

[8] Details can be found in People v. Kurbegovic (1982).

[9] Jenkins (1994).

Olympic Park) and more than 100 injuries (most at the Olympic Park). Unlike Kaczynski, who had shunned modern society, Rudolph fled into the wilderness to escape apprehension. He was apprehended after a chance sighting by an off-duty police officer in 2003[10].

When our American lone wolves have not chosen bombing as their attack method of choice, they have predominantly chosen armed attacks which mostly manifest themselves in the use of firearms to perpetrate either unique, serial or spree shootings. We pay some attention to shooting sprees because, in addition to having characterised the actions of a number of American lone wolf terrorists and in addition to confirming human tragedy as a primary objective of the terrorist, spree shootings also represent an important challenge to law enforcement and security agencies. In fact, one of the earliest examples of a lone wolf spree shooting was directed, in the first instance, at members of law enforcement. It was New Year's Eve 1972 when Mark Essex, a young black militant, inflicted 9 fatalities and 13 injuries in a one week spree of violence in 1973. In a photograph taken a few years earlier, upon his enlistment in the United States Navy, we see Essex's young face and stark white and blue navy uniform and sailor's cap. On New Year's Eve 1972 Essex deliberately targeted police officers in an attack that began at the New Orleans P.D. One officer was killed and one injured in the initial attack. Eight other police officers were killed or wounded in the ensuing spree of violence and police pursuit along with several civilians. Essex was shot and killed by police on January 7 1973, one week after his initial attack.

If we define a spree shooting as a time-concentrated violent incident involving firearms, the actions of Aimal Kansi, Colin Ferguson, Rashid Baz, Larry Shoemake, Ali Hasan Abu Kamal, Buford Furrow, Ronald Taylor, Richard Bauhammers, Hesham Mohammed Ali Hadayet, Naveed Afzal Haq and Nidal Malik Hasan may all be categorised as shooting sprees. The actions of these lone wolves involved shooting attacks directed against people who happened to be present at the time of the attack. In most cases the shootings were over within an hour. Typical of this sort of time-concentrated terroristic violence is Aimal Kasi who sneers darkly from his FBI photograph. In 1993, he used an assault rifle to kill two people and injure three others. The victims were sitting in their vehicles in traffic outside of the CIA building. After the shootings, Kasi fled in his vehicle and then travelled to Pakistan the following day. He remained at large for more than four years before being brought back to the United States. The calculated nature of attacks that leave victims nowhere to hide or flee similarly characterises the shooting spree undertaken that same year by Colin Ferguson. In December 1993, Ferguson boarded a commuter train in New York State and entered a car carrying ninety passengers. He used a 9 millimetre Ruger handgun to shoot them as he walked along the aisle. Before being overpowered by passengers, Ferguson had killed five people and injured eighteen more[11]. The shooting was over in a matter of minutes.

These types of time concentrated armed attacks may be contrasted with the serial shootings undertaken by some of the other lone wolf terrorists on our list. Among the most prominent examples are Neal Long, Joseph Paul Franklin, Joseph Christopher and Frank Spisak Jr. The terrorist activities of these men were not time-concentrated and lasted for many months or several years. It is probably the case that the attacks would have continued if the perpetrators had not been caught. Of those attacks that occurred over months rather than years, Joseph Christopher's series of shootings and stabbings between September 1980 and

[10] Fonda, Cuadros, Fulton, Land, Richards and Sikora (2003).
[11] Gibbs and Blackman (1993).

May 1981 and Frank Spisak's series of shootings in 1982 are good examples. Christopher was known as both the '22 Calibre Killer' and 'The Midtown Slasher'. In some ways, Christopher's attacks were a series of sprees or a spree followed by a series of other incidents. He sometimes had many victims on a single day and several of his murders were concentrated into a three-day period in September 1980. These victims were all shot. The young man, just twenty-five, who appears in a grainy black and white photograph with sleepy eyes arched by prominent eyebrows and an even more prominent mop of cropped wavy hair, then changed his weapon of choice to a knife and his armed attacks became stabbings rather than shootings. The very next year, Frank Spisak Jr, a Hitler idoliser with a similar moustache and prominent prescription glasses, engaged in a series of shootings at Cleveland State University between February and August 1982. He killed three people and injured two others. One of the victims was shot seven times but survived and was able to identify the shooter. Spisak was arrested in September of that year[12].

In at least several of the cases that we have discussed, the terrorist or his legal counsel have sought to demonstrate incapacity to stand trial on grounds of legal insanity. Spisak is among these. His defense offered expert testimony to the effect that Spisak was mentally insane at the time of the killings. Interestingly, though, Spisak himself took the witness stand and delivered testimony over a number of days outlining the rationale for his actions. The testimony regarding his mental insanity was struck from the record and Spisak was sentenced to death. Despite a number of appeals, this sentence was finally carried out in 2011. The sanity of those responsible for violent acts of terrorism is a theme that has emerged often in the psychological literature dealing with terrorist behaviour. Victoroff (2005) provides a comprehensive review. Documented investigations do not find substantial evidence of insanity and it is not surprising that terrorists have usually been declared mentally fit to stand trial and take responsibility for their actions. Although possibly psychopathic, lone wolf terrorists are usually not psychotic and irrational. Examples of careful planning are found in many cases that belie an underlying rationality, warped though it may be. Joseph Paul Franklin changed his assassination target because he thought security around his initial subject rendered success unlikely, Buford Furrow assessed three different Jewish institutions before choosing a community centre because it had the least security[13], Leroy Moody bombed and murdered a black councilman to lead authorities to believe that a white-supremacist group was responsible and, most obvious of all, lone wolf terrorists have chosen weapons designed to inflict human tragedy. Colin Ferguson loaded his gun with Black Talon bullets designed to inflict maximum damage[14]. His victims could not escape their railway car. Escape was not an easy option for Aimal Kasi's victims either. And so on it goes. A series of biographies of violence and the weapons used to perpetrate it and choices taken in order to ensure its effectiveness.

[12] Smith v. Spisak (2009).

[13] Gibney, Dawson, Grace, Jackson, Krantz, Tartakovsky and Thompson (1999).

[14] Gibbs and Blackman (1993).

LONE WOLVES IN EUROPE

Lone wolf terrorists have also been active in Europe. According to the Instituut voor Veiligheids en Crisismanagement (2007), between 1968 and 2007, there were 39 lone wolves active in Europe. Once more we find that armed attacks and bombing are the most commonly chosen attack methods. Nineteen of the forty European lone wolves deployed these attack methods. Unlike the lone wolves active in the United States, the European lone wolves have often chosen hijacking or hostage taking as an attack method. Fourteen of the lone wolves engaged in these activities. The remainder of the European lone wolves were engaged in assassination (2) and arson (4). Interestingly, hijackings are recorded in the 2000s and do not appear to be an obsolete attack method. Since 9/11, hijackings have been associated with aircraft. However, other public vehicles have been targets for hijackers and in Europe lone wolf terrorists have in recent years engaged in the hijacking of buses. In fact, there were two such hijackings within days of each other in Germany in 2003. Both events ended without injury or fatality.

When examining the activities of the European lone wolf terrorists at least one very interesting fact emerges. This is the relative absence of 'serial' lone wolves in Europe. In the United States, at least several lone wolf terrorists were active over an extended period of time much in the same way as a serial murderer is active over time. George Metesky, Theodore Kaczynski, Neal Long and Joseph Paul Franklin remained at large and active for periods of two years or more. Kaczynski remained at large for almost two decades. In Europe, examples of serial lone wolf terrorism are harder to find. The Italian Unabomber and Franz Fuchs are prominent examples of European lone wolves with activity extending beyond a single attack. The 36 other lone wolves associated with terrorist incidences between 1968 and 2007 engaged only in single attacks. This is due in part to their being apprehended, of course, but there is more separating the serial lone wolves from the single attackers than luck in avoiding apprehension. Much will depend on the planning processes and the types of attacks the lone wolves engaged in. This in turn will depend on various factors specific to the lone wolf, including his aversion or taste for risk.

Two examples of spree or time-concentrated violence emerge from the record of European lone wolf terrorism. In 1999 David Copeland embarked on a 13-day bombing spree through London that resulted in three fatalities and 139 injuries. On each of three successive weekends, Copeland placed bombs in public places. The bombs were packed with nails to maximise human tragedy. Copeland was twenty-two when he committed these acts of terrorism but in photographs he appears more drawn than a man of that age should, his eyes dulled with a burden of anger rather than illuminated with intelligence. Like some of the other lone wolf terrorists we have discussed he pled 'diminished responsibility' at trial due to mental illness and like some of the other lone wolf terrorists his plea was rejected by a jury. He was sentenced to at least 50 years in prison. A similar fate awaits the most recent perpetrator of lone wolf 'spree' terrorism, Anders Behring Breivik. In Norway in July 2011 Breivik engaged in a bombing and shooting spree that resulted in the deaths of 77 people. The attacks were undertaken in two parts. First, a car bomb was left outside the government building that housed the offices of the Prime Minister. The bomb was detonated and killed eight people. This is exactly what would be expected from an 'average' bombing attack. Breivik then travelled approximately 40 kilometres to a youth camp where he murdered another 69 people in an hour-long shooting spree. For a terrorist attack that might be categorised as an 'armed assault', 69 fatalities is many standard deviations from the mean number of fatalities historically generated in such attacks[15]. Breivik was arrested and tried. He was found to be sane and responsible for the deaths and injuries he inflicted during his attacks. He was given the maximum sentence under Norwegian law of 21 years but is unlikely to be released.

Concluding Remarks

The biographies of the lone wolf terrorists are written most clearly in the violence which they have perpetrated and the methods they *chose to use* to do so. Although the particular technical aspects of the equipment utilised in individual attacks may differ and although each deployment has its own unique characteristics, the attack methods available to lone wolf terrorists may be categorised under nine headings: armed attacks, arson, assassination, hostage, bombing, hijacking, kidnapping and unconventional with 'other' being reserved for the relatively few attack methods that are not categorised under one of these headings. These attack method categories encompass the attack methods that have been deployed throughout the latter half of the twentieth century and into the twenty-first century by transnational terrorists whose actions are recorded in the RAND-MIPT database. The actions of the transnational terrorist groups have produced a historical record of fatalities and injuries that have been associated with each of the ten attack methods deployed time and time again in terrorist activities. This historical record reveals a preponderance of armed attacks and bombing. These are overtly violent attack methods that have generated a very large number of injuries and fatalities. The historical record also reveals the lethality of less overtly violent attack methods. Most notably, the investigator, law enforcement and the terrorist must expect hostage taking to generate injuries and fatalities. Indeed, relative to number of hostage taking incidences that have been observed historically, hostage taking has proved to be a very potent contributor to the injuries and fatalities associated with transnational terrorism.

The transnational terrorism database records the injuries and fatalities for each type of attack method. This provides us with a statistical foundation for a determination of the injuries and fatalities that investigators can expect from the deployment of particular attack methods and a statistical foundation for what investigators can expect terrorists to expect. The expectations of lone wolf terrorists regarding the injuries and fatalities that may result from the deployment of a particular attack method almost certainly are formed from publicly available information regarding injuries and fatalities and other relevant details of particular attacks. This does not mean that the lone wolf will take all information into account. Information is scarce and imperfectly communicated. The lone wolf may falter in his calculations. On this point, the investigators might have the advantage of possessing better or more sophisticated knowledge of the injuries and fatalities likely to be generated by particular attack methods or combinations of attack methods. This informational advantage has potential

---

[15] What might be required is some estimate of an expected number of injuries and fatalities from shooting sprees in confined locations, such as schools, campuses or youth camps. The injuries and fatalities inflicted by lone shooters (though not necessarily lone wolf terrorists) have sometimes been very substantial. The mean and standard deviation of the injuries and fatalities inflicted by such specialised armed attacks may represent the statistical foundation for a new attack method category.

utility because the lone wolf terrorist cannot escape the statistical framework that characterises the injuries and fatalities generated by particular attack methods.

Lone wolf terrorists do not engage in completely unique categories of attack methods. The most commonly deployed attack methods among the transnational terrorists are armed attacks and bombing. Likewise, among the lone wolves active in the United States and Europe armed attacks and bombings are the most commonly deployed terrorist attack method. Although a particular lone wolf may generate injuries and fatalities that lay many standard deviations from the mean or expected level during any given attack, the two moments of the distribution (mean and standard deviation) of fatalities and injuries generated by particular attack methods provide a statistical foundation for an analysis of attack method choice. Overtly violent attack methods figure prominently in the historical record of attacks but law enforcement must not overlook the lethality of less overtly violent attack methods such as hostage taking and the lethal efficiency of assassination, which rarely fails to produce human tragedy. The pre-emption or prevention of the utilisation of these attack methods by lone wolves is an important objective. Failing this, finding and apprehending the lone wolf before further infliction of human tragedy the next most important objective. Encompassing the lone wolf's choices of attack methods within an economic analytical framework is our contribution to the achievement of these objectives. A first step is to realise that the lone wolf must choose from a set of categories of attack methods that has remained relatively stable over time and that in doing so he will expect particular outcomes on average from a deployment of any given attack method or combination of attack methods.

Chapter 5

THE CORRELATION STRUCTURE

One of the most important parts of the 'statistical structure', if we may call it that, of the injuries and fatalities that are inflicted by the different attack method categories is the correlation structure. The reason why the correlation structure is important is because it shapes the risk-reward payoff available to different attack methods and *combinations* of attack methods. The correlation structure, in short, is responsible for the fact that diversification or combination—the use of more than one attack method across attacks—increases the terrorist's payoffs at every level of risk. If we did not take the correlation into account we would underestimate the expected payoffs to terrorism. The correlation structure reveals the extent to which the injuries and fatalities generated by different attack methods move up and down together over time. The correlation structure is a component of the statistical structure of terrorist attack methods and combinations of attack methods. More importantly, the correlation structure reveals the extent of the gains from diversification that may be exploited by the lone wolf terrorist and the properties of the risk-reward relationship that characterises combinations of attack methods. When attack methods are imperfectly correlated, the risk-reward relationship that characterises combinations of attack methods exhibits important properties of which law enforcement and security agencies must be aware.

It is the economic model of choice called the 'mean-variance expected utility analysis' that leads us to consider the correlation structure that characterises the different attack methods. Like all economic models of choice, mean-variance utility analysis asks first what the opportunity set looks like and second what the optimal choice or choices from that set would be. If we portray an individual as choosing from among risky opportunities—the RAND-MIPT attack methods—on the basis of mean and variance and if those risky opportunities involve combinations of different opportunities—that combinations of the different attack methods—then we are forced to ask what the complete opportunity set will look like or, what amounts to the same thing, what shape the opportunity set all of the possible 'pairs' of mean and variance formed from all the possible combinations of attack methods will be. In order to figure out the variance of a combination of attack methods, however, it is necessary to take into consideration the correlation and covariance between the payoffs of each of the attack methods within a given combination. It is by this pathway that we are led to consider the correlation structure and it is with a great deal of appreciation for the economic-statistical logic that underlies the mean-variance approach developed by Markowitz and Tobin that we find the correlation structure of the injuries and fatalities associated with different attack methods and attack method combinations to be such as to produce the concave set of opportunities familiar to all those who have studied Markowitz's pioneering work on portfolio theory. This set of opportunities is characterised by gains to combination or, equivalently, higher payoffs at each level of risk. These payoffs emerge from combinations of imperfectly correlated attack methods and if law enforcement were to remain unaware of the relevance of the correlation structure it would consistently underestimate the payoffs expected to be obtained from terrorist activity.

The correlation structure becomes a factor when terrorists can combine attack methods within a single period or across periods. The terrorist group can do both and may even use two different attack methods simultaneously. A lone wolf terrorist operating on his own will find it more difficult to combine attack methods within a single period and, without the use of some technical device such as a 'timer', will probably find it impossible to deploy two or more attack methods simultaneously. He can, however, combine attack methods over time and the evolution or innovations that characterise his approach to terrorism may naturally involve this. What must not be overlooked is that law enforcement and the government's security agencies might view 'lone wolf terrorism' as a phenomenon in a holistic sense and detached from the independent lone wolf terrorists who contribute to it. In this case, lone wolf terrorism becomes a set of attack methods deployed by independent individuals but the outcomes of which represent the results of a category of terrorism. The outcomes of this category of terrorism, 'lone wolf terrorism', depend on the statistical structure of the injuries and fatalities that characterise the individual attack methods and the combinations of them that emerge, not perhaps deployed by one single lone wolf, but by the aggregate of lone wolf terrorists. If one lone wolf uses one type of attack method and another lone wolf uses another type, the expected injuries and fatalities at each level of variability will be higher in aggregate than we would be led to expect if each attack method was examined in isolation without reference to the correlation structure.

The Case of Perfect Correlation

Each individual attack method has a risk and a reward. The risks and rewards for each individual attack method are summarised in our table of means (payoffs) and standard deviations (variability or risk). The terrorist, in choosing from among the attack methods, must trade off risk against reward. Using RAND-MIPT data for 1968 to 2007, Table 5.1 presents the average or expected outcomes and the standard deviation or 'risk' that the actual outcome will diverge from that which was expected.

If the lone wolf terrorist can combine attack methods, each combination of attack methods exhibits its own risk and reward and the risk-reward trade-off characterising the entire set of opportunities (both single attack methods and combinations of attack methods) evolves into a more complex statistical structure. The nature of the risk-reward trade-off that emerges when combinations of attack methods may be formed depends on the correlation structure of the payoffs generated by each individual attack method that is included in each combination.

Table 5.1. Average Outcomes and Risk: RAND-MIPT Attack Method Categories 1968 to 2007

Attack Type	Average Fatalities and Injuries Per Attack Per Year	Standard Deviation
Armed Attacks	5.32	15.00
Arson	0.72	1.85
Assassination	1.54	0.71
Hostage	11.46	38.18
Bombing	5.88	6.09
Hijacking	3.91	10.82
Kidnapping	0.46	0.35
Other	1.14	3.02
Unconventional	7.48	42.94
Unknown	1.11	4.04

To see how the correlation structure influences the nature of the risk-reward trade-off that emerges when the terrorist can form combinations of different attack methods, let us explore the special case of perfect correlation between two individual attack methods. If the payoffs to individual attack methods are perfectly correlated and if these individual attack methods are combined into a combination of attack methods, the risk-reward trade-off will be a positively sloped straight line in risk-reward space (for a combination of any two perfectly correlated attack methods) or a positively inclined plane (for a combination of any three perfectly correlated attack methods) or a positively inclined hyper-plane (for a combination of more than three perfectly correlated attack methods). If, for example, the payoffs to bombing and arson were perfectly correlated, the risk-reward relationship for any combination of these two attack methods would be depicted by the straight line in payoff-risk space in Figure 5.1.

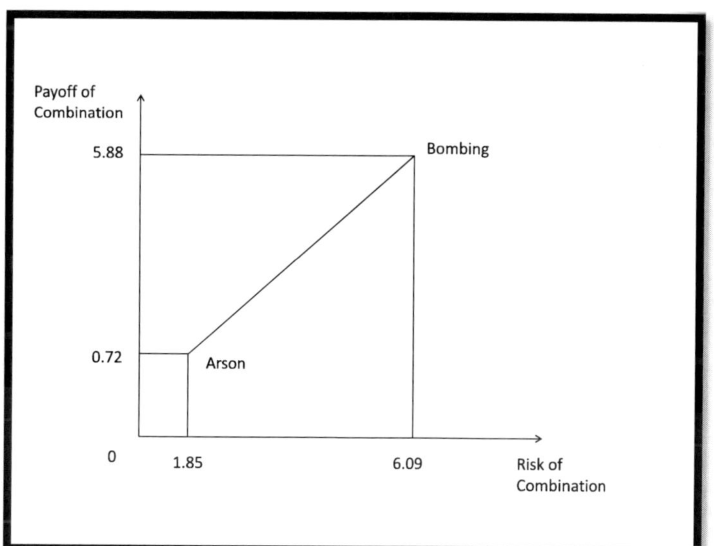

Figure 5.1. The Trade-Off Between Risk and Reward: Perfect Correlation.

Under such circumstances, the lone wolf terrorist could combine arson with bombing attacks by allocating some of his resources to each attack method. The payoff and risk associated with any such combination of perfectly correlated attack methods would lie on the straight line connecting the two single attacks. Depending on how much risk the lone wolf terrorist was willing to bear, a combination of arson and bombing could be used to generate the required amount of risk and reward. With perfect positive correlation each increment in the expected payoff of the combination of arson and bombing is associated with an exactly proportional increase in the risk of the attack method combination. The lone wolf cannot obtain a more favourable risk-reward trade-off by combining two (or more) perfectly positively correlated attack methods. With perfect positive correlation, the risk of an attack method combination is simply the weighted average of the risk of the attack methods included in the combination. There are no advantages to combining arson and bombing if the expected payoffs of the two attack methods are perfectly positively correlated.

From a law enforcement point of view, perfect positive correlation between the payoffs to different terrorist attack methods represents an ideal case. The terrorist group or lone wolf terrorist facing a situation where the payoffs to all attack methods are perfectly correlated confronts a situation where there are no advantages in terms of increased payoff and lower risk to combining different attack methods. With a zero allocation to bombing, the lone wolf generates an expected payoff of 0.72 fatalities and injuries with a risk of 1.85. If the allocation to bombing is increased to 50 percent, the lone wolf generates an expected payoff of 3.30 with a risk of 3.97. If the allocation is increased again to 60 percent, the lone wolf generates an expected payoff of 3.81 with a risk of 4.39 and so on. Each increment in the resource allocated to bombing yields a linearly proportional increment in the risk of the attack method combination. The terrorist group or the lone wolf terrorist cannot reduce the chances of a poor outcome by allocating resources to different attack methods when the payoffs to those attack methods are perfectly correlated. From an investigative perspective, such a situation is ideal because an important risk reduction mechanism is not available to the terrorist. Unfortunately, the payoffs to attack methods are not perfectly positively correlated.

The Consequences of Imperfect Correlation

As the correlations between the payoffs to different attack methods become less than perfect, the risk-reward relationship that characterises attack method combinations of now imperfectly correlated attack methods undergoes important changes. Specifically, the risk-reward relationship begins to exhibit concavity. If the payoffs to individual attack methods are imperfectly correlated and if these individual attack methods are combined into a combination of attack methods, the risk-reward trade-off will be a positively sloped concave line in risk-reward space (for a combination of any two imperfectly correlated attack methods) or a positively inclined concave plane (for a combination of any three imperfectly correlated attack methods) or a positively inclined concave hyper-plane (for a combination of more than three imperfectly correlated attack methods). If, for example, the payoffs to bombing and arson are imperfectly correlated, the risk-reward trade-off or relationship for any combination of these two attack methods would be depicted by the concave line in payoff-risk space in Figure 5.2.

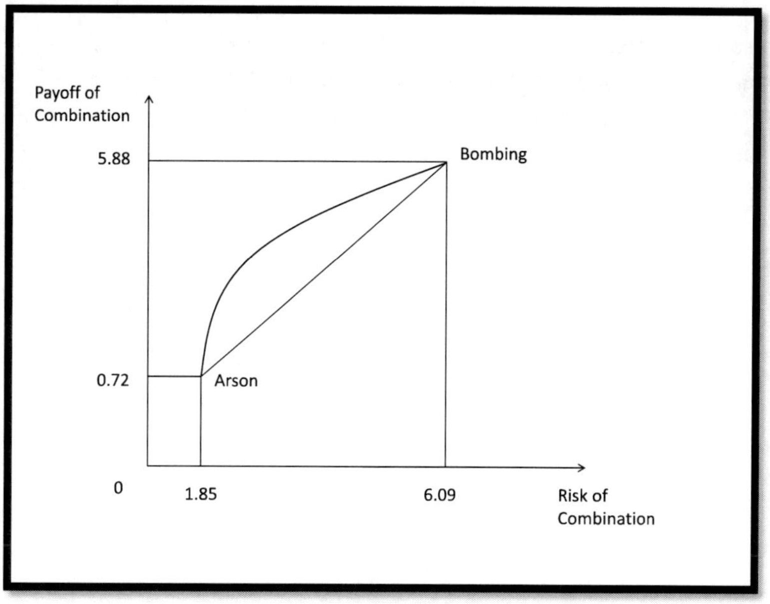

Figure 5.2. The Trade-Off Between Risk and Reward: Imperfect Correlation.

Under such circumstances, the lone wolf terrorist could advantageously combine arson with bombing attacks by allocating some of his resources to each attack method. The payoff and risk associated with any such combination of imperfectly correlated attack methods would lie on the concave line connecting the two single attacks. Depending on how much risk the lone wolf is willing to bear, a combination of arson and bombing could be used to generate the required amount of risk and reward. With imperfect correlation, the lone wolf can obtain a more favourable risk-reward trade-off by combining two (or more) imperfectly correlated attack methods. With imperfect correlation, the risk of an attack method combination is not simply the weighted average of the risk of the attack methods included in the combination. There are advantages to combining arson and bombing if the expected payoffs of the two attack methods are imperfectly correlated. This is demonstrated by the fact that the concave line lies above the straight line connecting the two attack methods under conditions of perfect correlation. Higher expected payoffs are obtainable at each given level of risk when imperfectly correlated attack methods can be combined.

The gains in expected payoffs at each given level risk that are obtainable by combining imperfectly correlated attack methods are embedded within the statistical structure of the expected payoffs and risks that characterise each attack method. That is, concavity is a property of the combination of imperfectly correlated attack methods. It is not an outcome that is restricted to the examples or attack methods that we have chosen to discuss. From the investigative point of view, understanding this component of the statistical structure of attack method combinations is fundamentally important. A terrorist group or lone wolf terrorist may choose to combine attack methods. When the payoffs that are expected to be generated by the chosen attack methods are imperfectly correlated, the terrorist can exploit imperfect correlations within the correlation structure to obtain higher expected payoffs without increases risk. From an investigative and law enforcement perspective, the expected payoffs that are available to the lone wolf would be underestimated by a failure to consider the implications of a choice by the terrorist to combine two or more attack methods where the payoffs to those attack methods are characterised imperfect correlation. The concavity of the risk-reward relationship under conditions of imperfectly correlated payoffs is an important component of the statistical structure of the payoffs and risks associated with terrorist attack methods.

Impossible Risk-Reward Trade-Off Relationships

From some perspectives, terrorism appears to be a completely random and unstructured activity that is analytically intractable. This is far from the case. There is a statistical structure that underlies the payoffs and variability associated with the outcomes of particular attack methods and attack method combinations. The choices of the lone wolf terrorist are undertaken within this structure. As such, components of the statistical structure of the payoffs and variability of attack methods are important guide-posts that allow the economic investigator to rule in and rule out particular attack method choice possibilities. When the payoffs to attack methods are perfectly correlated, the risk-reward trade-off or relationship that characterises combinations of those perfectly correlated attack methods is linear. A linear risk-reward trade-off rules out 'gains from combination' in the form of increased expected payoffs at each given level of risk or, equivalently, decreases in variability at each level of payoff. When the payoffs to attack methods are imperfectly correlated, the risk-reward relationship is concave and 'gains from combination' are possible.

Within the ideal case of perfectly positively correlated payoffs, the risk-reward relationship that characterises combinations of attack methods is linear. Within the more realistic case of imperfectly correlated payoffs, the risk-reward relationship that characterises combinations of attack methods is concave in payoff-risk space. The same analysis that allows us to 'rule in' these two possibilities (though perfect correlation will probably not be observed empirically) allows us to rule out a convex risk-reward relationship for combinations of attack methods. This allows us to rule out particular levels of risk that may be borne by the lone wolf terrorist. Combinations of perfectly positively correlated attack methods lie on the straight line (or plane or hyper-plane) that connects the attack methods. With imperfect correlation, higher levels of expected payoff can be obtained for each given level of risk and the risk-reward relationship exhibits concavity. The lone wolf terrorist cannot combine attack methods in such a way that he bears more risk than that which is found to characterise combinations of perfectly positively correlated attack methods. The risk-reward relationship must be a straight line or a concave line and can never be characterised by a convex line (or plane or hyper-plane) in payoff-risk space. The risk-reward trade-off depicted in Figure 5.3 is not possible.

The lone wolf terrorist cannot construct a combination of attack methods that is characterised by a higher level of risk than that which characterises combinations that lie on the straight line connecting the two attack methods. A convex risk-reward relationship is not possible. In payoff-risk space, therefore, the lone wolf cannot drift into a space that is characterised by a convex relationship. Rather, he is confined to a risk-reward relationship that is concave or, under the special circumstances of perfect positive correlation, linear. From the investigator's point of view, the risk that is borne by the lone wolf is restricted by this linear boundary. Without an understanding of the correlation structure of the payoffs to different attack methods it might be possible for law enforcement and security agencies to overestimate the risk that is borne by the lone wolf. Hand in hand with such a miscalculation of risk would be a miscalculation of the expected payoffs that may be generated by the lone wolf's terrorist activities. The lone wolf chooses attack methods or combinations of attack methods. Such combinations are characterised by a particular risk-reward relationship. This relationship cannot exhibit the property of being convex.

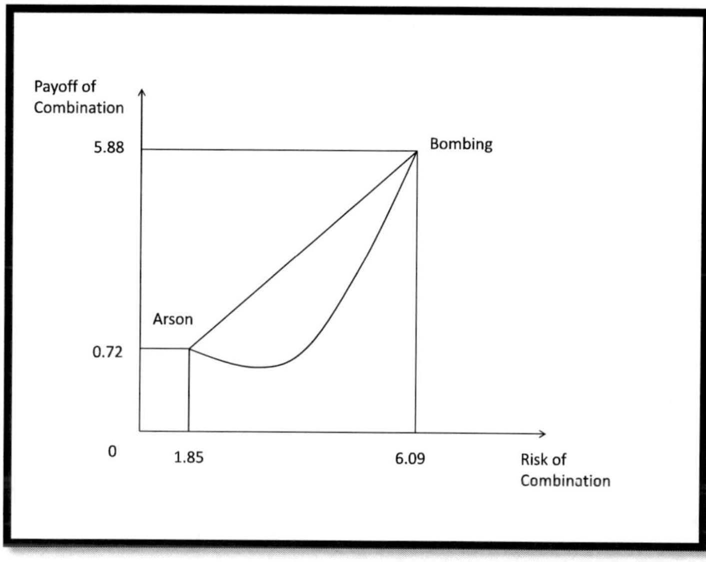

Figure 5.3. Impossible 'Convex' Trade-Off Between Risk and Reward.

THE HISTORICAL CORRELATION STRUCTURE OF ATTACK METHODS

For the transnational terrorism data contained within the RAND-MIPT database for the period 1968 to 2007, the correlation structure of injuries and fatalities generated by different attack methods reveals a set of less than perfectly positively correlated attack methods. The correlation coefficients, ρ, for each pair of attack methods are shown in the correlation matrix. The relevance of the correlation structure to the analysis of terrorism was highlighted by Phillips (2009 and 2011).

It is easy to see that the correlations between the injuries and fatalities generated by particular attack methods are less than perfectly positive and, in many cases, are negative. The correlations should be interpreted as the degree to which the fatalities and injuries per attack per year move together over time. A perfectly positive correlation, $\rho = 1$, between any two (or more) attack methods would mean that we would observe a perfectly proportional increase (or decrease) in the fatalities and injuries generated per attack by one attack method (say, bombing) when there was an increase (or decrease) in the fatalities and injuries generated per attack by another attack method (say, arson). Perfect positive correlations are not observed to constitute a part of the correlation structure. The correlation structure is constituted by less than perfectly positively correlated payoffs and less than perfectly negatively correlated payoffs. This rules out the possibility, empirically, of a linear risk-reward relationship for any attack method combination constructed by the lone wolf.

Less than perfectly positive correlations, $0 \leq \rho < 1$, constitute a large part of the correlation structure. Such correlations indicate that an increase (or decrease) in the fatalities and injuries generated per attack by one attack method (say, hijacking) is associated with a less than proportional increase (or decrease) in the fatalities and injuries generated per attack by another attack method (say, bombing). Less than perfectly negative correlations, $-1 < \rho < 0$, also constitute a large part of the correlation structure. Such correlations indicate that an increase (or decrease) in the fatalities and injuries generated per attack by one attack method (say, unconventional attacks) is associated with a less than proportional decrease (or increase) in the fatalities and injuries generated per attack by another attack method (say, armed attacks). The empirically observed correlation structure implies that the risk-reward relationship of any combination of attack methods constructed by the lone wolf will be characterised by concavity in payoff-risk space.

The risk-reward trade-off available to the lone wolf terrorist is a bounded set. Given the information revealed in the correlation structure, the boundaries can be defined. For any pair of attack methods this can be represented geometrically in two-dimensional payoff-risk space. Consider arson and bombing once more. As we have ascertained earlier, if these two attack methods were perfectly positively correlated, the risk-reward relationship would be a straight line in payoff-risk space. If these two attack methods were perfectly negatively correlated, $\rho = -1$, the risk-reward relationship would be two straight lines in payoff-risk space—A, C and C, B in Figure 5.4. These lines, together with the line A, B, represent the boundaries of the risk-reward relationship. If arson and bombing were perfectly negatively correlated it would be possible to construct a combination with zero risk (standard deviation) by allocating approximately 23 percent of resources to bombing and 77 percent to arson. This demonstrates by an extreme case the fact that combinations of less than perfectly positively correlated attack methods can generate a combination with lower risk than any of the individual attack methods contained within the combination. Because the empirically observed correlation between bombing and arson is 0.683, the risk-reward relationship of combinations of arson and bombing will exhibit concavity in payoff-risk space.

All of the empirically observed correlations in the attack methods correlation structure are imperfect. No two attack methods are characterised by perfectly negative or perfectly positive correlation. For any two pairs of attack methods, a combination of attack methods constructed by the lone wolf terrorist will exhibit a concave risk-reward relationship. This will also be the case for combinations of more than two attack methods. A combination of any two (or more) attack methods that has zero risk (standard deviation) will not be attainable by the lone wolf. All of the straight line boundaries of the risk-reward relationship are ruled out by the empirically observed correlation structure between attack methods. The lone wolf terrorist is encompassed within the statistical structure of the payoffs and risks of the available attack methods. Furthermore, the lone wolf's choices must see him drift towards the boundary of the concave risk-reward relationship. This is where the expected payoffs to attack method combinations are highest for each level of risk.

Table 5.2. The Correlation Structure of the RAND-MIPT Attack Method Categories: 1968 to 2007

	Armed Attacks	Arson	Assassination	Hostage	Bombing	Hijacking	Kidnapping	Other	Unconventional	Unknown
Armed Attacks	1									
Arson	0.222	1								
Assassination	-0.050	0.025	1							
Hostage	-0.042	0.224	0.035	1						
Bombing	0.162	0.683	0.089	0.092	1					
Hijacking	-0.064	0.291	-0.117	-0.090	0.22	1				
Kidnapping	0.116	0.096	0.475	0.185	0.12	-0.14	1			
Other	-0.070	-0.033	0.156	0.105	-0.05	-0.09	0.207	1		
Unconventional	-0.021	-0.052	0.059	-0.048	-0.04	-0.05	0.177	0.470	1	
Unknown	-0.066	-0.082	0.047	0.003	-0.10	-0.06	-0.018	0.050	0.102	1

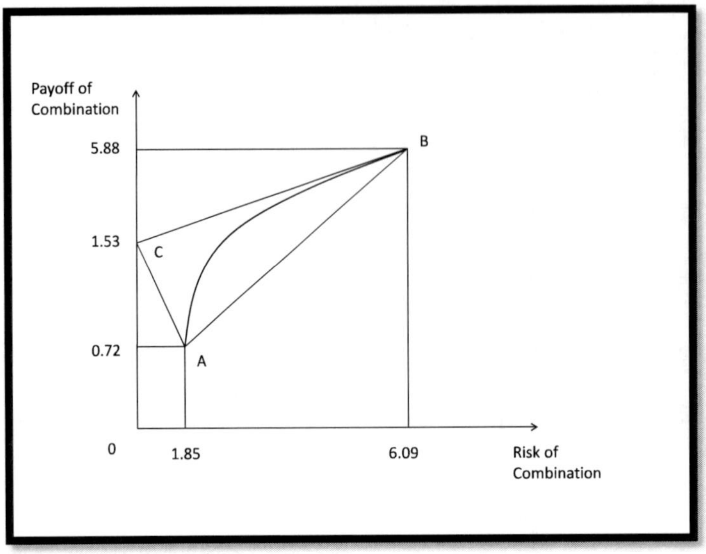

Figure 5.4. The Case of Perfect Positive or Negative Correlation.

Correlation Structure and Law Enforcement

The correlation structure is an important component of the statistical structure of lone wolf terrorism. As we have seen, it allows the investigator to rule in and rule out particular risk-reward relationships for attack method combinations and it reveals the possible investigative miscalculations that may result from failing to consider the correlation structure when analysing the lone wolf's choices. There is further reason to regard the correlation structure of the payoffs to attack methods as being more than a statistical artefact. The correlation structure must reflect particular empirical events such as decisions by terrorists, innovations in attack method technology and law enforcement efforts directed at curtailing particular methods. If law enforcement efforts are directed towards a particular attack method, effective law enforcement efforts may reduce the fatalities and injuries generated per attack whilst, simultaneously, terrorists reallocate resources to other attack methods where there are lower levels of law enforcement. Such events will affect the correlation structure over time. This is a richer way of describing the deterrence and substitution effects derived by traditional analysis. The analytical framework we are describing encompasses and adds a dynamic element to the conclusions of traditional economic analysis of terrorism.

The correlation structure is a set of empirical observations and it should be affected by and reflect empirical or historical events. The correlation structure will not be stable across time periods or sub-periods and will gradually change over time. The correlations between any two attack methods may be different in one time period than in another. This reflects the innovations in attack methods technology, law enforcement and terrorist choice. It is a dynamic structure. Information about the correlation structure will be embedded within news and media reports or communicated in other ways. The lone wolf's choices take place within this dynamic environment and evolve dynamically in response to relevant aspects of the environment. That aircraft security was significantly enhanced following the 9/11 terrorist attacks is not a piece of privately held information. A lone wolf terrorist may still take the risk of engaging in an aircraft hijacking. However, we could reasonably expect him to recognise the higher level of risk compared to other possible attack methods. The correlation structure is a relevant piece of investigative information that represents one piece of the analytical framework within which we are encompassing the lone wolf terrorist.

Concluding Remarks

The correlation structure of attack methods tells us how the fatalities and injuries generated by attack methods move up and down together. Rather than being a statistical artefact, however, the correlation structure is an important piece of investigative information and an important component of the analytical framework within which we are encompassing the lone wolf terrorist. The correlation structure allows us to rule in and rule out particular risk-reward trade-offs or relationships for the possible ways in which the lone wolf terrorist may combine attack methods. When correlations are not perfectly positive or perfectly negative, the risk-reward relationship between any combinations of attack methods must be concave in payoff-risk space. This concavity implies that the lone wolf terrorist may benefit by combining attack methods. He may obtain higher payoffs without increased risk or lower risk for same payoffs. These 'gains from combination' must be considered by law enforcement and security agencies if they are to avoid underestimating the lone wolf's payoffs or overestimating the risk that he bears. When it is possible for him to do so we may expect the lone wolf to attempt to obtain the 'gains from combination'. He need not be particularly calculating to make this attempt. He needs only to believe like many other people engaged in many other activities that putting all his eggs in one basket is unwise. It should be noted, however, that within a single time period and the shorter that time period is, a lone wolf terrorist will experience more difficulty in combining different attack methods than will a terrorist group that can potentially send different operatives with different attack methods to different locations simultaneously. Hence, we may expect the lone wolf terrorist to experience more difficulty in obtaining gains from combination than a terrorist group.

If the lone wolf terrorist is to engage in violent terrorism he must choose an attack method from one of the available attack method categories. He must choose armed attacks, arson, assassination, bombing, hostage taking, hijacking, kidnapping or unconventional attacks. In doing so, he must confront a trade-off between risk and reward. Additional expected payoffs, additional human tragedy, is obtained by bearing additional risk. The more risk the lone wolf bears, the more chance there is that the actual outcomes of his violent terrorist attacks will diverge from those outcomes that he expected. There is no way out of this statistical structure. Each attack method exhibits expected payoff and risk. But there are aspects of the statistical structure that might be exploited by the lone wolf. Following nothing more complicated than an inclination to observe a simple maxim—eggs should be kept in separate baskets—the lone wolf may extract 'gains from combination'. When attack methods may be combined an important component of the statistical structure is brought into play. The expected payoffs of the various attack methods are not perfectly positively correlated. Additional expected payoffs may be obtained without additional risk by combining attack methods. Fortunately, we are aware of this and we are also aware that despite this embedded advantage, the lone wolf terrorist's opportunities are bounded on all sides of the concave set.

Chapter 6

THE LONE WOLF'S OPPORTUNITY SET AND CHOICES: THEORY

The lone wolf terrorist's opportunities to inflict human tragedy must emerge out of the attack method categories that are available to him. These attack methods do not present the opportunity to inflict a completely random and independently distributed amount of human tragedy. Each attack method has an average (mean) or expected number of injuries and fatalities that the lone wolf terrorist may expect to inflict and each attack method is attended by the risk that the injuries and fatalities that are actually inflicted may diverge from the lone wolf's expectations. The outcomes of attack methods are variable. An attack method is an opportunity to inflict an expected amount of human tragedy while bearing the risk that the actual outcome will be different from that which was expected. When the lone wolf terrorist can combine attack methods within a time period or across time periods his opportunities are broadened to include the mean-variance or reward-risk 'pairs' of all of the permissible combinations of attack methods. Furthermore, the opportunity set reflects the increments in expected payoffs at each level of risk that accompany the combination of attack methods whose payoffs are not perfectly correlated. That is, the property of 'concavity' and the resulting 'gains from combination'.

The lone wolf terrorist's opportunity set is important because he is bound by it and within it. It is the set of all the possible attack methods and attack method combinations from which the lone wolf terrorist can choose. We know that this should be a concave set that reflects both the trade-off between risk and reward and the correlation structure that characterises the expected payoffs to each attack method. This statistical structure is what makes the economic theoretical framework feasible. What we need to do is derive the opportunity set theoretically so that we have the complete statistical structure and a logical economic structure with which to encompass the opportunities and choices of the lone wolf terrorist. The lone wolf makes choices under risk and uncertainty. If the lone wolf makes these choices on the basis of the two moments of the distribution of fatalities and injuries generated by the attack methods, mean and variance, then he orders his preferences and makes his choices on the basis of mean and variance, reward and risk. The complete opportunity set is therefore the set of mean-variance 'pairs' that can be generated from the available attack methods and the various ways of combining those attack methods. If the lone wolf can combine attack methods, then the complete opportunity set will be formed from the means and variances of the individual attack methods and the means and variances of the multiplicity of possible combinations of attack methods.

In economic science, the principles and theoretical framework for the mean-variance analysis of the opportunity set were worked out by Markowitz (1952). Markowitz recognised that choice will not simply be made on the basis of the greatest expected payoff. Not only would this imply that the individual would choose without regard to risk but it also implies that there is never a combination of attack methods that is preferred to a single attack method. This would rule out diversification or combination as a strategy with which to increase expected payoffs and decrease risk. Markowitz argues correctly that diversification is both observed and sensible. In the context of terrorism, this is also the case. Terrorist groups do not restrict themselves to particular attack methods but may combine attack methods over time (or simultaneously). Although the (simultaneous) combination or diversification options for the lone wolf terrorist are more restricted due to his individual nature, we must not ignore the possibility that the lone wolf terrorist may decide to combine attack methods over time (including very short periods of time). This does not require any sophisticated calculation on the part of the terrorist nor does it require any special insight on his part to recognise combination as a 'strategy'. Rather, it is simply the old maxim advising against putting all eggs in one basket manifesting itself in the choices that are made. The fact that this can be treated formally within a mean-variance analytical framework simply means that we can encompass this possible choice-making heuristic that individuals may be expected to use in making their decisions. The opportunity set that includes or allows for combinations of attack methods is broader than that which would prevail if terrorists were only able to choose a single attack method.

The Complete Opportunity Set: Single Attack Methods and Combinations

With a single attack method, the calculation of mean (expected payoff) and variance (risk) is a straightforward matter. When attack methods can be combined, it is necessary to consider the expected payoffs and risks of combinations of attack methods when they can be combined in various proportions. For example, it is possible to combine armed attacks, bombings and hostage-taking in different proportions. One such combination may be characterised by 50 percent of resources allocated to armed attacks, 25 percent allocated to bombings and 25 percent allocated to hostage-taking. Another such combination may be characterised by 90 percent of resources allocated to armed attacks, 7 percent allocated to bombings and 3 percent allocated to hostage-taking. There is a multiplicity of such combinations and each will have a different expected payoff and risk. The terrorist may not only choose among attack methods on the basis of expected payoff and risk but among combinations of attack methods. All such combinations constitute the complete opportunity set of attack methods from which the terrorist can choose.

Phillips (2009) explains the computation of the terrorist's opportunity set. The computation of the expected payoff or mean for a particular combination of attack methods is relatively straightforward. The expected payoff of a combination of attack methods is the weighted average payoff of the payoffs of each individual attack method that is contained within the combination. If the mean or expected payoff of a particular attack method, *i*, is given by x_i and the proportion or weight of each attack method within the combination—in the first example above, the proportions or weights are 0.50, 0.25 and 0.25—is given by w_i, then the mean or expected payoff from a combination, *C*, of attack methods is given by:

$$E(R_C) = \sum_{i=1}^{n} x_i w_i$$

Although the expected payoff of any combination of attack methods is relatively easy to compute, the calculation of the variance or risk for a combination of attack methods is less straightforward. When attack methods are combined, the variances of each attack method interact and the variance of the combination is not simply the weighted average of the variances of each individual attack method contained within the combination. The variances of attack methods when combined together may reinforce or dampen each other. For this reason, it is necessary to consider not only the variances of each individual attack method but also the covariance or correlation structure between each possible pair of attack methods. We know that the fatalities and injuries generated by the different attack methods exhibit less than perfect correlation. As a result, the combination of attack methods has the potential to increase the expected payoffs and decrease the risk of a terrorist operation. That is, in a world where terrorists can combine attack methods, the expected fatalities inflicted by terrorism are higher at each level of variability than would be the case if terrorists could not combine attack methods. This is the gain from the deployment of diversification or combination of attack methods as a strategy. Reflecting the importance of covariance, the risk or variance of a combination of attack methods is given by:

$$\sigma_C^2 = \sum_{i=1}^{n} \sum_{j=1}^{n} w_i w_j \rho_{ij} \sigma_i \sigma_j$$

$$= \sum_{i=1}^{n} w_i^2 \sigma_i^2 + \sum_{\substack{i=1 \\ i \neq j}}^{n} \sum_{j=1}^{n} w_i w_j \rho_{ij} \sigma_i \sigma_j$$

In this formula, ρ_{ij} is the correlation coefficient that expresses the degree of correlation between attack method *i* and attack method *j*. It should also be noted that $\rho_{ij}\sigma_i\sigma_j$ is equal to the covariance between attack methods *i* and *j* (σ_{ij}). The double summation sign simply implies that all possible pairs of attack methods must be accounted for in the calculation. Once the computation for all possible combinations of attack methods has been undertaken, the complete opportunity set for the lone wolf terrorist emerges. When each of the mean-variance 'pairs' for each of the attack methods is plotted in expected payoff-risk space, the expected structure emerges. There is a positive relationship between risk and reward and there are no 'convex' sections within the opportunity set. The opportunity set is a concave set as depicted in Figure 6.1.

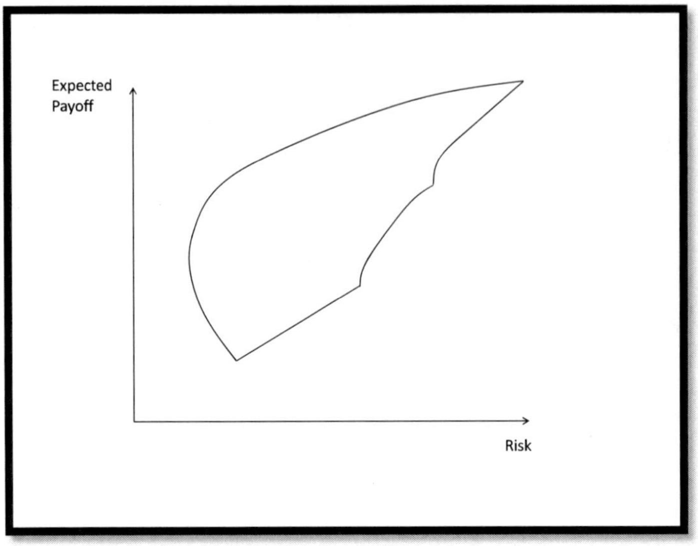

Figure 6.1. Theoretical Representation of the Opportunity Set.

This shape emerges from the statistical structure, especially the correlation structure, of the payoffs to the different attack methods. At the uppermost boundary, the opportunity set is concave because the payoffs to attack methods are imperfectly correlated. The boundary exists because there is some level of fatality at each level of risk which is the maximum that can be expected to be inflicted given the historical record of the outcomes of terrorist incidences. At the lowermost or eastern boundary, the opportunity set is either linear if some attack methods exhibit perfect correlation or a series of 'concave waves' reflecting the imperfect correlations among the attack methods used to form those combinations. There cannot be a bowed-outwards section for the reasons given above. There is no such thing as 'more than perfect correlation' and a combination cannot be more risky or variable than the attack methods that it contains and combination cannot be used to increase risk or variability. It is worth noting that the shape emerges from the historical data and the statistical structure embedded within it. It is not a purely theoretical or abstract construct invented by economists or statisticians. As we shall see, when we start with the mean and variance of the fatalities inflicted over time by each attack method, form combinations of attack methods and determine the combinations that have the highest expected payoffs at each level of risk and plot the results in expected-payoff-risk-space we get the sort of u-shape that we have drawn above.

One might wonder what use it is to know the payoffs and risks for every combination of attack methods. We have already explained how it is only through such an analysis that we know about the gains from combination and the fact that we should expect payoffs to be higher at each level of risk when imperfectly correlated attack methods are combined. Obtaining the complete opportunity set serves an even more important purpose. It provides us with an indication of the lone wolf terrorist's most dangerous opportunities. Although the lone wolf terrorist may roam in search of opportunities, he must do so within the boundaries of the complete opportunity set. It is somewhere within the opportunity set that we shall find him. Even so, this could be a very large area. Deciding where to look would appear to be another impossible task. Ideally, we need some way of narrowing down the search area to a set of attack methods and attack method combinations that is smaller than the set containing every possible attack method combination (every possible combination of expected payoff and risk). Fortunately, a solution is at hand. There will be many attack method combinations that are suboptimal. They will have a lower level of expected payoff than other attack method combinations with the same level of risk or they will have a higher level of risk at the same level of expected payoff. The lone wolf will discard these opportunities and concentrate on pursuing those opportunities that dominate the others. He will find his way towards the set of choices contained on the uppermost boundary of the complete opportunity set. He might make a mistake but we will be prepared for his most dangerous choices.

THE EFFICIENT OPPORTUNITY SET

The set of attack method combinations that dominates the others is called the 'efficient opportunity set'. It contains all of the attack methods and combinations that have the highest expected payoff for each level of risk. The efficient opportunity set emerges, like the complete opportunity set, from the structure of the means and variances of the attack methods and their combinations. When it is sketched, the efficient set is the set of attack methods and attack method combinations that lie on the upper-most boundary of the complete opportunity set in expected payoff-risk space. This is represented by the dashed line in Figure 6.2. If particular attack method combinations are not available to the lone wolf terrorist, then his ability to diversify or combine is restricted and the gains from combination are curtailed. The efficient set will therefore lie in the interior of the complete opportunity set. In general, when particular choices are unavailable, the lone wolf terrorist cannot roam as far to the north-east in expected payoff-risk space as he would be able to if all attack methods and combinations were available. Again, the ability of the analytical framework to deal with these different scenarios is what makes the analytical framework a powerful tool with which to work.

Of course, it is all very well to say that the efficient opportunity set lies at the upper-most boundary of the complete choice but if we are in pursuit of the lone wolf terrorist or if we are attempting to pre-empt him, we will need a way of computing the attack method combinations that lie in the efficient set and a way to determine where particular combinations in the efficient set may lie. The actual determination or computation of the attack methods and attack method combinations that lie in this set involves solving what is called a 'quadratic programming problem'. Randomly select any possible attack method or attack method combination (that is, an attack method or combination that lies anywhere in the complete opportunity set). It will have an expected payoff of $E(R_C)$ and risk of σ_C^2. It will lie somewhere within the complete opportunity set. Now it is possible to find the attack method or attack method combination that yields the maximum expected payoff at the same level of risk, σ_C^2, as our randomly selected combination or, to put it another way, to find the combination that lies directly above the randomly selected combination on the boundary of the complete opportunity set. This is accomplished by solving the quadratic programming problem:

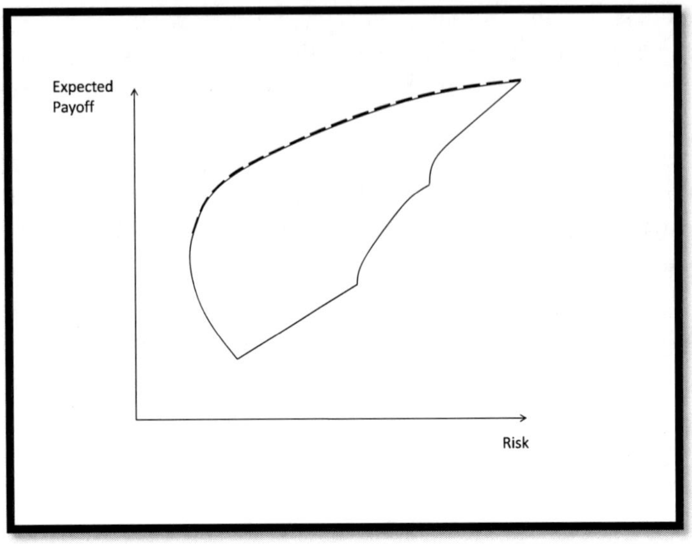

Figure 6.2. The Efficient Frontier or Uppermost Boundary.

$$\max E(R_C) = \sum_{i=1}^{n} w_i E(R_i) = R^*$$

Subject to a target level of return variance (risk), σ_C^2 *:

$$\sigma_C^2 * = \sum_{i=1}^{n}\sum_{j=1}^{n} w_i w_j \rho_{ij} \sigma_i \sigma_j$$

And the constraints:

$$\sum_{i=1}^{n} w_i = 1$$

$$w_i \geq 0$$

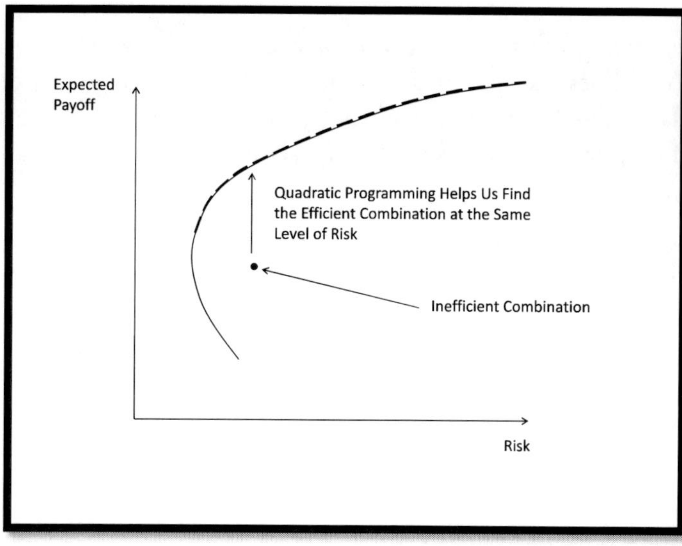

Figure 6.3. Finding the Efficient Frontier or 'Boundary Points'.

Given any particular randomly selected (or purposely selected) combination of attack methods, the efficient counterpart for the selected combination is computed by solving the quadratic programming problem. This gives us the combination that provides the highest payoff at the level of risk exhibited by the randomly selected combination. This is depicted in Figure 6.3. The entire efficient set or uppermost boundary of attack method combinations emerges by applying this approach repeatedly. That is, select combinations at random and compute the efficient counterpart for it (the combination that lies on the boundary of the complete opportunity set directly above—which means at the same level of risk—the randomly selected combination). By doing this we race the lone wolf terrorist to the efficient or optimal set of choices. The lone wolf may not always operate within the efficient set. We might find him before he is able to roam that far. He is learning and planning. He may make choices that are less than perfectly optimal. However, this does not mean that we pass the lone wolf terrorist by and overlook some of his possible choices. It means that we are waiting for him at his most efficient combinations where the level of human tragedy is highest for a given level of risk. From the boundary we can pursue the lone wolf inwards, step by step, restricting him and pushing him into less dangerous combinations until he is no longer a threat or until he is within the grasp of law enforcement.

More About the Statistical Structure

There is a statistical structure characterising the expected payoffs and risks of attack methods and attack method combinations. If something like the geometrical objects depicted in Figures 6.1, 6.2 and 6.3 did not emerge, it would be more difficult to build any sort of theoretical framework. Even purely qualitative theoretical work requires some underlying logic to provide the 'traction' necessary for the theory to take hold. The structure that we have identified does not emerge by some trick and it is not purely a product of abstract reasoning with no grounding in reality. Rather, the statistical structure is inherent within the mean-variance structure of the attack methods and attack method combinations. When attack methods can be combined, a statistical structure emerges in both the means (expected payoffs) and variances of those combinations. This is reflected in the formulas for the expected payoff and variance of an attack method combination:

$$E(R_C) = \sum_{i=1}^{n} x_i w_i$$

$$\sigma_C^2 = \sum_{i=1}^{n} \sum_{j=1}^{n} w_i w_j \rho_{ij} \sigma_i \sigma_j$$

$$= \sum_{i=1}^{n} w_i^2 \sigma_i^2 + \sum_{i=1}^{n} \sum_{\substack{j=1 \\ i \neq j}}^{n} w_i w_j \rho_{ij} \sigma_i \sigma_j$$

If there are three attack methods, the statistical structure can be depicted in a manner that is analogous to Markowitz's explanation (1952, pp.84-85). In this case $i = 3$ and $j = 3$. When the means or expected payoffs of the attack methods are not equal, the set of all combinations with a particular expected payoff is a system of parallel straight lines. Markowitz calls these *isomean* curves. The set of all combinations with a particular level of risk is a system of ellipses. Markowitz calls these *isovariance* curves. The isomean and isovariance curves for combinations of attack methods x_1 and x_2 can be depicted in two-dimensional space[1]. The two-dimensional diagram that emerges from Markowitz's analysis (1952, p.85) is depicted in a simplified form without some aspects of Markowitz's geometry in Figure 6.4.

x_1, x_2 and x_3 can be combined in a multiplicity of different ways. It will be possible to collect together all combinations that have a particular expected payoff. These collections are a system of parallel isomean curves. Each isomean curve consists of the various combinations (weighting schemes) that yield the same expected payoff. The system is not infinite because not all combinations are feasible and there will be an upper limit to the expected payoff that can be generated by combinations of the three attack methods. Similarly, it will be possible to collect together all combinations of x_1, x_2 and x_3 that have the same risk (variance). The collections are a system of ellipses or isovariance curves. There will be an inner-most ellipse that represents the lowest possible variance that emerges from a combination of these three attack methods and there will be an outer-most ellipse that represents the highest possible variance that emerges from a combination of x_1, x_2 and x_3. Working with the feasible combinations given by the constraints of the quadratic programming problem (above), a minimum-variance combination and a maximum expected payoff combination emerges along

[1] The attack method x_3 emerges from the proportion or weighting of resources allocated to x_1 and x_2. That is, $w_3 = 1 - w_1 - w_2$.

with a set of feasible combinations of x_1, x_2 and x_3 that represent combinations everywhere in between. The way in which the means or expected payoffs of the combinations increases with risk depends on the expected payoffs of each individual attack method contained within the combination.

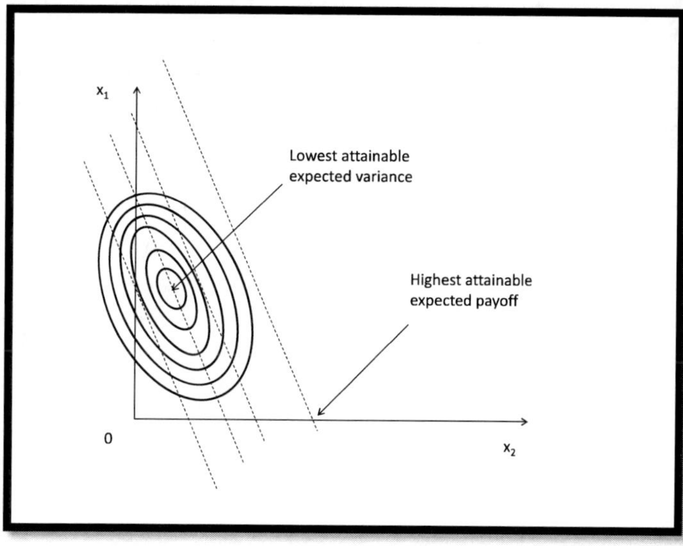

Figure 6.1. Markowitz's Isomean Curves and Isovariance Ellipses.

It is true that the outcomes of terrorism—the injuries and fatalities that result when an attack method is used—are 'random variables'. Nothing is certain and the lone wolf terrorist cannot be assured of a particular outcome and, therefore, neither can those in law enforcement who would attempt to pre-empt him. But there is structure. There is a statistical structure that emerges from the expected payoffs, the variances of those payoffs and the correlation or covariance structures that characterise the payoffs of different attack methods. All we need is for the lone wolf terrorist to behave as if he has an inkling of this structure, for him to sense it and to be aware of the possible payoffs to be expected from particular attack methods and the possibility that for some attack methods the actual payoffs may be quite a bit different from those that he expects. Much, if not all, of the information that he needs is reflected in media reports about the outcomes of terrorist activity. If the lone wolf terrorist's knowledge or understanding of this structure is incomplete or his actions that take place within this structure are more unconscious than consciously calculated, it means that he may choose sub-optimally or less dangerously than he could have. By being aware, however, of the potential impact of optimal choice, we are prepared for the most dangerous choices and we do not rely on the lone wolf terrorist's alleged 'irrationality' to act as a barrier or obstacle between him and the efficient set of opportunities.

Choosing from the Opportunity Set

The opportunities available to the lone wolf terrorist have statistical structure and so do his choices from the opportunity set. Before choices can be analysed we need to determine the set of opportunities from which the individual can choose. Once the opportunity set has been delineated, further economic analysis is undertaken to determine what choices will be made. The traditional approach within economic science is to work on the basis that the individual whose choices are being analysed tries to make the best or optimal choice. He chooses rationally. All this approach does is to identify a 'best' or 'optimal' way to achieve the given objective. This does not mean that the individual is immune from making a mistake or that he only bases his decisions on cold calculation. Critics of economic analysis have misunderstood this point. An economic analysis of choice that works on the basis that the individual tries to make the best or optimal choice does not rule out any of the sub-optimal choices. All possible choices from the opportunity set are encompassed by the analysis. Delineating the optimal does not mean ignoring the sub-optimal. The entire opportunity set is considered. In the context that we have been describing, the optimal choices are also the most dangerous ones. Critics would, by their own logic, have us ignore the most dangerous opportunities on the grounds that the lone wolf is irrational and would never choose them. This is one of the most pernicious, though no-doubt unintentional, implications of cross-disciplinary methodological criticism in a context characterised by a considerable degree of miscommunication or misunderstanding.

Choices from the opportunity set are analysed within orthodox economics by using an expected utility function. The utility function 'represents' the individual. It is a metaphor for him. It reflects how relevant factors such as expected payoff and risk affect his expected utility or satisfaction. The expected utility function or, rather, the indifference curves associated with it, are 'superimposed' onto the opportunity set. The set of indifference curves reflect various sets of choices for which expected utility is the same. Indifference curves that are situated towards the north-west in expected payoff-risk space are associated with greater amounts of expected utility. The steepness of the indifference curves is a reflection of the individual's preference for risk. Steep curves indicate a very risk averse individual while flatter curves indicate a less risk averse individual. While an individual will prefer a choice on the highest indifference curve, the opportunity set delineates the boundary of feasible choices. If our starting point is that the lone wolf terrorist attempts to make the best or optimal choice from the opportunity set then he will choose a point on the upper boundary of the opportunity set that is tangential to his highest indifference curve. This is the point at which expected utility is optimised given the available opportunities and the preferences of the lone wolf terrorist.

Any utility function is simply a mathematical object that allows us to represent formally the 'weighing up' or the preference ordering that individuals undertake when making a choice from the opportunity set. When the choices are made on the basis of mean (expected payoff) and variance (risk) of the possible outcomes of the choices, the individual considers the average payoff and the possibility that the actual outcome will be different from the outcome that was expected. The individual's risk preference plays an important role in shaping this choice-making process. If he is risk averse, more risky or variable choices must be compensated with higher expected payoffs. A utility function merely formalises this preference ordering process and allows us to see how much satisfaction or utility an individual obtains from a particular choice and how utility or satisfaction may change when circumstances change. The mathematical form of the utility function may be different depending on the type of analysis being undertaken. When choices are being examined within a mean-variance framework, the quadratic utility function is usually chosen as a starting point because it guarantees that choices are consistent with the von Neumann and Morgenstern axioms. That is, the individual's choices will not be intransitive. If A is preferred to B is preferred to C, A will be preferred to C rather than the other way round[2].

In mean-variance analysis, the quadratic utility function acts as a framework or a structure that prevents the analysis from yielding results that are inconsistent with the von Neumann and Morgenstern axioms. Because the individual whose choices we are analysing within a mean and variance context will, no doubt, make mistakes here and there (remembering that we said that rational decisions need not be perfect or free from error) and because the sanctity of the von Neumann and Morgenstern axioms is probably overstated within economic science, the use of the quadratic utility function within a mean-variance analysis should not be too controversial. However, in finance, the use of mean-variance analysis came under considerable criticism when it was discovered that a quadratic utility function is necessary to *guarantee* that the choices made on the basis of the mean-variance criteria are consistent with the axioms. The quadratic utility function was found to imply certain things about choice that financial economists found distasteful. Most important among these is the implication of 'satiation'. Economists had been brought up on the idea that more is always desired. Too much is never enough. This is despite the possibility of satiation being embedded deep within the analytical frameworks of indifference curve analysis[3].

A number of economists of substantial note, including James Tobin (1969), criticised the critics in no uncertain terms and argued strongly in favour of the computable results generated by mean-variance analysis, though they may come with some limitations, over the non-computable or 'empty' existence theorems of alternative models of choice (Tobin 1969, p.14). Tobin makes several very important points that should be noted by those who would, having seen it written in a text book that the quadratic utility function has some weaknesses and failing to consult the academic literature, argue that mean-variance analysis is flawed:

1. The von Neumann and Morgenstern axioms will not by themselves tell us anything about how an individual chooses among combinations (portfolios). Some restrictions must be placed on the utility function to obtain useful results.
2. Although the restriction to quadratic utility can be avoided if the individual regards the payoffs to particular combinations to be normally distributed, this is not always the case.
3. In fact, non-log-normally distributed payoffs emerge from the very choices that become available to individuals. It is not an inconvenience for the analyst or an imperfection but something that lies at the heart of the choice problem to be analysed.

---

[2] If C were preferred to A, the choices would be intransitive and violate the von Neumann and Morgenstern axiom of transitivity.

[3] They are never drawn as such but indifference curves can be drawn as complete and closed circles rather than open-ended curves.

4. Even if there are combinations that exhibit log-normally distributed payoffs, the payoffs of linear blends of those combinations will not be log-normally distributed. Tobin notes that these combinations are the 'very essence' of the combination choice problem.
5. The quadratic utility function, unlike the logarithmic utility function, can handle rankings or preference orderings for such combinations. An analytical apparatus that could not "... handle this essential fact is as useless as a model of consumer choice that does not allow the consumer to move within his budget constraint to any market basket of goods he wants" (p.14).

In short, mean-variance analysis is less general than state preference theory but the generality of the latter is sacrificed in favour of computable results. Given that state preference theory has just as many detractors, mean-variance analysis has all the more to recommend it as an analytical tool. Every analytical tool has weaknesses but as Tobin suggests, critics must do better than point out the problems with the quadratic utility restrictions that mean-variance analysis places on choices. They must suggest a better and more general approach. However, this is "... satisfied neither by the elegant but nearly empty existence theorems of state preference theory or by the normative prescriptions to the individual that he should consult his utility and his subjective probabilities and then maximise" (Tobin 1969, p.14). Computable results are desirable and mean-variance analysis provides a method by which to obtain them.

In addition to Tobin's defence of mean-variance analysis, it has been demonstrated that mean-variance analysis frequently 'holds' even when payoffs are not normally distributed or when agents are not described by quadratic utility. That is, the preference orderings that emerge when it is assumed that the decision-maker bases his choices on mean and variance coincide at least approximately with those obtained by a full expected utility analysis where it is assumed that the decision-maker bases his choices on all possible outcomes and the probabilities associated with them. Furthermore, even if quadratic utility is assumed, the quadratic utility function approximates the results from a broad range of utility functions (see Elton *et al.* 2003, p.232; Kroll, Levy and Markowitz 1984; Levy and Markowitz 1979). The criticisms of mean-variance analysis and its underlying assumptions, especially the quadratic utility function, are undermined considerably by these results. Mean-variance analysis provides an approximation for a full expected utility analysis. If quadratic utility is assumed, the mean-variance approach will coincide exactly with a full expected utility analysis. Although quadratic utility has some undesirable properties, especially satiation, it will approximate a broad class of utility functions.

It is interesting to note, also, that the quadratic utility function may actually be quite useful for our purposes. The criticisms directed towards it by financial economists cannot simply be mapped into the economic analysis of terrorism. Although financial economists have been wary of a utility function that allows for satiation, this property may apply with more relevance in the analysis of the lone wolf terrorist. Indeed, it is analytically sound to leave the possibility of satiation open. A lone wolf terrorist seeking to optimise injuries and fatalities from his attacks may, after a series of successful attacks, become temporarily satiated with the level of human tragedy that his attack methods have generated. At this point, he might drift away for a period of time and return to his terrorist activity at a later time. Certain lone wolves appear to have demonstrated this tendency. After a series of successful attacks, Theodore Kaczynski drifted away for some time before remerging at a much later time. The quadratic utility function may, in combination with mean-variance analysis, permit some of the boundaries of satiation to be computed. Unlike financial economics where more and more money or wealth is always assumed to be preferred, inflicting human tragedy is an activity that may, at least for a period of time, satiate the lone wolf terrorist and lead to his disengagement from terrorism. To be able to account for this behaviour is a positive aspect of the quadratic utility function.

CONCLUDING REMARKS

The lone wolf terrorist is bound by an opportunity set. The complete opportunity set consists of all of the possible combinations of attack methods. The lone wolf chooses from among the possible combinations of attack methods on the basis of the two moments of the distribution of injuries and fatalities generated by the attack methods. He chooses on the basis of expected or average payoff and variance or risk. Somewhere within the complete opportunity set is where we shall find the lone wolf terrorist. He will be seeking attack methods and attack method combinations that yield higher payoffs for a given level of risk. He will be making his way towards the efficient set of attack methods. The efficient set of attack methods contains the attack method combinations that have the highest expected payoff for each given level of risk. The attack methods and attack method combinations in the efficient set dominate all of the others. By using a mean-variance analysis, we can compute the efficient set and lie in wait for the lone wolf terrorist. We can prepare for his most dangerous actions by securing against particular attack method combinations. A lone wolf terrorist with an objective to inflict human tragedy is steadily encompassed within a theoretical framework that permits computable results to be generated. These results are of direct relevance to the law enforcement efforts designed to pre-empt or pursue the lone wolf.

The statistical structure of the attack methods and attack method combinations provides a foundation for the analytical framework that encompasses the actions of the lone wolf terrorist. From some perspectives, terrorism appears to be a random act and the results of terrorism—fatalities and injuries—equally random. Although there is no certainty, there is a statistical structure. The lone wolf terrorist does not drift aimlessly. The outcomes of his terrorist attacks are not independent. The lone wolf must choose from attack methods that have expected payoffs and expected levels of risk. The actual outcomes of attacks may diverge from those which were expected. This is the risk involved in undertaking a terrorist action. The mean-variance approach makes these expected payoffs and risks the basis for terrorist choice. This asks nothing more of the lone wolf terrorist except that he has some idea about the expected outcomes of particular terrorist actions and the possibility that the actual outcomes may diverge from those which he expected. The results of a mean-variance analysis will coincide exactly with full expected utility analysis when quadratic utility is assumed or when payoffs are normally distributed. The results will coincide approximately with full expected utility analysis when expected payoffs are not normally distributed or if quadratic utility fails to hold. The computable results of mean-variance analysis provide a distinct advantage over purely logical results and allow more concrete investigative advice to be provided. Step by step, the goal is to encompass the lone wolf terrorist's opportunities and choices within this analytical framework.

Chapter 7

THE LONE WOLF'S OPPORTUNITIES: PRACTICE

Pursuing the lone wolf terrorist begins with a determination of the constituents of the opportunity set. If we know what the dominant set of attack methods and attack method combinations consists of we are in a better position to anticipate the lone wolf as he drifts towards his optimal and most dangerous allocation of his resources. Perhaps the most appropriate data set to use is the RAND Corporation's transnational terrorism database. This data set depicts the fatalities and injuries that can be expected from particular attack methods in settings that most closely align with the type of lone wolf activity that we wish to pre-empt. A complete set of terrorist attack data would include the 'localised' attacks that have taken place in Iraq and Afghanistan, for example. However, domestic law enforcement agencies and security agencies will be most concerned with lone wolves that penetrate the security structures of Western targets either in Western countries or against Western targets in other parts of the world. Although terrorism is a problem that must be fought on many fronts, a lone wolf attack in a Western city or on a commercial aircraft en-route to a Western country or on a Western embassy in a foreign country is the front that concerns us here. The RAND-MIPT database of transnational terrorist attacks is the data set that most accurately reflects the injuries and fatalities that might be inflicted by a lone wolf terrorist operating against Western targets or within a Western country.

Using the RAND-MIPT transnational terrorism database has the additional advantage of being 'independent' of any specifically lone wolf terrorist data series. We could use the series of fatalities and injuries generated by our lone wolves but this could potentially undermine the analysis. What we are after is a data set that provides a good indication of the average fatalities and injuries that may be expected to be generated by particular attack methods. If a lone wolf terrorist is to undertake a bombing attack, for example, we require a sound estimate of the average number of fatalities and injuries that can be expected to result. The series of fatalities and injuries generated by lone wolf terrorist attacks is quite small by comparison and would possibly introduce data sample bias into the analysis if we were to use lone wolf attack data as the basis for estimating the mean and variance of attack methods that may be deployed by lone wolves and then as the basis for analysing lone wolf choices. When we come to an examination of the actual activities and choices of lone wolves, it will be useful to have estimates of mean and variance of attack methods obtained from an independent data source. In this chapter, we move beyond the purely theoretical work of the previous chapter and use actual historical data and the equations and method that we discussed to compute the lone wolf terrorist's opportunity set. It contains all the attack methods and combinations of attack methods and their associated payoffs and risks.

COMPUTING THE LONE WOLF'S EFFICIENT SET: THE 'SPECIALIST' LONE WOLF

We call the lone wolf who allocates all of his resources to attack methods the 'specialist' lone wolf terrorist. He specialises in terrorism. The specialist lone wolf terrorist's efficient set of attack method opportunities is computed by solving the quadratic programming problem:

$$\max E(R_C) = \sum_{i=1}^{n} w_i E(R_i) = R^*$$

Subject to a target level of return variance (risk), σ_C^2 *:

$$\sigma_C^2 * = \sum_{i=1}^{n} \sum_{j=1}^{n} w_i w_j \rho_{ij} \sigma_i \sigma_j$$

And the constraints:

$$\sum_{i=1}^{n} w_i = 1$$

$$w_i \geq 0$$

Such a computation places no additional constraints on the lone wolf terrorist's resource allocation beyond the constraint that all (i.e. 100 percent) of his resources must be allocated and no attack method can be allocated a negative resource allocation. Our first computation of the lone wolf's efficient set does not exclude the possibility that the lone wolf terrorist may allocate resources across all possible attack methods and engage effectively in complete diversification or combination. That is, he may allocate 100 percent of resources in any proportion across all of the available attack methods. Because a lone wolf terrorist operates alone, his opportunities for diversification or combination might, in practice, be limited. At any single point in time, the lone wolf terrorist must be at a single location engaged in a single attack method. On the other hand, the lone wolf might engage in a timed bombing attack and simultaneously be engaged in perpetrating another type of attack when the bomb device detonates. Also, the lone wolf terrorist can use different attack methods over time and the degree of combination that is feasible for him depends on how we define our time periods. Our first computation leaves open all diversification or combination opportunities. We will place restrictions on these opportunities in subsequent applications of the analysis in order to explore the implications for restricted attack method combination on the lone wolf's efficient set and for scenarios where the lone wolf may not specialise in terrorism but allocate time and resources to other activities.

The lone wolf who specialises in terrorism will allocate all of his resources to attack methods (i.e. terrorism). He is not interested in other forms of non-violent expression. The sum of the weightings of his allocations to attack methods and attack method combinations is equal to 1.00 or 100 percent. To identify the efficient set of opportunities available to this specialist lone wolf terrorist, we must solve the quadratic programming problem outlined above with a constraint that says that the lone wolf terrorist allocates all of his resources to terrorism. The sum of his resource allocations to attack methods is equal to 1.00. This may mean that he allocated 100 percent of his resources to bombing or it may mean that he divides 100 percent of his resources among, say, bombing, arson and armed attacks. The objective of the analysis is to determine the set of opportunities that have the highest expected payoff for each level of risk and to identify the attack method combinations that constitute that set. For a lone wolf terrorist who allocates 100 percent of his resources to terrorism and who has no restrictions placed on his ability to diversify among or combine attack methods, the efficient set may potentially contain any combination of the attack methods identified by RAND-MIPT. Importantly, it also gives the lone wolf terrorist access to the global minimum variance combination of attack methods. This is the attack method combination that has the lowest risk of any of the possible combinations of the available attack methods.

The specialist lone wolf's efficient set of attack method opportunities has several important properties:

1. It lies as high in expected payoff-risk space as is feasible given the available attack methods from which to choose and form combinations.
2. The specialist lone wolf terrorist's efficient set contains those attack method combinations that have the highest expected payoffs given the available attack methods. It is not possible to combine attack methods in such a way that yields higher expected payoffs than those contained in the specialist lone wolf's efficient set.
3. Assassination dominates the resource allocation weightings of the lowest risk combinations.
4. Bombing, hostage taking and unconventional attacks dominate the resource allocation weightings of the highest risk combinations.
5. Arson is largely ruled out of the efficient set of attack method opportunities. It only figures in a very minor way in some of the combinations. This is due to the very low number of casualties historically associated with this attack method. It is not an attack method that will generally be chosen by a lone wolf seeking to inflict significant human tragedy and such a lone wolf terrorist may be expected to soon learn to move onto other attack methods.

Apart from the fact that the specialist lone wolf's efficient set of attack method opportunities is situated as far to the north-west in expected payoff-risk space as is feasible, another of its important properties is that it contains the global minimum variance combination. This is the attack method combination that has the lowest risk of any possible combination available to the specialist lone wolf terrorist. That is, when 100 percent of resources are allocated to the attack methods, the global minimum variance combination is the combination with the lowest possible risk. It is obtained by solving the slightly different quadratic programming problem:

$$\min \sigma_C^2 * = \sum_{i=1}^{n} \sum_{j=1}^{n} w_i w_j \rho_{ij} \sigma_i \sigma_j$$

Subject to the constraints:

$$\sum_{i=1}^{n} w_i = 1$$

$$w_i \geq 0$$

The resource allocation weightings that characterise the global minimum variance combination of attack methods are dominated by kidnapping (96.4 percent), with small amounts of the remaining resources allocated to assassination (1.17 percent), arson (0.921 percent), hijacking (0.514 percent) and the miscellany of attack methods that constitute the RAND-MIPT's 'unknown' classification (0.958 percent). A specialist lone wolf who allocates 100 percent of his resources to the available attack methods cannot obtain a combination with a lower level of risk than this global minimum variance attack method combination. A lone wolf terrorist who chooses this combination will be predominantly engaged in the activity of kidnapping. The global minimum variance combination may be contrasted with the combination that has the maximum risk for a 100 percent allocation of resources. Not surprisingly given what we know about the risk-reward characteristics of the attack methods, the riskiest combination is an allocation of 100 percent of resources to hostage taking or to unconventional attacks. For the hostage taking lone wolf, human tragedy is a likely outcome. The possibility that the actual level of human tragedy may diverge significantly from that which was expected is very high. The hostage taking lone wolf bears considerable risk.

The Opportunities of the Non-Specialist Lone Wolves

The lone wolf may choose not to specialise in attack methods (i.e. terrorism). He may instead allocate some part of his resources to attack methods and some other part of his resources to less violent methods of expression. The type of individual that we are attempting to ensnare within the analytical framework when we speak of the 'non-specialist' lone wolf is an individual who will engage in terrorism but who may not allocate all of his time and resources to terrorism. He is also interested in attempting to further his objectives, whatever they may be, by non-violent forms of expression. If we speak of political objectives, then the non-specialist lone wolf may engage in the political process to some extent. He may allocate resources including time to such activities as attending political rallies and demonstrations, engaging in online dissemination of his views and developing longer treatises or manifestos.

These non-violent activities are only a part of the 'means' that he is willing to deploy to achieve his objective. He is also willing to do violence and in this regard his immediate objective becomes one of inflicting human tragedy. This allocation of time and resources between legitimate and illegitimate activities is reminiscent of Ehrlich's (1973) theoretical framework. It allows us to capture within the analytical framework the opportunities and choices of a lone wolf individual who does not allocate all of his resources to the available attack methods (i.e. to terrorism).

Non-specialisation reduces the lone wolf's opportunities to inflict human tragedy and has the direct effect of reducing the expected payoffs that are possible at each level of risk. The non-specialist lone wolf terrorist is less 'dangerous' than the specialist lone wolf terrorist but still far from being harmless. For the non-specialist, the efficient set of attack method combinations that may be formed with less than 100 percent allocation to terrorist activities will lie inside the efficient set that may be formed when 100 percent of resources are allocated. To determine the opportunities available to the non-specialist lone wolf terrorist we must solve the by-now-familiar quadratic programming problem with a constraint that restricts the total allocation of resources to the attack methods to some fraction of 100 percent. While this exercise can be taken to any level of detail, much can be learned about the non-specialist lone wolf's opportunities by concentrating the analysis on several indicative levels of specialisation. The ones that we have chosen are 10 percent, to represent a very non-specialist lone wolf who allocates most of his resources to non-violent activities, 25 percent, 50 percent and 75 percent. These several degrees of specialisation can be compared with each other and with the opportunities available to the specialist lone wolf who allocates all (i.e. 100 percent) of his resources to violent activities.

Formally, the opportunity sets of the non-specialist lone wolves are computed by solving the quadratic programming problem with resource allocation constraints of 0.10, 0.25, 0.50 and 0.75:

$$\min \sigma_C^2 * = \sum_{i=1}^{n} \sum_{j=1}^{n} w_i w_j \rho_{ij} \sigma_i \sigma_j$$

Subject to the constraints:

$$\sum_{i=1}^{n} w_i = 0.10; 0.25; 0.50; 0.75$$

$$w_i \geq 0$$

Our very non-specialist lone wolf who allocates only 10 percent of resources to terrorism has significantly less opportunity for exploiting the gains from combination. As a consequence, his efficient set of opportunities is situated relatively farther to the south-west in expected payoff-risk space. Even the riskiest combinations do not have expected payoffs that exceed 1.00 fatalities and injuries. Of course, the risk is relatively lower as well. Even the riskiest combinations do not have standard deviations much exceeding 2.00. This does not mean that the non-specialist lone wolf is harmless. Depending on the attack method combination that is chosen, the non-specialist lone wolf who allocates only 10 percent of his resources to terrorism may still inflict some level of human tragedy. The expected level is less than 1.00 but it would not be surprising to find that this non-specialist lone wolf is able to inflict a higher level of human tragedy over time (or even during a single attack). Like the specialist lone wolf, the riskiest combinations that can be formed on the basis of a 10 percent allocation of resources are characterised predominantly by hostage taking, bombing and unconventional attacks. The least risky combinations are characterised predominantly by combinations of assassination and bombing. Like the global minimum variance combination for the specialist lone wolf, the lowest risk combination for the lone wolf who allocates 10 percent of resources to terrorism is dominated by kidnapping (9.75 percent).

Our 'mid range' specialist lone wolves allocate (a) 25 percent; (b) 50 percent; and (c) 75 percent of resources to terrorism. As the allocation increases—as the degree of specialisation increases—more opportunities become available to generate higher expected payoffs at each given level of risk. This is the exploitation of the underlying statistical structure and correlation structure of the attack methods. The benefits from combination begin to become apparent when the expected payoffs at each level of risk are compared at different levels of specialisation. Where the very non-specialist lone wolf terrorist could not form an attack method combination with an expected payoff in excess of 1.00 fatalities and injuries, the 25 percent allocation is mostly characterised by attack method combination opportunities with expected payoffs in excess of 1.00 fatalities and injuries. Furthermore, even at the same level of risk there are feasible combinations at the 25 percent level of resource allocation that yield higher fatalities and injuries. Of course, a further increase in specialisation to 50 percent resource allocation to terrorism yields a similar increment in the expected level of human tragedy for each level of risk, as too does a further increase to 75 percent. Each time, the opportunity set moves higher in expected payoff-risk space.

At all of these levels of specialisation—10 percent, 25 percent, 50 percent and 75 percent—familiar patterns emerge to characterise the lone wolf terrorist's opportunities to inflict human tragedy. A combination of assassination and bombing dominates the lowest risk combinations. This is interesting because bombing, on its own, has relatively variable outcomes. One might have thought that assassination and bombing would be 'mutually exclusive' in the sense that either a high risk or a lower risk attack method is chosen but not both. The analysis points out the flaws that may emerge in drawing such conclusions without the benefit of the theoretical framework that we are attempting to use to encompass the lone wolf. It is precisely the benefits from combination of attack methods that law enforcement must be aware of in order to pre-empt, anticipate or understand the lone wolf's choices. At lower levels of risk, therefore, it is not the case that simply the least risky attack method is chosen and that law enforcement may expect a particular level of human tragedy to be inflicted. If the lone wolf can combine attack methods, the correlation structure may produce an opportunity to inflict a higher level of human tragedy at the same level of risk by combining two attack methods with quite different expected payoffs and risks. In this case, the combination of a lower risk attack method (assassination) and a relatively higher risk attack method (bombing) produces a combination with an expected payoff and risk structure that is relatively low risk but which inflicts a higher level of human tragedy for the level risk that is borne than would be possible taking either attack method individually.

The higher risk combinations are dominated by bombing, hostage taking and unconventional attacks across all of the levels of specialisation. Arson is all but ruled out because it is not usually a constituent attack method in any efficient combination. Armed attacks feature in a large proportion of the attack method combinations across all levels of specialisation. However, the resource allocation weighting is always relatively low. For lower risk combinations, assassination and bombing dominate the combinations. At higher risk combinations, bombing, hostage taking and unconventional attacks dominate. Armed attacks do not dominate the attack method combinations at any level of risk but they are present. When full diversification or combination among the attack methods is available to the lone wolf terrorist, the statistical structure of the attack method combinations diminishes or enhances the expected prevalence of any particular attack method. Fundamentally, the statistical structure highlights the benefits that may accrue to the lone wolf by combining attack methods and reveals the structure of the opportunities available to the lone wolf at each level of risk. As the lone wolf becomes more specialised, his opportunities for inflicting human tragedy increase at each level of risk.

THE OPPORTUNITIES AT DIFFERENT DEGREES OF SPECIALISATION

We have discussed the additional opportunities and 'gains from combination' that become available as the lone wolf's degree of specialisation increases. We spoke of the opportunity set moving gradually upwards as the degree of specialisation increases. We spoke of higher expected payoffs at each level of risk. Most of these ideas are reflected in a single picture. Figure 7.1 shows how the degree of specialisation determines the opportunities that are available to the lone wolf terrorist.

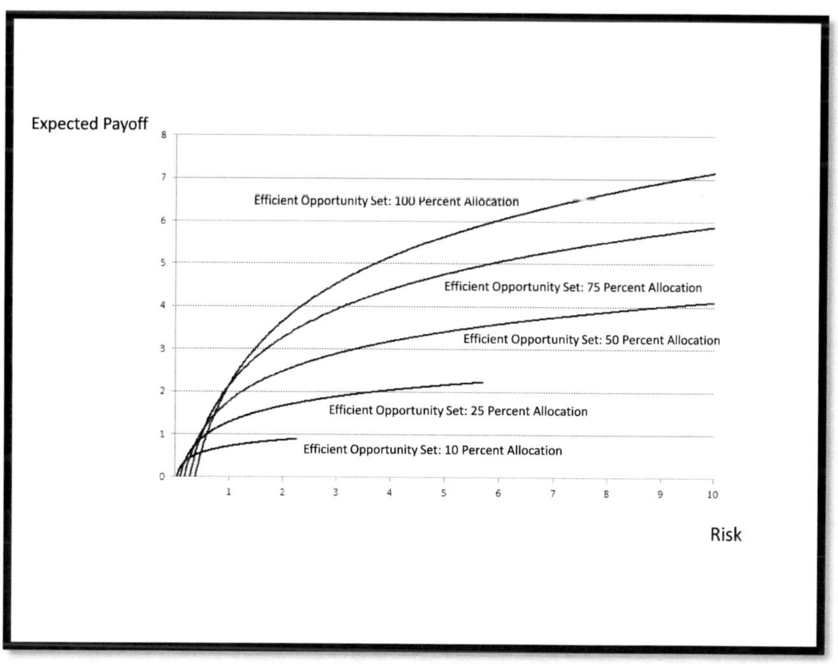

Figure 7.1. The Lone Wolf's Efficient Frontier at Each Level of Specialisation.

Figure 7.1 contains a family of efficient opportunity sets. Each set is formed from attack method combinations that solve the quadratic programming problem at each level of risk and at each level of specialisation. The historical RAND-MIPT data underlies the analysis and the shapes that you see are the result of the application of the analytical method that we have been discussing to data that contains an inherent statistical structure. A very non-specialist lone wolf is very constrained. A specialist lone wolf has the widest array of combinations. At each given level of risk, the more specialised lone wolf inflicts a higher level of human tragedy. This can be shown most clearly in Table 7.1 which shows the set of combinations at various levels of specialisation that are dominant at a level of standard deviation or variability of 5.00 injuries and fatalities. The numbers in each of the rows corresponding to each attack method are the resource allocation weightings for that attack method. We have chosen a mid-range level of standard deviation or risk of 5.00. At various levels of lone wolf terrorist specialisation, the expected payoff is maximised at this precise level of risk by a particular combination of attack methods. At each level of specialisation, the composition of the dominant attack method combination at this level of risk varies according to the availability of combination opportunities. At complete specialisation, the benefits from combination are fully exploitable. As a consequence, the specialist lone wolf terrorist is able to inflict human tragedy at a level that is more than 60 percent higher than the lone wolf terrorist who allocates only 25 percent of resources to attack methods and spends the remainder of his time and resources to other forms of activity. At all levels of risk this discrepancy in favour of the specialist lone wolf exists and must be considered by the law enforcement agencies.

Table 7.1. Resource Allocations and Average Outcomes at Each Specialisation Level: 5.00 Level of Risk

Specialisation Level	**0.25**	**0.50**	**0.75**	**1.00**
Armed Attacks	0	0	0	0.042
Arson	0	0	0	0
Assassination	0	0	0	0.042
Hostage	0.1324	0.1312	0.13	0.123
Bombing	0	0	0.62	0
Hijacking	0	0	0	0.043
Kidnapping	0.1176	0.368	0	0.66
Other	0	0	0	0
Unconventional	0	0	0	0.044
Unknown	0	0	0	0.042
Expected Payoff	1.57	1.68	1.79	2.56
Risk	5.00	5.00	5.00	5.00

When Combination Is Not Possible

The lone wolf terrorist is a lone individual and he cannot be in two places at once. For this reason, Phillips (2011) works from the position that the lone wolf terrorist does not combine attack methods. The lone wolf has restricted 'diversification' or combination opportunities. At any given point in time, the lone wolf must be engaged in only one activity. Over time, he may vary his attack methods. Apart from the special case where a timed bombing device, for example, is used to execute an attack at one location whilst another attack method is deployed at a different location it would seem quite sensible to consider the lone wolf to have restricted opportunities for combination within a single time period. If this is the case, then for each level of specialisation that characterises the lone wolf, he will allocate some portion of his resources to a single attack method. For example, the specialist lone wolf may allocate 100 percent of his resources to armed attacks. The non-specialist may allocate 10 percent of his resources to armed attacks. If it were this clear cut, the opportunity set becomes characterised by a limited number of points. However, it is possible that the lone wolf's choice of level of specialisation will be influenced by the availability or lack thereof of the possibility of combining attack methods. If combination is restricted, the lone wolf may explore his specialisation options more carefully.

There are a number of ways in which this may be analysed. One way is as follows. At each level of risk, we may determine which degree of specialisation and which attack method yields the highest expected payoff when only one attack method can be chosen. Formally, at different levels of risk solve the quadratic programming problem:

$$\max E(R_C) = \sum_{i=1} w_i E(R_i) = R^*$$

Subject to a target level of return variance (risk), σ_C^2 *:

$$\sigma_C^2 * = \sigma_i^2$$

And the constraints:

$$\sum_{i=1} w_i = 1$$

$$w_i \geq 0$$

The levels of risk at which this quadratic programming problem was solved are: 0.1, 0.2, 0.3, 0.5, 1.0, 1.5, 2.0 ...42.5. The degrees of specialisation and the attack methods that correspond to the solution of the quadratic programming problem at these levels of risk are presented in Table 7.2. 'Plunge points' where resource allocations approach or equal 100 percent are shaded. At the lowest levels of risk, assassination dominates across a range of degrees of specialisation. For example, if the lone wolf bears a very small standard deviation (risk) of 0.5 fatalities and injuries per attack, a 71.5 percent degree of resource allocation (specialisation) is the optimal choice. As the level of risk that will be borne increases, assassination no longer remains an optimal choice and bombing emerges as the optimal choice of attack method. For example, at a 4.5 level of risk, a 74.9 percent degree of specialisation in bombing is optimal. At still higher levels of risk, the lone wolf will find that it is optimal to switch from bombing to hijacking and then to armed attacks. Finally, hostage taking and unconventional attacks come to dominate. At each level of risk, there is a single attack method and a degree of specialisation that produces the highest expected payoff.

Table 7.2(a). Risk, Specialisation Level and Dominant Attack Method

Risk (Standard Deviation)	Degree of Specialisation	Attack Method	Expected Payoff
0.1	0.143	Assassination	0.22
0.2	0.286	Assassination	0.441
0.3	0.429	Assassination	0.66
0.4	0.572	Assassination	0.883
0.5	0.715	Assassination	1.10
1.0	0.166	Bombing	0.97
1.5	0.249	Bombing	1.46
2.0	0.333	Bombing	1.96
2.5	0.416	Bombing	2.45
3.0	0.499	Bombing	2.94
3.5	0.582	Bombing	3.43
4.0	0.666	Bombing	3.92
4.5	0.749	Bombing	4.41
5.0	0.832	Bombing	4.90
5.5	0.915	Bombing	5.39
6.0	0.999	Bombing	5.88

Table 7.2(b). Risk, Specialisation Level and Dominant Attack Method

Risk (Standard Deviation)	Degree of Specialisation	Attack Method	Expected Payoff
6.5	0.609	Hijacking	2.38
7.0	0.655	Hijacking	2.56
7.5	0.702	Hijacking	2.74
8.0	0.749	Hijacking	2.93
8.5	0.796	Hijacking	3.11
9.0	0.843	Hijacking	3.29
9.5	0.890	Hijacking	3.47
10.0	0.936	Hijacking	3.66
10.5	0.983	Hijacking	3.84
11.0	0.743	Armed Attacks	3.95
11.5	0.777	Armed Attacks	4.13
12.0	0.810	Armed Attacks	4.31
12.5	0.844	Armed Attacks	4.49
13.0	0.878	Armed Attacks	4.67
13.5	0.912	Armed Attacks	4.85
14.0	0.945	Armed Attacks	5.03
14.5	0.979	Armed Attacks	5.21

If a lone wolf terrorist can choose just one single attack method and cannot combine attack methods, his optimal opportunities become a set characterised by a single attack method and a particular level of specialisation at particular levels of risk. For the most part, complete specialisation emerges as an optimal choice only at small number of points. At very low levels of risk, complete specialisation is not expected at all. At the mid-range of risk, we do observe complete specialisation—100 percent allocation of resources—in bombing at 6.0 standard deviation of fatalities and injuries. At the mid-to-high ranges of risk we observe almost complete specialisation in hijacking at a 10.5 standard deviation of fatalities and injuries and almost complete specialisation in armed attacks at 14.5. At the very highest levels of risk, complete specialisation will be observed in hostage taking and, ultimately, in unconventional attacks. Quite simply, a lone wolf terrorist seeking to bear the highest levels of risk will find that these highest levels can only be reached through a complete specialisation in the riskiest attack methods.

Concluding Remarks

The lone wolf terrorist has opportunities. It is our task to assist law enforcement efforts designed to determine what these opportunities consist of. Obviously, there will be a limit on how far this determination can be taken but even a very partial determination that rules in some opportunities, rules out other opportunities or more carefully and completely describes facets of the lone wolf terrorist's opportunity set may constitute the basis for useful investigative advice. The opportunity set available to the lone wolf must be feasible. An individual can only do what the world allows him to do and there will be some boundary to his set of opportunities. When deployed, each terrorist attack method that has revealed itself in the historical record is expected to inflict a particular level of human tragedy at a particular level of risk. A statistical structure underlies the attack methods. The statistical structure provides an expected payoff and risk for each opportunity. The utilisation of these attack methods represents a set of opportunities from which the lone wolf terrorist may choose. The lone wolf may not be limited to a single attack method. He may be able to combine attack methods. In this case, the statistical structure, particularly the correlation structure, becomes a critically important consideration for law enforcement. By combining attack methods the lone wolf gains increments in the level of human tragedy he is expected to inflict without increasing the level of risk that he bears. An alternative way of putting this is that the lone wolf obtains increments in the expected payoffs to attacks at all levels of risk.

The combination of attack methods expands the opportunities available to the lone wolf. Opportunities are also expanded or contracted by the degree of specialisation that characterises the lone wolf. As we saw earlier, our adaptation of Ehrlich's (1973) model of criminal behaviour portrays the lone wolf as allocating resources (including time) to terrorism and to other forms of expression. The specialist lone wolf allocates 100 percent of his resources to terrorism. The non-specialist allocates some portion less than 100 percent of his resources to terrorism. The opportunity set for the very non-specialist lone wolf who allocates just 10 percent of his resources to terrorism is a very constrained opportunity set in expected payoff-risk space. As the level of specialisation increases and the amount of resources that are allocated to terrorism rises, the opportunity set available to the lone wolf shifts upwards in expected payoff-risk space. More opportunities for combination emerge. At each level of risk the lone wolf can expect to inflict a higher amount of human tragedy. A lone wolf who engages in very low risk attacks may be expected to inflict a varying degree of human tragedy depending on the degree of specialisation that characterises him. A specialist operating in the same range of risk may be expected to inflict a higher level of human tragedy than his non-specialist counterpart operating at exactly the same range of risk.

At each level of specialisation there are patterns that emerge in the combinations that are formed at particular levels of risk. At the lower levels of risk, assassination and bombing dominate the attack method combinations. This is an interesting characteristic of the opportunity set because bombing is a relatively high risk attack method. Law enforcement operating without an investigative-analytical framework that considers the statistical structure of attack methods and the combinations of attack methods that may be formed may have fallen into the error of disassociating bombing from lower risk terrorist attacks. Combined with assassination, however, bombing figures prominently in the combinations that constitute the efficient set of opportunities at lower levels of risk. At higher levels of risk, the attack method combinations are dominated by hostage taking, bombing and unconventional attacks. Armed attacks, which have been a prominent choice of lone wolves operating in the United States, are present across a range of attack method combinations. They do not dominate but they are present. We must expect the lone wolf to utilise this type attack method.

Indeed, if the lone wolf cannot combine attack methods, armed attacks become dominant at particular levels of risk and may be the attack method of choice for 'spree' lone wolves. When the lone wolf cannot combine attack methods, each level of risk is associated with a particular single attack method and a particular level of specialisation that inflicts the maximum human tragedy at that level of risk. At the lower ranges of risk, this single attack method is assassination. At intermediate ranges of risk, this single attack method is bombing and then hijacking and then armed attacks. At the highest levels of risk, hostage taking and unconventional attacks dominate the choices of a lone wolf who cannot combine attack methods. One of the key contributions that we can make is to provide analysis of the opportunities available to the lone wolf terrorist. Once these opportunities are analysed, we see that there is structure and that there are certain facets of the lone wolf's opportunities that might not have been properly considered without the analytical approach we have taken. Identifying the opportunities is a part of the task. The next step is to determine how the lone wolf will choose once he is confronted with these opportunities.

Chapter 8

THE LONE WOLF'S CHOICES: PRACTICE

If there is one thing that we could say that economics 'is about' it is *choice*. However, in order to be able to choose an individual must have something to choose from. The less prominent but equally important part of economic analysis is the determination of the opportunity set from which choices are made. It would be more correct to say, then, that economics is concerned with the analysis of *opportunities and choices*. The world provides particular opportunities. These are things that can be done if one chooses to do them. These are the things that are feasible. Other opportunities are not available or not feasible. These are the things that cannot be done. The lone wolf terrorist must choose from the available combinations of attack methods and he must confront the risk-reward trade-off that characterises these attack method combinations. Up to a limit, higher expected payoffs are available only by taking more risk or exploiting the 'gains from combination'. Once the maximum risk is borne, the world provides no opportunities that generate higher expected payoffs. There are individual attack methods that are each expected to inflict a particular level of human tragedy. Each attack method has a particular level of risk. The set of opportunities available to the lone wolf includes these attack methods and combinations of them. The set of opportunities is a set of expected payoffs and risks. In the previous chapter we computed this set at various levels of specialisation. We must now consider how the lone wolf terrorist will choose his attack method or attack method combination from the set of opportunities and, in particular, which attack method or attack method combination he will choose.

If the optimal choice in this case means the choice of attack method or attack method combination that inflicts the highest level of human tragedy at a particular level of risk, then the optimal choice is also the most dangerous one. Critics of economic analysis may argue that it is not relevant to investigate optimal choice when people do not act rationally or do not have resources or the intellectual capacity to choose optimally. Although this point of view is almost always based on a mistaken conception of the notion of rationality which tends to view it as some sort of perfect ability to calculate, it loses much of its relevance as a criticism of the economic analysis of terrorism and terrorist choice when the optimal choice is also the most dangerous one at the particular level of risk. When the optimal choice is also the most dangerous one, it is obviously important to know what that optimal choice is. If the lone wolf terrorist makes a mistake and chooses sub-optimally, he also chooses less dangerously. A criticism of the analysis of optimal choice in this case is a criticism of an approach that determines the most dangerous choices. These choices are obviously important to determine.

If the lone wolf terrorist corrects his mistakes over time, then he will choose more optimally and more dangerously with each successive attack. Whether he chooses optimally or sub-optimally, he must choose from the opportunities that are available to him and which are feasible. He must choose from somewhere within the complete opportunity set.

In the previous chapter we showed how the complete opportunity set of attack methods and attack method combinations could be computed using actual historical data. Although we have a computational advantage over the lone wolf terrorist, it is to be expected that the lone wolf terrorist is aware of what level of human tragedy might be associated with particular acts of terrorism and the fact that the actual outcomes vary somewhat from incident to incident and, therefore, from expectation to actuality. There is no doubt that a lone wolf terrorist interested in perpetrating an act of terrorism will form his expectations on the basis of publicly available information about terrorism and terrorist attacks which he will actively seek from media reports about terrorism and terrorist attacks and, perhaps, other forms of violence where similar attack methods have been deployed. Determining the opportunity set on the basis of averages and variability of the injuries and fatalities inflicted by the different attack methods ensures that we are working with the same sort of information that is available to the lone wolf terrorist. We are not asking him to calculate a series of probability estimates for every possible outcome of every potential type of terrorist attack. When we used the RAND-MIPT data to compute the opportunity set, we found that particular attack methods dominated others in attack method combinations formed at different levels of risk or variability. The attack methods that will dominate the lone wolf terrorist's choices will depend on the level of risk that he chooses to bear. The lone wolf's risk preference will play a most important role in shaping the choices of the lone wolf terrorist. If he chooses rationally and selects an optimal attack method or attack method combination, he also chooses most dangerously at the level of risk. We need to know what these choices will be.

So, we proceed with good reason to determine the lone wolf terrorist's optimal choices under different conditions. This is done by analytically confronting the lone wolf terrorist with the opportunity sets that we have determined. The lone wolf terrorist is 'reflected' in the analytical framework as the quadratic expected utility function:

$$U(R) = c + aR - d\sigma_R^2$$

If the lone wolf happens, for a given payoff, to prefer a smaller variance of payoffs to a larger variance, then $d > 0$. The size of d will depend on how averse to variance or risk the lone wolf happens to be. The function is the analytical reflection of the lone wolf terrorist. If the lone wolf terrorist was able to gaze into the analytical framework he would see himself reflected in the expected utility function. What is more, he would see that reflection encompassed within an economic theoretical framework, the boundaries of which he could not traverse.

If he could see his reflection represented by the geometry that is used in this type of economic analysis, the lone wolf terrorist would see his opportunities as concave efficient sets and he would see himself as a set of 'indifference' curves. Indifference curves are the set of points, derived from an expected utility function, that represent 'points of indifference' at a particular level of expected utility. For example, in Figure 8.1 the individual who is represented by the indifference curves in payoff-risk space is indifferent between choices A and B. Point A provides a lower return with lower risk. Point B provides a higher return with higher risk. Either combination, A or B, will give the individual the same utility. Because both points A and B reside on higher indifference curves, the individual would prefer either A or B to C. This is a simple geometrical representation of the preferences of an individual decision-maker.

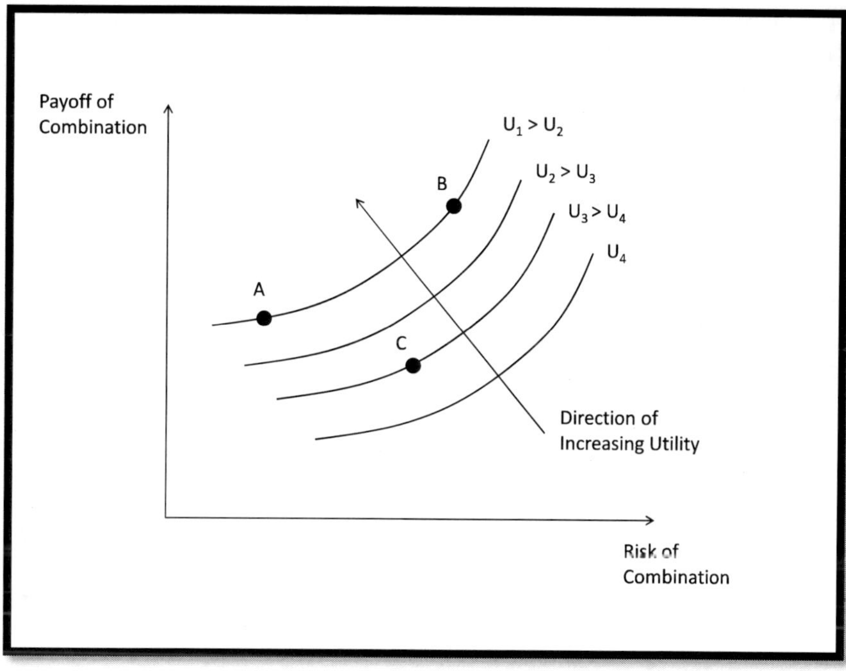

Figure 8.1. Utility, Indifference Curves and the Choice Between A, B or C.

If we may continue with the metaphor, the lone wolf terrorist sees an analytical reflection of himself as a set of indifference curves superimposed over a set of opportunities depicted as concave efficient sets. The indifference curves slope upwards because the lone wolf terrorist, as we have currently defined him and as he now sees himself, must be rewarded with additional expected payoff if he is to bear additional risk. Utility is higher on the higher indifference curves because at each given level of risk the lone wolf terrorist prefers more expected payoff to less. The lone wolf would like to make choices that lie on his highest indifference curve. The world presents him with limited opportunities and limited resources. He is constrained. His best choices must correspond to the highest indifference curve at the highest point of feasible opportunity. This is a point of tangency between the highest indifference curve and the relevant opportunity set. In the diagram, when all possible opportunities to combine attack methods are available, the uppermost opportunity set is the relevant one. The optimal choice will be the point of tangency between that efficient set and the indifference curve. The preferences reflected by indifference curves that are higher than this one are not possible or feasible given the opportunities that are available.

An individual's indifference curves are steeper or flatter depending on whether the individual is more or less averse to risk. To illustrate the interaction of opportunities and choices and the idea of 'optimal' choice, we choose a lone wolf terrorist with a moderate level of risk aversion in the first instance. In Figure 8.2, the lone wolf's map of indifference curves contains upward sloping indifference curves to reflect risk aversion—more risk requires a higher expected payoff as compensation. The curves are neither very steep nor very flat in order to reflect a moderate level of risk aversion. More utility is obtained by moving to a higher indifference curve. Such a movement is restricted by the opportunities that are available to do so. In the previous chapter we computed the set of opportunities that correspond to different levels of specialisation. Each opportunity set is concave and upward sloping reflecting both correlation structure and the gains from combination that are implied by it and the positive trade-off between risk and reward that characterises the attack methods. As more resources are allocated to terrorism, up to a limit of 100 percent, more opportunities become available and the efficient set moves upwards. Given the available opportunities, the lone wolf terrorist tries to get to a maximum of injuries and fatalities at the level of risk that he feels comfortable with. He tries to get to the highest indifference curve given the available opportunities. In this case, if he specialises completely in terrorism and allocates 100 percent of his resources to it, his optimal choice is the tangency between the '100 percent allocation efficient opportunity set' and his highest indifference curve. Although he would like to be on an even higher indifference curve, he cannot move any higher given the available opportunities.

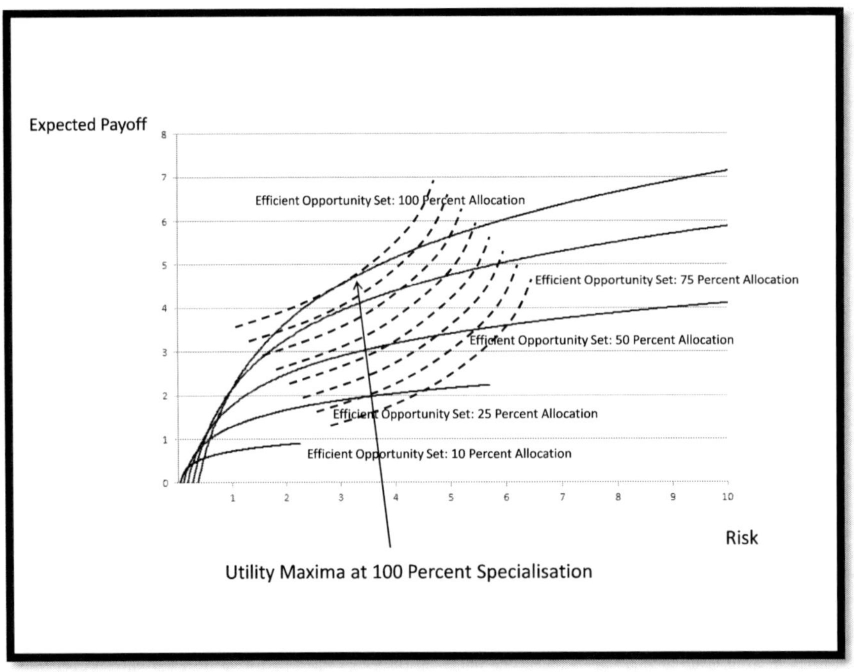

Figure 8.2. Moderate Risk Aversion: Opportunities and Choices.

The lone wolf's optimal choice—where his expected utility function is optimised or maximised—is the choice of attack method or attack method combination from the relevant set of efficient attack method combinations at the point of tangency between that set and the lone wolf terrorist's highest indifference curve. The optimal choice at a given level of risk will be that optimal intersection of the lone wolf's preferences and the opportunities that the world presents to him. Given that we have determined or delineated the opportunities, it is now our task now to examine the lone wolf terrorist's preferences vis-à-vis these opportunities. Although these preferences may be revealed by the serial lone wolf over time, a topic we shall discuss later, we can somewhat delineate the lone wolf terrorist's preferences and determine the types of opportunities the rational optimising lone wolf will choose under a small number of alternative preference configurations. As we said before, the lone wolf terrorist's risk preferences play an important role in shaping his choices. We shall work through each of the levels of specialisation under three different risk preference configurations: (1) very low risk aversion; (2) moderate aversion to risk; and (3) very high aversion to risk. Under these different configurations, the lone wolf will be found to occupy different regions of the efficient set of opportunities.

It is important to note, before we get started on taking a closer look at these three cases, that particular attack methods dominate others at particular levels of risk. The attack methods that constitute the efficient attack method combinations are not all 'mixed up' at each and every level of risk such that a small adjustment of risk introduces or excludes many different attack methods. Therefore, if we say that there are, broadly, three types of lone wolf terrorists defined by their risk preference: very low risk aversion, moderate risk aversion and high risk aversion, we would expect to be able to allocate each type of lone wolf terrorist to a particular range of risk and, because we know which attack methods dominate at each particular risk range, determine which attack methods will dominate his optimal choice of attack method combination. Approximately, the attack methods that dominate particular ranges of risk are identified in Figure 8.3.

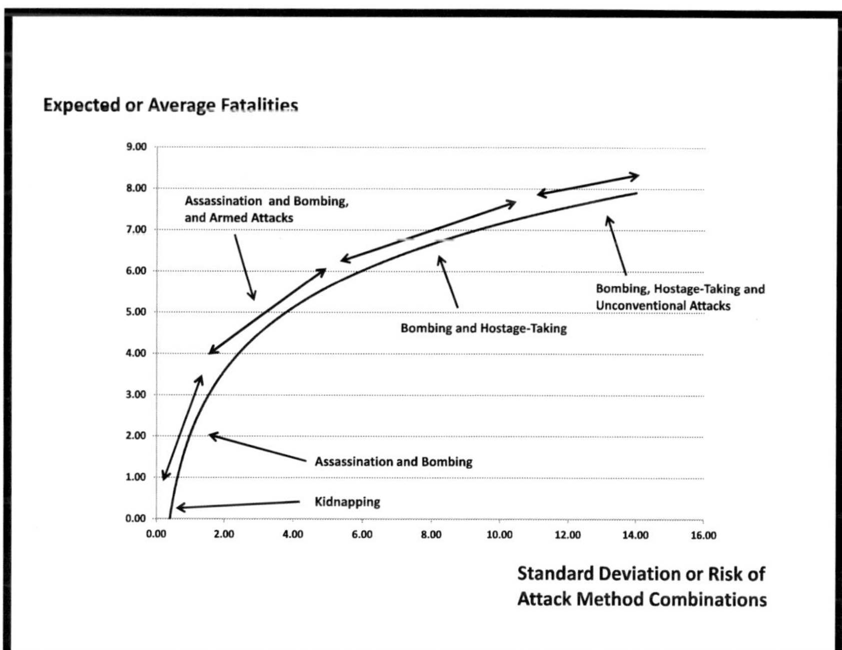

Figure 8.3. Attack Methods and Risk Ranges.

Assassination and bombing dominate attack method combinations formed at the lowest range of risk and will therefore dominate the choices of very risk averse lone wolf terrorists. At the highest range of risk bombing, hostage taking and unconventional attacks dominate and will dominate the choices of the more risk seeking lone wolf terrorist. As we shall see, the analysis can be inverted such that we start from the details of an attack that has just taken place. When a lone wolf terrorist selects an attack method or combination and carries out a violent action, he reveals something about his risk preference. A lone wolf terrorist who undertakes an assassination-type attack reveals a higher level of risk aversion. Because there are certain characteristics we expect lone wolves with different levels of risk aversion to exhibit, we can draw inferences about the lone wolf terrorist based on the risk preferences that he reveals when he selects an attack method. This is the source of investigative advice that may be generated from the economic model of choice that we have been developing. As we shall explain, it complements the approach used by offender profilers in the determination of 'offender risk'. However, because we have both a precise definition for risk—variability of possible outcomes—and a precise measurement for variability we can determine the riskiness of a terrorist action without conflating the choice of attack method and the lone wolf terrorist's approach to its deployment. For now, let us concentrate on determining where in expected-payoff-risk-space a lone wolf terrorist with a particular level of risk aversion will be found and which opportunities he may be expected to favour.

VERY LOW RISK AVERSION: WITH COMBINATION OF ATTACK METHODS POSSIBLE

The lone wolf terrorist who has a very low degree of risk aversion is represented by a map or group of very flat indifference curves in expected-payoff-risk-space. These indifference curves are superimposed onto the opportunity sets in Figure 8.4. When he has very low risk aversion he does not require very much additional expected payoff to compensate him for bearing additional risk. The indifference curves are flatter, less steep. What is more, the lone wolf terrorist with very low risk aversion will be attracted to those attack methods that have a higher risk and a higher expected payoff. He is also attracted by a higher degree of specialisation in terrorism rather than other forms of expression. As such, his group of indifference curves will be further out to the east when we draw them in expected-payoff-risk-space. When it is possible to combine attack methods, specialisation provides access to combinations with higher risk and higher expected payoffs. When the lone wolf terrorist can combine attack methods, a lone wolf terrorist with very low risk aversion will engage in those attack method combinations that have relatively higher risk and he will exhibit a tendency towards specialisation in terrorism. We know from our delineation of the opportunities that this must involve the allocation of a high percentage of resources to the attack method combinations constituted mainly by bombing, hostage taking and unconventional attacks.

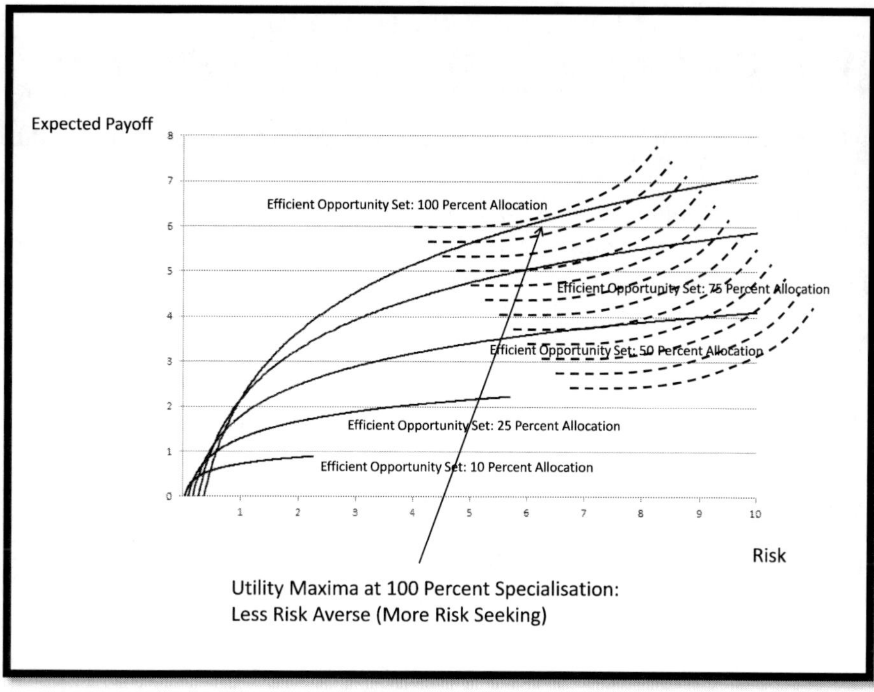

Figure 8.4. The Flat Indifference Curves of a More Risk Seeking Lone Wolf.

The attack methods that mainly constitute the attack method combination to which this lone wolf terrorist is attracted are bombing, hostage taking and unconventional attacks. Examples of resource allocation weightings for these attack methods are as follows. For an attack method combination with an expected payoff of 6.91 injuries and fatalities and a standard deviation (risk) of 8.42 injuries and fatalities, the lone wolf allocates approximately 6 percent of resources to unconventional attacks, 76 percent to bombing and 17 percent to hostage taking and a small amount armed attacks. At a slightly higher level of risk of 9.03, an expected payoff of 7.04 injuries and fatalities emerges from a similar resource allocation. The difference is a slightly higher weighting in each of unconventional attacks, bombing and hostage taking with a reduction to a 0.00 percent allocation to armed attacks. Although there are slight variations, therefore, these variations are not very significant from a law enforcement point of view. A lone wolf terrorist with very low risk aversion and the opportunity to combine attack methods will drift towards combinations that are predominantly characterised by high weightings to bombing, hostage taking and unconventional attacks. Since these attack methods dominate over the 'range' of higher risk attack method combinations, it is possible to conclude that a lone wolf terrorist with very low aversion to risk will allocate his resources to these attack methods rather than to other attack methods, such as assassination, which bombing, hostage taking and unconventional attacks dominate at higher levels of risk. Attack methods are not 'mixed up' across all ranges of risk. As we progress to higher levels of risk, some attack methods become dominant. So, a lone wolf terrorist who has a very low level of risk aversion will not find it optimal to 'mix up' attack methods but to concentrate on those that dominate the others at the higher level of risk that he wishes to bear vis-á-vis lone wolves with a higher degree of risk aversion.

MODERATE RISK AVERSION: WITH COMBINATION OF ATTACK METHODS POSSIBLE

When the lone wolf terrorist has a moderate level of risk aversion his map of indifference curves is characterised by curves that are steeper than those that characterise the lone wolf with very low risk aversion. This is depicted in Figure 8.5. The indifference curves for this lone wolf terrorist are steeper because a terrorist with a higher degree of risk aversion requires more compensation in the form of higher expected payoffs if he is to bear a higher level of risk. He will not be drawn towards the very riskiest attack methods or attack method combinations and he will not be drawn into complete specialisation in terrorism. As such, the indifference curve map or grouping sits further to the left than the case we have just examined and his optimal choice is more likely to be at the tangent between his indifference curve and one of the non-specialist efficient sets. The lone wolf terrorist who is moderately averse to risk will be drawn to attack methods and attack method combinations of a moderate level of risk. While the less risk averse lone wolf is prepared to deploy attack method combinations with levels of standard deviation (risk) perhaps 8.00 or higher, the moderately risk averse lone wolf may perhaps be unprepared to venture to a higher level of risk. Conversely, he may also not be prepared to venture into lower levels of risk, perhaps below 5.00 or 4.00. Being attracted to neither the highest or lowest risk attack methods, this may mean that he will avoid hostage taking and unconventional attacks on the one hand and assassination on the other (or allocate a smaller percentage of his resources to them). He may allocate more of his resources to bombing and armed attacks.

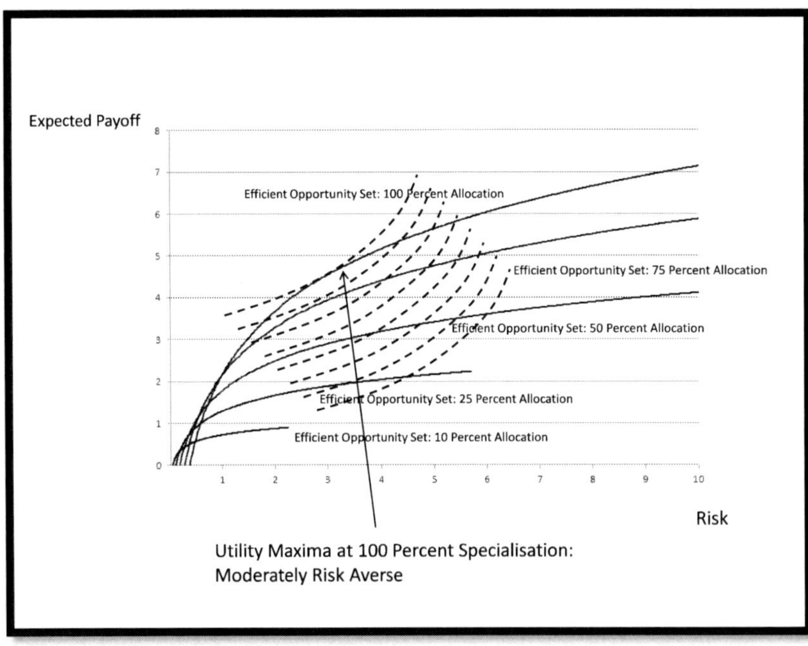

Figure 8.5. The Steeper Indifference Curves of a Moderately Risk Averse Lone Wolf.

The attack methods that mainly constitute the attack method combinations that attract this lone wolf are unconventional attacks, hostage taking, bombing and armed attacks. Examples of resource allocation weightings for these attack methods are as follows. For an attack method combination with an expected payoff of 4.84 and a risk of 4.95, the lone wolf operating at 75 percent specialisation allocates 3.40 percent to unconventional attacks, 60.60 percent to bombing, 7.20 percent to hostage taking and the remainder of around 4.00 percent to armed attacks. At a slightly higher level of risk of 5.68, an expected payoff of 5.04 is generated by allocating 4.20 percent to unconventional attacks, 58.50 to bombing, 10.30 to hostage taking and around 2.00 percent to armed attacks. If the lone wolf engages in a lower level of specialisation of 50 percent allocation of resources to terrorism and 50 percent to some other form of expression, attack method combinations with middle range levels of risk are also generated by allocations to these four attack methods. For example, with 50 percent specialisation, at a 4.19 level of risk and 3.45 expected payoff, the lone wolf allocates 3.10 percent to unconventional attacks, 38.00 percent to bombing, 8.30 percent to hostage taking and about half of one percent to armed attacks.

High Risk Aversion: With Combination of Attack Methods Possible

When the lone wolf terrorist has a very high level of risk aversion his analytical reflection is a map or group of indifference curves that are much steeper than those that characterise the reflection of the lone wolf with very low risk aversion. This type of lone wolf terrorist is depicted in Figure 8.6. He does not avoid risk altogether but he requires much more compensation in the form of higher expected payoff for bearing additional risk. He will be averse to the riskiest attack methods and attack method combinations and prefer to allocate resources to attack methods or combinations that yield a lower expected payoff and a lower risk. If he is to venture into a region of higher risk, he will expect considerable additional expected payoff for doing so. He may also be expected to be a non-specialist and prefer not to allocate a large percentage of his resources to terrorism. As such, his indifference curves map will be situated more the left-hand side than either of the two cases we have examined previously and his optimal choice is likely to be located at the tangent of his indifference curve and one of the very non-specialist efficient sets. He will prefer levels of risk, perhaps in the range below 4.00. We know from our delineation of the lone wolf terrorist's opportunities that this will mean limiting his exposure to the riskier attack methods such as hostage taking and unconventional attacks and allocating more resources to less risky attack methods such as assassination and armed attacks.

The attack methods that dominate the attack method combinations that attract the very risk averse lone wolf terrorist are assassination and bombing. Remember, bombing still figures prominently in many of the lower risk opportunities that are available to the lone wolf terrorist. Examples of resource allocation weightings are as follows. For a non-specialist lone wolf who allocates 25 percent of his resources to violent terrorism, an attack method combination that has a risk of 2.09 and an expected payoff of 1.72 requires an allocation of 1.60 percent of resources to unconventional attacks, 19.00 percent to bombing, 4.2 percent to hostage taking and a small allocation to armed attacks. At a lower level of risk still, an attack method combination with a risk of 0.72 and an expected payoff of 0.95 requires an allocation of 9.7 percent of resources to bombing, 12 percent to assassination, 1.00 percent each to armed attacks and hijacking and very small amounts of less than one-half of one percent to unconventional attacks and hostage taking. At the lowest level of specialisation of 10 percent resources allocated to terrorism the pattern is similar. Bombing remains a prominent inclusion in most attack method combinations. At the very lowest levels of risk, assassination dominates.

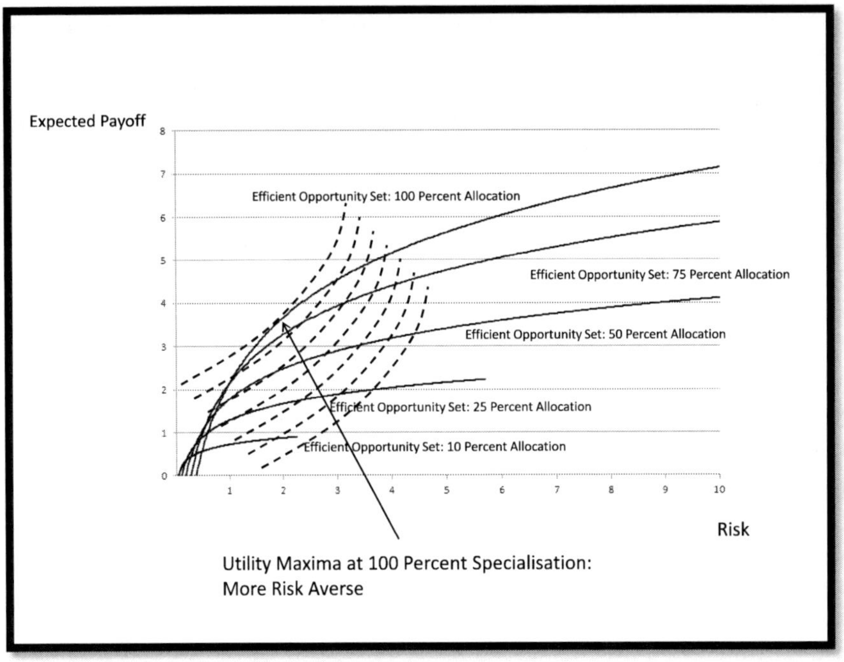

Figure 8.6. The Steep Indifference Curves of a More Risk Averse Lone Wolf.

There are opportunities available to the lone wolf terrorist. Although the lone wolf's opportunities may seem intractable, they are subject to important delineations. Some opportunities are not available. From the opportunities that are available, the lone wolf terrorist makes choices. These choices depend on the exact specification of a utility function that characterises the lone wolf. In general, an appropriate utility function to use is the quadratic utility function. Depending on the level of the lone wolf's aversion to risk, the lone wolf will make choices from among the attack methods and attack method combinations on the basis of risk and expected payoff. If he is very averse to risk, he will only venture to the higher risk combinations if he is substantially rewarded with additional expected payoff. If he is less averse to risk, the higher risk combinations will attract him. An optimal choice is one that has the highest level of expected payoff for a given level of risk. This will be a choice from the efficient set of opportunities. The lone wolf might make a sub-optimal choice. He might make mistakes. His sub-optimal choices are less dangerous than his optimal ones. An error from the lone wolf leads to a less dangerous choice but we do not rely on him making errors. We are prepared for his most dangerous choice.

Choice When No Combination Is Possible

We will not rule out the possibility that the lone wolf terrorist cannot combine attack methods. When this is the case, the lone wolf cannot obtain the 'gains from combination' that derive from the statistical-correlation structure that characterises the payoffs to the different attack methods. He is restricted to allocating some portion of his resources, depending on his level of specialisation, to a single attack method during any given time period. In this case, the lone wolf terrorist will optimise his expected utility function under the additional constraint that only one attack method can be deployed. Again, the lone wolf terrorist who is not averse to risk will tend to choose a riskier attack method such as hostage taking or unconventional attacks and will also be more inclined towards the riskier activity of specialising in terrorism rather than allocating time and resources to other activities. The more risk averse the lone wolf is, the more likely it becomes that he will avoid the riskier attack methods and focus instead on attack methods such as armed attacks, bombing and assassinations. He is unlikely to be a specialist in terrorism and will reserve some resources, perhaps the overwhelming majority of his resources, for other forms of expression. As risk aversion decreases, we expect specialisation to increase and we can determine which attack method dominates particular ranges of risk and particular levels of specialisation.

The opportunities for the lone wolf terrorist who cannot combine attack methods are restricted. When combination is not possible, the lone wolf cannot obtain the 'gains from combination'. He must choose to allocate his resources to a single attack method. Under these conditions, an optimal choice once more means allocating resources to the attack method that has the highest expected payoff for a given level of risk at a given level of specialisation. We computed a schedule of these choices showing which attack methods we would expect to be chosen at particular levels of risk and particular levels of specialisation. This was presented in Table 7.2. Lone wolves with higher risk aversion will shy away from the riskiest activities and may also tend to avoid specialisation. If the very risk averse lone wolf avoids levels of risk (standard deviation) that are above, perhaps, 4.00, he will allocate some of his resources to bombing or, if he is very risk averse, to assassination. If he is less risk averse and decides to allocate all of his resources to one of the available attack methods he might specialise in assassination. For the lone wolf terrorist with moderate risk aversion who is attracted to the expected payoff-risk trade-off in the region where standard deviation is around 4.00 to around 8.00, bombing and hijacking are enticing. At a standard deviation of around 6.00, more and more resources will be allocated to bombing and the lone wolf terrorist with moderate risk aversion may specialise in bombing. Beyond this level of risk, the allocation of some resources to hijacking becomes the preferred choice. At levels of risk beyond 8.00 we will more than likely find the lone wolf with very low risk aversion. He will allocate more and more resources to armed attacks and may even come to specialise in them. If he desires even more risk, hostage taking and unconventional attacks will entice him until finally we leave the domain of the risk averse lone wolf terrorist and enter the domain of the risk seeking lone wolf. It is here that we will find risk seeking lone wolf allocating all of his resources to the riskiest attack method.

One of the more interesting aspects of our schedule of specialisation and attack methods that we presented in Table 7.2 are those 'inflection' points where a lower level of specialisation in a more risky attack method might be preferred to a higher level of specialisation in a less risky attack method. A more risk averse lone wolf terrorist might be expected to allocate less of his resources and time to terrorism than he does to other activities. This does not necessarily mean that he will not 'test' or experiment with some slightly more risky attack methods and allocate a small amount of his resources to them. The other interesting aspect of our schedule of attack method choice and specialisation under conditions where attack methods cannot be combined are those points at which the lone wolf terrorist of the more risk seeking type might be expected to plunge all of his time and resources into a single attack method. These 'plunge points' occur at various points across the ranges of variability encompassed by our opportunity sets. Throughout the schedule of specialisation we will expect lone wolf terrorists with different levels of risk aversion to allocate some amount of their time and resources to a particular attack method (if they cannot combine attack methods). Only the most risk averse would 'experiment' with assassination and only the risk seeking 'plunger' would allocate all of his resources including time to an armed attack. One the more interesting points of inflection is where bombing melds with assassination approximately between a standard deviation of 0.5 and 2. When targeted, as in the Kaczynski case, bombing resembles assassination. Our schedule of specialisation along with our definition and measurement of risk allows us to incorporate these subtleties into our analysis of the behaviour and choices of the lone wolf terrorist.

Concluding Remarks

For a lone wolf seeking to inflict some level of human tragedy, the lone wolf terrorist's optimal choice is also his most dangerous choice. The critics of economic analysis often focus on the popular conceptions of ideas such as 'rationality' and 'self interest' without fully uncovering the meanings that have been attached to these concepts within economic science. The lone wolf can be rational and still make serious errors of judgement. Rationality is not the same as perfect decision making. Within the economic framework that we have used to ensnare the lone wolf or to encompass his opportunities and choices, the lone wolf terrorist makes choices on the basis of risk and expected payoff. These are the two moments of the distribution of the possible outcomes of attack method deployment. The analysis of choice on the basis of these two moments of the distribution is a simpler alternative to a 'full expected utility approach' where the expected utility of each possible outcome of a choice must be assessed. The mean-variance analysis not only approximates such a full expected utility analysis for a wide range of utility functions but has the added advantage of providing computable results. If the goal of the economic analysis of terrorism is to provide anything beyond purely logical arguments to law enforcement then an approach that yields computable results is essential.

The lone wolf terrorist is ensnared within the analytical framework by two important steps. The first of these is the delineation of the lone wolf terrorist's opportunities. Certain opportunities are ruled in and others are ruled out. Although the world seemingly offers an endless array of opportunities, this is not the case. Among other things, the risk-reward trade-off available to the lone wolf is a concave set and this set has an upper bound beyond which no attack method combination offers a higher expected payoff for the given level of risk. The second step is the delineation of the lone wolf's choices. The lone wolf optimises an expected utility function. His optimisation problem consists of choosing the attack method or attack method combination that inflicts the optimal level of human tragedy at the chosen level of risk. A lot depends, then, on the lone wolf's preferences for risk. If he has very low aversion to risk, he will be enticed by the higher expected payoffs of the riskier attack method combinations. If he has a higher aversion to risk, he is enticed by the lower expected payoffs of the less risky attack method combinations. The lone wolf's choice is a risk-reward trade-off. This must take place within the boundaries of the opportunities that we have delineated. The lone wolf is ensnared within the economic analytical framework. His analytical reflection—his indifference curves—is encompassed within expected-payoff-risk-space.

Confronted with the available opportunities and his preferences, the lone wolf sees that the optimal choice at a given level of risk is some point of tangency between the uppermost indifference curve and the uppermost boundary of the relevant set of opportunities. This single point is the optimal choice. It has the highest expected payoff at the particular level of risk. We know from the examination of the lone wolf's opportunities that certain attack methods dominate attack method combinations at particular ranges of risk. Often within a range of at least a few points of risk (standard deviation) the dominant attack methods are found to constitute attack method combinations in very similar weighting schemes. For example, with complete specialisation, an attack method combination that has a risk of 8.39 and an expected payoff of 6.91 is obtained by combining unconventional attacks (6.4 percent), bombing (76 percent), hostage taking (16.7 percent) and a very small allocation to armed attacks. An attack method in the same risk range, with a risk of 9.12 and an expected payoff of 7.06, is obtained by combining unconventional attacks (6.9 percent), bombing (74 percent) and hostage taking (19.1 percent). It is not the case that the attack methods and the weightings that are assigned to them change dramatically within ranges of risk and that the attack methods are 'mixed up' at each and every level of risk. We do not need to know the lone wolf's exact optimal choice to be able to reach useful conclusions about the type of attack methods that he will choose if he has a particular level of risk aversion.

When the lone wolf is not very averse to risk, he will not require very much additional enticement in the form of increments to expected payoff to be engaged in a more risky attack method combination. He is more likely to specialise in violent terrorism and his attack methods will largely be some combination of bombing, hostage taking and unconventional attacks. Lone wolves with higher levels of risk aversion will require larger incremental increases in expected payoffs for a given increase in risk than our less risk averse lone wolf. These lone wolves are likely to engage in a lower level of specialisation in violent terrorism and for a lone wolf in the mid-range of risk aversion resources are likely to be allocated to bombing, hostage taking, unconventional attacks and armed attacks. When the lone wolf has a high degree of risk aversion, much higher increments in expected payoffs are required for each increment in risk. The lone wolf with a high degree of risk aversion is less likely to be a specialist and allocate all of his resources to terrorism and when he does allocate resources to terrorism he will tend to allocate most of his resources to assassination, armed attacks and bombing. Although opportunities may seem endless and choices impossible to delineate, the behaviour of the lone wolf can be analysed within an economic analytical framework that encompasses him, his choices and his opportunities. Opportunities and choices constitute the foundation for a framework that ensnares the lone wolf. He cannot roam freely in expected-payoff-risk-space.

The lone wolf terrorist's choices are more restricted if he cannot engage in the combination of attack methods. Once more, the lone wolf's aversion to risk plays a large part in determining which (single) attack method he will choose. If he is very risk averse, he will avoid complete specialisation in violent attack methods or terrorism. When he does attack, assassination dominates his choices at the lowest levels of risk. Lone wolves with lower levels of risk aversion may increase their level of specialisation and direct their resources to attack methods such as bombing and hijacking. We may see a specialist lone wolf bomber at an intermediate level of risk and risk aversion. At still lower levels of risk aversion, the lone wolf will exhibit more of a tendency towards specialisation in the violent attack methods of terrorism. At these lower levels of risk aversion (and higher levels of risk) we are likely to find lone wolves allocating resources to hijacking, armed attacks and, at very high levels of risk, hostage taking and unconventional attacks. At various points along the way, as we consider lone wolves with lower and lower levels of risk aversion, we may find specialist lone wolves allocating all of their resources to hijacking, armed attacks, hostage taking or unconventional attacks. At all steps along the way, we can follow because all of the lone wolves must be found to inhabit the delineated regions of expected-payoff-risk-space.

Chapter 9

SUMMARY: THE LONE WOLF'S OPPORTUNITIES AND CHOICES

The economic analysis of any situation or behaviour is based on two things: opportunities and choices. Opportunities are not limitless. There are limits to what the world offers, particularly within certain contexts. Given these limited opportunities, the individual makes a choice. Economic science usually operates by determining the best or optimal choice that could be made under particular circumstances. This has attracted a great deal of criticism because people are usually perceived to be incapable of making optimal choices. Rational choice is a prime target of the critics of economic analysis. To make things clear, though, while people may not be perfect calculating machines, they are far from completely hapless decision makers. Good decisions do get made every day. Second, economic science does not require people to be perfect calculating machines. People may make mistakes or errors of judgement. The same is true of our lone wolf terrorist. He has a set of available opportunities and he must make choices. In making his choices he may err but it would be very foolish to rely upon any terrorist making consistently poor decisions let alone assuming that all terrorists are incapable of making an optimal choice from a set of opportunities. After all, terrorist attacks have been planned and executed with the utmost care, attention and calculating cunning. The way in which we have constructed our economic framework ensures that we treat the optimal decision of the terrorist as the most dangerous one. If the lone wolf terrorist errs he may be less dangerous than we have allowed for. This is a better situation than allowing for an error-prone 'irrational' lone wolf terrorist and finding out later that he was in fact far more calculating.

The opportunities available to the lone wolf terrorist can be narrowed down step by step within an expected-payoff-risk or mean-variance analytical framework. The attack methods available to the lone wolf terrorist are the attack methods that have been deployed by lone wolves and transnational terrorists over the past four decades. These include armed attacks, arson, assassination, bombing, hostage taking, hijacking, kidnapping, unconventional attacks and the miscellaneous 'unknown' and 'other' categories. Each of these attack methods has been utilised to inflict human tragedy and a large time series of data exists that allows us to draw some conclusions about the expected brutality of the various attack methods. What was most noticeable from our first broad discussion of attack methods is the brutality of some of the attack methods that are seemingly not overtly violent. Hijacking and hostage taking generate large numbers of injuries and fatalities. If the lone wolf terrorist seeks to cause injuries and fatalities, he might not restrict his activities to overtly violent forms of attack such as bombing or armed attacks. Rather, he may engage in hostage taking expecting to inflict human tragedy in the event that his demands are not conceded to by the government. This implies, of course, that even if demands are made by a lone wolf during a hostage situation, the attainment of the substance of any such demands may not be his primary objective.

Within a mean-variance framework, assassination too stands out. Assassination is an overtly violent attack method and there is little doubt that the lone wolf terrorist assassin aims to inflict some level of human tragedy when he uses this attack method. Indeed, inflicting one or more fatalities is the clear objective. What is important for us to consider is the fact that assassination attempts are characterised by a low level of expected payoff and a very low level of risk. There are usually only a few injuries and fatalities resulting from an assassination attempt but the time series of injuries and fatalities associated with assassination does not display a great deal of variability or risk. In fact, assassination attempts have rarely failed to cause injury and fatality even though the primary target of the assassination may not have been harmed during an assassination attempt. Although the press will normally report on an 'unsuccessful' assassination attempt, especially of the archetype kind, it is our goal to pre-empt or pursue the lone wolf terrorist who would be responsible for *any* level of human tragedy. Whether the primary target has been struck or not, assassination has been associated with a consistent infliction of human tragedy. The lone wolf terrorist who decides to deploy assassination as an attack method must be expected to inflict some level of injury and fatality. Like hostage taking, law enforcement must consider the possibility that the lone wolf terrorist plans an assassination expecting to inflict a level of human tragedy even in the event that the primary target or targets is not struck.

The first step that we took in delineating the lone wolf terrorist's attack method opportunities was to identify the categories of attack methods that would encompass the attack methods that are available to the lone wolf terrorist. The RAND Corporation's transnational terrorist database (RAND-MIPT) is characterised by ten attack methods or categories. This dataset provides a statistical picture of the lethality of the various categories of attack methods. Overtly violent attack methods such as bombing and armed attacks have generated a significant number of injuries and fatalities over the past four decades. However, less overtly violent attack methods have also been very harmful. Elements of this statistical picture are embedded within the extant news reports that covered the terrorist activities. Casual attention may be insufficient to obtain a reasonable estimate of the possible outcomes to a terrorist attack but we must expect those for whom terrorism is an all encompassing objective to have devoted much more than casual attention to the information embedded within the popular press. The most common attack methods among transnational terrorists are bombing and armed attacks. Likewise, lone wolves have predominantly tended to choose these two attack methods. Lone wolves have not chosen completely unique attack methods. They are, like the transnational terrorist, unable to escape from the two moments of the distribution that characterises the injuries and fatalities generated by the deployment of terrorist attack methods.

Each attack method has a historical statistical record that tells us the average level of injury and fatality that may be expected to result from the deployment of that attack method. This is the expected payoff. When deployed in a particular instance an attack method may generate more or less injury and fatality than expected. The possibility that the actual outcomes will vary from the expected outcomes is the risk that is associated with the deployment of an attack method. This risk is measured by the variance or standard deviation of the payoffs. The lone wolf terrorist must confront the risk-reward trade-off and cannot escape from its implications. If a higher payoff is desired, a higher risk must be borne. The riskiest attack methods will normally have higher expected payoffs but these attack methods are attended by a higher probability that the actual outcome of an attack will vary from the outcome that was expected. This variability works on the upside and the downside and is not asymmetrical. For example, an attack method may be expected to generate 5.00 injuries and fatalities with a standard deviation also equal to 2.00. When deployed, the most likely outcome will lie in the range of between 3.00 and 7.00 injuries and fatalities. The lone wolf terrorist's attack may inflict more or less human tragedy than he expected. The lone wolf terrorist must face the trade-off between variability and reward and make a choice between higher risk and higher reward or lower risk and lower reward such that his choice is in accordance with his risk preference or the level of variability of the possible outcomes that he feels comfortable with given the payoff he expects to obtain.

A mean-variance analytical framework depicts this trade-off between risk and reward in the lone wolf's choices as preference ranking based on mean (expected) payoffs and variance (risk) and it does so in a manner that is computable in the sense that intermediate assumptions do not enter in subsequent steps of the ordering of attack methods on the basis of mean and variance. Each attack method has an expected payoff and risk. A mean-variance analysis of choice among the different attack methods involves depicting the lone wolf terrorist as an individual who ranks his preferences for attack methods on the basis of payoff and risk. He then chooses the attack method that he has ranked the highest. Although this is a formal way of depicting the choice, it does not require any special intelligence from the lone wolf terrorist. In choosing among some possible options, an individual will select the one that he likes the best. When the options are subject to risk and uncertainty, he has to make some allowance for risk and will probably expect a higher expected payoff from a riskier option. Mean-variance analysis simplifies the analysis of the choice scenario. Rather than weighing up the likelihood of all the possible outcomes of the utilisation of a terrorist attack method, attack methods are ranked and chosen on the basis of risk and reward. Not surprisingly given the inherent soundness of this approach, mean-variance analysis approximates a full expected utility analysis.

It is here that we start to realise how important the lone wolf terrorist's preferences for risk are likely to be in shaping his choices from among attack methods and attack method combinations. Each attack method has a risk and a payoff. To obtain a higher payoff, the lone wolf will need to explore riskier attack methods the outcomes of which are more variable. If the lone wolf terrorist prefers risk or is enticed by risk, he will be enticed by the riskier attack methods and their relatively higher expected payoffs. If the lone wolf terrorist dislikes or is deterred by risk, he will drift towards the less risky attack methods and their relatively lower expected payoffs. The mean-variance analytical framework paints a very clear picture of risky choice and the trade-off between variability of possible outcomes and expected reward. In delineating the lone wolf's opportunities, our first step was to identify the attack methods or categories towards which resources might be allocated. Our second step was to identify the risk-reward trade-off that characterises those attack methods or attack method categories. Step by step, the opportunities are delineated and aspects of the opportunities that are relevant to the analytical structure are highlighted. Where the lone wolf terrorist may appear, on the surface, to confront a large array of disorganised and complex opportunities, we find that he confronts attack methods or attack method categories with well-defined risk-reward trade-offs.

The risk-reward trade-off that characterises attack methods and attack method combinations has a statistical-correlation structure. If the lone wolf terrorist can combine attack methods, the correlation among the expected payoffs to each attack method becomes an important part of the analytical-statistical structure. Indeed, the nature of the correlation structure among attack methods determines the nature of the risk-reward trade-off and allows the law enforcement to rule in or rule out particular risk-reward structures. If the expected payoffs of different attack methods were perfectly positively correlated, the risk-reward trade-off would be linear. From a law enforcement point of view, this is the ideal case. Perfect positive correlation means that there are no advantages in terms of increased expected payoffs or lower risk associated with combining attack methods. Perfect positive correlation restricts and constrains the risk-reward trade-off. With perfect positive correlation between the payoffs to attack methods the lone wolf terrorist cannot reduce the chances of a poor outcome by combining attack methods. Unfortunately, the payoffs to attack methods are not perfectly positively correlated and it would be a short-coming in the investigative process if this were overlooked.

With imperfect correlation between the payoffs to attack methods there are gains from combination that may be obtained by the lone wolf terrorist who combines attack methods. Since it might occur to the lone wolf that 'spreading risk' or avoiding 'putting all eggs in one basket' is a good idea, it does not take any special level of rationality or insight for the lone wolf terrorist to obtain the 'gains from combination'. Furthermore, he may combine attack methods over time by altering his choice of attack method from period to period. If he were to choose arson in one period and bombing in another, then ex ante his overall level of risk and reward could exhibit gains from combination. It need not necessarily be a simultaneous combination. If the lone wolf does combine attack methods whose expected payoffs are not perfectly correlated, he will be able to generate higher expected payoffs at each level of risk or, similarly, reduce his risk at each level of expected payoff. Obviously, these are important considerations for law enforcement because the risk-reward relationship facing the lone wolf terrorist is shaped by the correlation structure. Fortunately, there are some bounds that characterise a feasible risk-reward relationship and there are some risk-reward relationships that are not possible. With imperfectly positive or negative correlation between the expected payoffs of the available attack methods the risk-reward relationship must be concave in expected payoff-risk space. A convex risk-reward relationship is impossible.

The lone wolf's opportunities for trading risk against reward in his planning and execution of terrorist attacks are bounded and some opportunities are impossible. With two or more attack methods that are perfectly positively correlated there is no incentive to combine attack methods and no advantages to doing so. When two or more attack methods are imperfectly negatively or positively correlated there is an incentive to combine attack methods and there are advantages to doing so. These 'gains from combination' provide the lone wolf with a higher expected payoff for a given level of risk or a lower risk at a given level of expected payoff. If law enforcement overlooked the correlation structure of attack methods and the 'gains from combination' of attack methods there would be a miscalculation of the risk-reward relationship facing the lone wolf and erroneous assessments of the type of risk preference that characterises the lone wolf. There are categories of attack methods and each attack method or category has a risk and an expected payoff. The lone wolf cannot escape the risk-reward trade-off. The more risk he takes, the higher his expected payoff. The relationship between risk and reward is not random or without structure. With imperfect correlations between expected payoffs the risk-reward relationship will be concave. It cannot be convex and can only be linear if correlations are perfectly positive. Unfortunately, the concave risk-reward relationship contains the inherent possibility of 'gains from combination'.

When attack methods can be combined, the risk-reward relationship will have certain properties depending on the nature of the correlation structure that characterises the expected payoffs of the various attack methods. We have observed from the historical data that the expected payoffs to attack methods have imperfect correlation with each other. The risk-reward trade-off will not be linear. Our next step is to determine which attack methods and attack method combinations have the 'optimal' risk-reward relationship. That is, provide the highest level of expected payoff at a given level of risk. This determination is made by solving the relevant quadratic programming problem. Under a number of different constraints that may confront the lone wolf terrorist in different circumstances, the solution to the quadratic programming problems provides the weighting or resource allocation schemes that define the optimal or efficient combinations of the available attack methods. These efficient combinations have the highest expected payoff at each level of risk. Over particular ranges of risk—say, low, moderate and high—particular attack method dominate others and the attack methods are not all 'mixed up' within risk ranges. This allows us to consider ranges of risk and ranges of risk aversion and identify the attack methods that dominate optimal choices over these ranges.

At lower levels of risk, the efficient attack method combinations are dominated by assassination and bombing attacks. At higher levels of risk, efficient attack method combinations are dominated by bombing, hostage taking and unconventional attacks. Arson is practically ruled out when the lone wolf terrorist can combine attack methods. Armed attacks are present across many of the attack method combinations but do not attract large resource allocations. The amount of human tragedy that the lone wolf can expect to inflict will vary with his degree of specialisation in these attack methods, in terrorism. At lower levels of specialisation the lone wolf terrorist has restricted opportunity for combination. Although the lower risk attack method combinations remain dominated by assassination and bombing and the higher risk attack method combinations remain dominated by bombing, hostage taking and unconventional attacks at all levels of specialisation, the non-specialist lone wolf is expected to inflict fewer injuries and fatalities at all levels of risk than his more specialist counterparts. Within our economic-theoretical mean-variance framework, the specialist lone wolf terrorist is the most dangerous because he may exploit the statistical-correlation structure of the attack methods most fully but he is, at the same time, encompassed by it.

If the lone wolf cannot combine attack methods, he must choose a single attack method within the given time period. He will then specialise to some degree in that single attack method[1]. The optimal allocation of resources at a particular level of risk is once again determined by the solution of the relevant constrained quadratic programming problem. At very low levels of risk the lone wolf will specialise to some degree in assassination, then

[1] Note that we do not equate the use of a single attack method with specialisation. Specialisation refers to the amount of resources devoted to terrorism (an attack method or combination) compared with the amount of resources devoted to other activities.

bombing at medium-low to medium ranges of risk, then hijacking, then armed attacks, then hostage taking and unconventional attacks as the level of risk that he is willing to bear increases. At various points we may see complete specialist lone wolves who allocate 100 percent of resources to a particular attack method at a particular level of risk. At a medium level of risk a specialist lone wolf allocating 100 percent of resources to bombing may well emerge. At higher ranges of risk we may see specialists or near-specialists in hijacking, armed attacks, hostage taking or unconventional attacks. Specialisation in violent terrorism carries more risk than non-specialisation. The unavailability of combination heightens that risk. Specialist lone wolves will be enticed by it.

A lone wolf can be depicted as choosing between attack methods and attack method combinations on the basis of expected payoff and risk. The actual preference ordering that results from a mean-variance analysis will approximate a full expected utility analysis even when quadratic utility is not assumed *and* payoffs are not normally distributed. If a quadratic utility function is assumed *or* if the payoffs are normally distributed the preference orderings will accord exactly with the von Neumann-Morgenstern axioms. In either case, quadratic utility approximates the preference orderings of a broader class of utility functions. A lone wolf who chooses optimally chooses from the efficient set of attack method opportunities. To be precise, he chooses that attack method or combination that best suits his preference for risk and reward. The lone wolf's preferences for risk play a significant role in shaping his choices of attack methods and combinations. Because we have been able to delineate the opportunities, we know which attack methods dominate attack method combinations across particular ranges of risk. Indeed, across ranges of risk that may be broadly labelled as low, medium and high (with more precision being accorded where necessary to, say, medium-low risk) the attack methods that constitute the efficient attack method combinations are characterised by stable and consistent patterns. The riskiest attack method combinations will be chosen by a lone wolf who is more risk seeking or not very risk averse. Lone wolves that exhibit higher levels of risk aversion will choose from attack method combinations that occupy less risky ranges of the efficient opportunity set. The lone wolf's preferences for risk shape his choice of attack method combination and, thereby, his choice of particular attack methods (which constitute the combination).

If the lone wolf terrorist is not very risk averse he will choose relatively high risk attack method combinations. These attack method combinations will be predominantly constituted or dominated by bombing, hostage taking and unconventional attacks. A not-very-risk-averse lone wolf terrorist will also be more likely to specialise in terrorism and allocate a large percentage (or all) of his resources to the available attack methods. A more risk averse lone wolf will choose lower risk attack method combinations. These attack method combinations will be constituted by unconventional attacks, hostage taking, bombing and armed attacks. Again unconventional attacks, hostage taking and bombing figure prominently but there will be lower resource allocations to hostage taking and unconventional attacks and increases in the resources allocated to bombing and armed attacks. This more risk averse lone wolf is also likely to specialise to a lesser degree and may allocate a relatively large percentage of his resources to activities other than attack methods and terrorism. The very risk averse lone wolf will choose the least risky attack method combinations. These attack method combinations will be constituted predominantly by armed attacks, assassination and bombing. This type of lone wolf is the least likely to specialise in violent attack methods and terrorism and is more likely to allocate a large percentage of his resources to other activities. The complete opportunity set presents the lone wolf terrorist with attack methods and combinations across all available ranges of risk. At particular risk ranges and particular ranges of risk aversion particular attack methods dominate the optimal attack method combinations. It is by this approach that we determine the type of attack method that will most likely be chosen by a lone wolf terrorist with a particular type of risk aversion.

CONCLUDING REMARKS

For a seemingly hopelessly complicated environmental context we have defined a structure. A lone wolf terrorist must choose attack methods. He makes his choice on the basis of the two moments of the distribution of injuries and fatalities that are expected to be generated by the attack method. In a formal manner of speaking, the lone wolf orders his preferences for attack methods on the basis of their expected payoff (mean) and variance (risk). He chooses the attack method that he ranks the highest. This may or may not be an optimal choice. The lone wolf can make mistakes. The axioms of rationality only refer to the consistency of the preference orderings. An optimal choice will be one that optimises the lone wolf's expected utility. An expected utility function that guarantees that the preferences formed on its basis are consistent with the von Neumann-Morgenstern axioms is the quadratic utility function. Although this type of function has been the subject of controversy within financial economics, it has been found to approximate a broad class of utility functions and mean-variance preference ordering has been found to approximate full expected utility analysis. The approximation with computable results—that is, all of the numerical-type conclusions that we have been able to reach without intermediate assumptions—would seem to be a more desirable path than an abstract mathematical-economic path that produces neat models but which are so abstract as to be operationally worthless. The latter path has no direct value for the investigative process.

The lone wolf is an unidentified subject (UNSUB) encompassed by a set of opportunities and faced with the task of making a choice. If he can combine attack methods and if he is enticed by risk, he will choose some combination of bombing, hostage taking and unconventional attacks. If he can combine attack methods but is deterred slightly by risk, he will choose some combination of bombing, hostage taking, unconventional attacks and armed attacks. The combinations chosen by this lone wolf will be characterised by lower resource allocations to hostage taking and unconventional attacks. He may also be less of a specialist and allocate less than 100 percent of his resources to terrorism. If he can combine attack methods and if he is quite deterred by risk, he will choose some combination of bombing, assassination and armed attacks. The very risk averse lone wolf is the least likely of our three lone wolves to be a specialist. He will allocate a low percentage of his resources to terrorism. In making all of these choices, each type of lone wolf aims to optimise his expected payoff for a given level of risk and obtain the highest level of utility available to him given his preferences for risk. This behaviour is best described analogously as the tangency between the efficient set of opportunities—those that have the highest expected payoff for a given level of risk—and the lone wolf's analytical reflection—his indifference curves.

The result of the analysis is that we understand more about the nature or statistical-correlation structure of attack methods and attack method combinations. The set of opportunities confronting the lone wolf terrorist is characterised by a trade-off between risk and reward and an inherent possibility for 'gains from combination'. The set of opportunities is also characterised by attack method combinations that are dominated by particular attack methods over particular ranges of risk. The attack methods are not all mixed up in the combinations at every level of risk such that a small change in risk leads to a wholesale change in the types of attack methods that constitute the optimal attack method combinations. The constituents of the attack methods are stable across ranges of risk. When the lone wolf terrorist chooses an attack method or attack method combination on the basis of the injuries and fatalities he expects to inflict and the variability of the possible outcomes from those which were expected, his risk preference plays a very important role in shaping his choice. Because some attack methods dominate the opportunity set across different ranges of risk they also dominate the lone wolf terrorist's optimal choices across different ranges of risk aversion. It is because of this that we can say that a lone wolf terrorist with a particular type of risk aversion will choose particular attack method combinations which are dominated by particular attack methods. In the second part of the book we explore this opportunity-choice scenario from another perspective. When the lone wolf makes his choice and undertakes a particular type of attack he reveals to us his particular type of risk aversion. If the type of risk aversion that characterises the lone wolf terrorist would lead us to expect him to exhibit other characteristics we may draw inferences that may provide us with investigative advice that may be communicated to law enforcement agencies that are in pursuit of the active and still-at-large lone wolf terrorist.

PART TWO: THE LONE WOLF PROFILE

> [There should be] a much broader use of scientific expertise... economics, accountancy or anthropology in cases in which ethnic minorities are involved. Not all disciplines are required in all cases (sometimes even none of them), but they must be available and there must be a sufficient mutual intellectual understanding of the contents of each other's work to enable a correct assessment of the expected role and contribution——Petrus van Duyne 1999, p.79.

How do we know what 'type' of lone wolf terrorist we are pursuing? We have an idea about how many injuries and fatalities can be expected and we understand the importance of the correlation structure and 'gains from combination'. But if a lone wolf can be any type of lone wolf—very risk averse, moderately risk averse, less risk averse (more risk seeking)—have we narrowed things down enough? Here we face a problem that is familiar to law enforcement. Quite simply, until the offender strikes, we do not know that he exists and cannot know what 'type' of offender he is. After the offender strikes once, we may still be unable to profile him with any degree of confidence. After the offender strikes twice or three times, his 'signature' becomes clearer and a profile may be constructed with more confidence. This is the case for other serial offenders and the serial lone wolf will not be different. It is usually only after two or three incidences that law enforcement and investigators are able to conclude that the incidences are probably the work of a single offender and not two or three separate offenders. So we may not know we are dealing with a lone wolf terrorist until he has struck more than once. No analytical framework—psychological or economic—can pinpoint an individual offender before he is engaged in any illegitimate activity. All that we can do before the lone wolf terrorist strikes is to delineate the prospective offender's opportunities and optimal choices. Our next step is to 'invert' this type of analytical process and imagine that we start from the moment when a terrorist activity has been undertaken and a lone wolf UNSUB is at large. What do the characteristics of the terrorist activity—the crime scene and type of attack method—tell us about the lone wolf terrorist?

Once a lone wolf strikes or a threat is made, the 'profiler' attempts to infer the characteristics of the offender from the characteristics of the crime. The profile of the offender is used as part of the investigative process and constitutes what may be called 'behavioural investigative advice' to assist in the pursuit of the lone wolf UNSUB[1]. Our

[1] UNSUB is 'unidentified subject', in the FBI's terminology (Douglas and Olshaker 1996).

position throughout this book has been that arguments about definitions and philosophical categories of terrorist activity are less important than finding a way to provide operationally relevant analytical results. Once a terrorist action has been perpetrated, there exists an UNSUB or UNSUBs who must be apprehended. Time will be of the essence because the individual or individuals responsible for a violent act of terrorism may strike again. Psychology, through what is now called investigative psychology and forensic psychology, has shown itself to be capable of contributing to the evolving investigative process that begins when an offence is committed or threatened and law enforcement commences its pursuit of the offender. Our task is to contribute to this process in a similar manner using our economic analytical framework. Together, investigative psychology and investigative economics may provide some additional insights about the UNSUB that assist law enforcement in their pursuit of the lone wolf.

The profiling exercise involves the drawing of inferences about the lone wolf UNSUB from the characteristics of his terrorist activity and any other available evidence. To do this, we need to work from the characteristics of terrorist activity, especially the chosen attack method or attack method combination, and other available evidence towards a narrowing down of the risk preference of the lone wolf terrorist. Remember, each attack method and attack method combination has a particular level of risk and sits in a particular region of the opportunity set in expected payoff-risk space. Choices from particular regions or risk ranges of the opportunity set are indicative of a particular level of risk aversion. Once we have identified the risk preference of the lone wolf we can work from that risk preference to aspects of criminal behaviour that may be associated with that risk preference and, finally, to a list of characteristics that may describe the lone wolf UNSUB. This list will be small but not insignificant. The aim, for the time being at least, is to contribute to other efforts directed towards identifying the lone wolf. The reason why we may expect to provide at least some useful behavioural investigative advice is because the Becker and Ehrlich economic models of criminal behaviour and the related work on the economic analysis of terrorist behaviour and choice yield empirically verifiable and verified results. As too does the much broader expected utility theory of choice and its mean-variance approximation. The theoretical structure is sound. Instead of working from observation to theory to empirical test, in part two of this book we work from crime scene evidence (characteristics of the terrorist's activities) to key aspects of the individual's preferences and from preferences to other aspects of behaviour that are associated with those preferences. In doing so, we squeeze the established economic analytical structures for information that may be operationally relevant. We squeeze the analytical structures for pieces of behavioural investigative advice. The characteristics of the lone wolf's terrorist activity and the other available evidence are filtered through the economic analytical framework that encompasses the opportunities and choices of the lone wolf. Terrorist activity reveals preferences. Preferences reveal other aspects of behaviour.

One preference that has not been adequately captured in the existing profiling or investigative psychology methodologies is preference for risk. This is mainly due to the fact that these methodologies do not include a definition and measurement for risk. The risks that are taken by an offender are important and shape our picture of him as an individual and an assessment of the risks involved in undertaking an illegitimate activity enter into the considerations of the offender profilers. However, profilers and investigative psychologists use very informal methods for deciding how much risk an individual has taken in perpetrating a particular attack. For example, if a crime takes place in broad daylight in an area adjacent to a busy a thoroughfare, it will be deemed more risky than if the crime takes place at night in a secluded location and the offender will be deemed to be more risk seeking. This approach, apart from being informal, conflates the planning and approaches of the offender with the riskiness of the offense itself. Let us say, for example, that robbery is characterised by a certain level of risk that each offender must bear if he wishes to partake in a robbery. The location that the offender chooses is part of his management of the risk inherent in the illegitimate activity. A risk-averse offender may very well choose to undertake a robbery in broad daylight and the risk-seeking offender may very well choose to undertake a robbery under the cover of darkness. It depends on the risks inherent in robbery itself. Choice of location, victim, time and so on are risk management processes. It is the riskiness of robbery as a class of illegitimate activity vis-a-vis other potential legal or illegal activities that is the key to determining the risk preference of the offender and not the characteristics of the specific robbery. A person who chooses robbery reveals a particular preference for risk over someone who reveals a preference for, say, insurance fraud.

The economic analysis of illegitimate behaviour is built on the foundations of the economic analysis of choice under risk and uncertainty. Opportunities that are available to an individual may be classed as more or less risky by the amount of variance their outcomes display over time. One opportunity will be riskier than another if its outcomes are more variable and this variability can be measured by variance. The fundamental choice confronting terrorists and lone wolf terrorists is the choice of attack method. Each attack method represents an opportunity to do violence and inflict some amount of human tragedy. Each attack method is risky in the sense that its outcomes are uncertain and variable. When a particular attack method is chosen, the lone wolf terrorist may expect to inflict some number of fatalities and injuries but there is a possibility that the actual outcomes will fall short or exceed that which was expected. This is the risk that is borne when a lone wolf terrorist chooses a particular attack method. When the lone wolf terrorist chooses an attack method, he reveals a preference for risk or a tolerance or intolerance for variability and uncertainty. Because we have a definition of risk and a measure for it, we have been able to classify particular attack methods as being more or less risky than others and when a lone wolf terrorist chooses one type of attack method or a particular combination of attack methods he reveals to us his preference for risk. The ways in which he may deploy his armed attack or the ways in which he may seize hostages or the targets he may choose for a bombing are his methods for approaching the risks inherent in each attack method. His preference for risk, however, is revealed by his choice of attack method, the riskiness of which is a function of the variability of its outcomes.

In a sense, then, economic analysis augments a particular aspect of the overall approach to offender profiling. This is the stage in the profiling process when the profiler thinks about the type of risk preference—though these words may not necessarily be used—that may characterise the offender. This is important because it not only tells us about the sort of person we might be dealing with but also allows us to draw other inferences about his likely future actions. Although the precise definition of risk and a way to measure it are points of strength that distinguish economic analysis from other approaches, there is no reason why traditional approaches cannot be used alongside an approach that first determines the risk associated with a particular type of terrorist attack method and then draws inferences about the type of lone wolf terrorist that may have perpetrated the act of terrorism using that attack method *within an economic analytical framework*. If profilers have identified the risk of the offender's choice and the risk preference of the offender as important components of the profile, additional insights from the viewpoint of economic analysis might be useful and complementary. In the second part of this book we use what we know about the relative risk of each attack method within the context of our economic analytical framework but instead of attempting to narrow down the optimal and most dangerous choices of different types of lone wolf terrorists, we start from the time of the attack and work backwards, determining what the choice of attack method implies about risk preference and what other characteristics we might expect of a lone wolf terrorist who has revealed a particular type of risk aversion.

Chapter 10

OFFENDER PROFILING

A criminal may reveal what shoes he was wearing from his footprints. His blood-type can be determined by body-fluids left at the scene. But as well as *material* traces, he also leaves *psychological* traces, tell-tale patterns of behaviour that indicate the sort of person that he is... They cannot be taken into a laboratory and dissected under a microscope. They are more like shadows which undoubtedly are connected to the criminal who cast them...[1]

The offender will be as follows[2]:

- Male (because most bombers are male)
- Has knowledge of metalworking, pipefitting and electricity
- Suffered an injustice by Consolidated Edison, which had rendered him chronically ill
- Suffers from an insidious disorder, paranoia and has a persistent and chronic disorder
- Is pathologically self-centred
- Has no friends, male or female, is a loner
- Symmetric athletic body type, neither fat or skinny
- Is middle-aged (due the onset of illness and duration of bombings)
- Good education, likely high school education but not college
- Unmarried, possibly a virgin
- Distrusts and despises male authority, hates father
- Never progressed past the Oedipal stage of love for his mother due to her early death or separation from him
- Lives alone or with female mother-like relative
- Lives in Connecticut, is of Slavic descent, Roman Catholic and attends church
- Neat, tidy and clean-shaven
- Quiet, polite, methodical and prompt
- Has chronic illness, either heart disease, cancer or tuberculosis, most probably heart disease
- Would be wearing a buttoned double-breasted suit when caught

---

[1] Canter and Gregory (1994).
[2] Profile of the 'Mad Bomber' by Dr James Brussel (cited by Canter and Youngs 2009, p.68).

Offender profiling is the drawing inferences about the offender from evidence left at the crime scene. Investigative psychology encompasses profiling but constitutes a broader framework for dealing with the psychological aspects of crime and criminal investigations. Investigative psychology and offender profiling are characterised by a tension between the practices and processes of field agents and the attempts by academics to place investigative psychology on a firm theoretical and empirical footing. The tension very clearly runs through the literature produced by both sides. On the one hand, the FBI profilers rely on individual judgement built from a mixture of research and law enforcement experience to make inferences about an offender. On the other hand, the academic investigative psychologists seem unlikely to concede that profiling is something that only certain people are good at. Rather, they are searching for a psychological theoretical-empirical framework that can be applied to the investigative process in a detached scientific manner by *any appropriately trained person*. This should also be the underlying principle of an application of economic analysis to the task of making inferences about an offender from the nature of the crime scene and the evidence left behind, though we will not rule out the possibility that an individual profiler's intuition might add unique value to the process. Someone might see far deeper within an analytical structure than others.

OFFENDER PROFILING

The criminal profiler character has been a main-stay on television for at least twenty years not least because it is only by having a character that can 'get inside the mind' of the criminal, usually a serial killer, that the otherwise scant evidence can be pieced together and the killer caught all within a primetime hour. The special gifts of the profiler enter prominently in these stories. He or she possesses more or less unique insight into the mind of the criminal. Using the available evidence at the crime scene the profiler draws inferences about the criminal that no-one else could draw. These could include where the criminal lives, the type of car he drives and where he will next commit a crime. The profiler can say things like, "He drives a dark coloured van. It's all beat up. Only one headlight works. He works a menial job, maybe a janitor. He drives aimlessly through the streets at night. He cannot rely on his charm or talk. He must surprise his victims..." and the film segues from the investigators to a darkened alley where a dark coloured, dilapidated van with a broken headlight is slowly approaching another unsuspecting victim. Whatever one might think of the television shows in which the profiler is portrayed, one must admit that the profiler makes for an intriguing character.

Not far behind all of the make-believe of television programming, there lies the actual profession of offender profiling and the academic field of investigative psychology. These are inextricably linked but they are far from being the same thing even though offender profilers write articles about their work and investigative psychologists participate in real investigations. The most notable representatives of these two groups are John Douglas who played a leading role in the establishment of the FBI's criminal profiling unit and who is the author of scholarly articles such as "Criminal Profiling from Crime Scene Analysis[3]," published in *Behavioural Sciences and the Law* and of entertaining books written for a more

[3] Douglas, Ressler, Burgess and Hartman (1986).

popular audience such as "*Mind Hunter*" (Douglas and Olshaker 1996). David Canter is the leading representative of the academic field of investigative psychology. He is the author of many scholarly articles which detail studies into the key part of the profiling process: the drawing of inferences about the offender from evidence left at the crime scene. He is also the co-author of the first authoritative textbook on the subject[4].

The point of disagreement, if it may be described as such, between the two 'camps' turns on the matter of the ability of the profiler to get inside the criminal mind. Criminal profiling is about drawing inferences about the criminal from the evidence that is left at the crime-scene. If one reads Douglas's books and articles, it seems to be the case that the profiler has a special, instinctive ability to perform this task. It may be built on or complemented by years of law enforcement experience and training and education in psychology but, nevertheless, a large part of it is instinctive. That this cannot be accepted fully by the academic side is clear. If profiling is more or less a skill that relies on individual abilities or, what would be worse, instincts, then investigative psychology as an academic or scientific field of inquiry is at least partially undermined. That the construction of a valid and useful criminal profile relies not on the instinctive ability of the profiler as such but on the detached 'laws' of inference obtained by careful academic study of crimes and offenders and which can be applied by *any appropriately trained person* must be the desirable state of affairs for the academic side of the profiling community. The problem is that there is still so much doubt about the validity of criminal profiling that it is unclear who will ultimately be proved correct on this particular point.

Within some parts of the literature serious doubt has been cast upon the very possibility, academic or otherwise, of offender profiling. According to some authors there are no 'patterns' between crimes, crime scenes and offenders that are consistent enough to form the basis for any rigorous academic or rigorous practical offender profiling process. In short, the idea of profiling is better left in the television script than applied in real investigations. This point of view has found its strongest expression in the articles of Snook et al. which portray criminal profiling as plain fantasy. In an article entitled "The Criminal Profiling Illusion: What's Behind the Smoke and Mirrors?" Snook et al. (2008) argue there is an absence of 'compelling' scientific evidence that offender profiling is reliable, valid or useful and the belief that offender profiling 'works' is an illusion deriving from the mixture of fact and fiction that has characterised offender profiling since its inception. They say that the anecdotal evidence in favour of offender profiling is given too much weight relative to the scientific-empirical support for offender profiling and that this has led to the premature acceptance of offender profiling as an investigative technique (Snook et al. 2008, p.1270).

The state of affairs that characterises offender profiling and investigative psychology is interesting to say the least. On the one hand, offender profiling has been applied in numerous real-world investigations and appears only to show signs of continuing the growth that the practice has experienced over the past two or three decades. On the other hand, the younger academic discipline of investigative psychology—its dedicated journal is only around ten years old—is struggling to establish its identity in the face of the possibility that the literature's ultimate contribution may be to one day conclude that the whole idea of criminal profiling is, as Snook et al. argue, an illusion deriving from the entertaining, exciting and compelling but, in the end, entirely fictional notions that have attended the development of

[4] Canter and Youngs (2009).

offender profiling and investigative psychology since its beginnings. This whole enterprise, not least the academic investigative psychology part of it, is sustained not only by the pursuit of an answer to the question about the possibility of offender profiling and the multiplicity of secondary research questions that derive from this but by something that may be encapsulated in a single word: 'pragmatism'.

From its inception, investigative psychology has emerged and evolved in an environment where 'the market' for profiling has been on the up and in which each new approach to inference imagined and tried successfully in practice or developed through academic inquiry has been added to a set of tools that have come to be valued by law enforcement professionals. This value may be ephemeral but so might be the value of many things. Whether 'successful' profiles have really contributed substantively to critical breakthroughs in tough cases and whether this success, even if substantive, is due to luck, innate and unique skill on the part of the profiler, guesswork, experience or science is beside the point if real law enforcement professionals believe that the profile has been useful. Not surprisingly in a context such as this both the practice of profiling and the academic field of investigative psychology have become characterised by a noticeable pragmatism that keeps both sides developing new ideas rather than grinding to a shuddering halt pending 'further investigation'. Alison et al. (2010) argue that this scientific pragmatism must be embraced.

How Does Profiling 'Work'?

Offender profiling is about drawing inferences about the offender from the crime and crime scene. Within the investigative psychology literature, which has been considerably shaped by the contributions of Canter (1989, 1994, 2004)[5], this process has been described by what are called the **A** → **C** equations. **A** are the actions that occur in and are related to a crime and **C** are the characteristics of the offender (Canter 2004, p.5). The drawing of inferences for **C** from **A** is encompassed within the symbol '→'. This is where all of the scientific modelling and processes underlying offender profiling sit (Canter 2004, p.5). This is also the place where economic analysis would sit. Within '→', a typology or classification plays a very important role. The idea is that the crime scene reveals things about the offender as a criminal and these things reveal further things about the criminal as a person. To facilitate the drawing of inferences about the offender, profilers use some sort of typology or classification scheme. Roughly speaking, the typology or classification scheme contains a set of characteristics of the offender as a criminal that 'map' into the set of characteristics of the offender as a person. The profiler uses information about the crime scene to classify the UNSUB as a particular 'type' of offender and uses the typology or classification scheme as the basis for drawing inferences about what sort of person the offender is likely to be.

As Canter (2004, p.8) explains, "A recurring consideration in the emerging investigative psychology literature is therefore the development of classification schemes, often in the form of typologies, into which offences and offenders can be assigned." If the crime or crime scene can be classified as a particular type, the offender will have the characteristics associated with

[5] These references represent only a fraction of the work produced by Canter and his co-researchers. See Canter and Youngs (2009), for example. This is the first comprehensive textbook produced in the field of investigative psychology.

that type. Canter (2004, p.8) identifies two critical assumptions that underlie the typologies: (1) within each type, the characteristics that define that specific type are likely to co-occur with one another with regularity; and (2) specific characteristics of one type are assumed not to co-occur with the characteristics of an alternative type. As may be expected from a field that is both scientific and pragmatic in nature, a dominant typology retains a place of prominence within both the academic literature and law enforcement practice even in the absence of strong empirical-statistical support. This is the organised/disorganised typology. The organised/disorganised typology is identified by Canter et al. (2004, p.293) as one of the "...most widely cited classifications of violent, serial offenders." This is probably due to the fact that although direct empirical support for the organised/disorganised typology is weak, empirical investigations of this and related typologies have revealed at least some support for the possibility of using crime and crime scene information to analyse the 'themes of actions' and linking these 'themes' to the characteristics of the offender and some evidence that may be interpreted as 'glimpses of structure' (Canter 1994; Salfati and Canter 1999, p.405; Canter et al. 2004)[6].

Douglas et al. (1986) and Douglas and Olshaker (1996) include among the characteristics that may be inferred from a typology like the organised/disorganised typology the offender's likely type of automobile, the condition in which it has been maintained, its colour, the presence or absence of a speech impediment, law enforcement or military background, age, employment, marital status, intelligence, education, personality, race, criminal record and even whether the individual might have passed a lie detector test during the investigation. As explained by Douglas et al. (1986) the process of classifying the crime and the offender as organised or disorganised may also shed light on motivation. For example, what appears to be a disorganised crime may have been staged deliberately to give exactly that impression or to hide the primary intent of the crime. Douglas et al. (1986) give the example of an investigation where the 'staged' intent of the crime was extortion or kidnapping for ransom. The real intent of the crime was sexually motivated rape and murder. The profilers were able to determine that the probable staging was an organised attempt to divert attention from the real nature of the crime by drawing on knowledge of law enforcement procedures. The profile, which included the conclusion that the individual may have been employed in law enforcement, was accurate in many respects.

The problem is that much of the evidence about classification schemes or typologies is not very supportive of the idea that a robust typology is possible. Of course, the offender profilers would argue that this is not a critical flaw because such evidence overlooks the role of the instinctive ability of the profiler in piecing together the puzzle. Unfortunately, there are problems with this argument too. Some studies which have compared the profiles constructed by professionals with profiles constructed by ordinary people suggest that no such innate ability exists. On a positive note, there does appear to be a semblance of structure in the crime scene and offender characteristics. There is not much to suggest something as neat as the organised/disorganised dichotomy but in a study of serial killings Canter et al. (2004) found that the murders were almost always characterised by a set of 'organised' characteristics (from the organised side of the disorganised-organised typology). These could prove to be interesting, particularly if all serial murderers exhibit similar 'organised' features but only particular 'disorganised' features. There may be structure conducive to some typology

[6] See Phillips and Pohl (2012) for a longer discussion on this point.

embedded in the different ways in which serial killers exhibit disorganised aspects of their activities but as yet nothing so clear-cut as that implied by the organised/disorganised typology (Canter et al. 2004, p.313). Whether this means that offender profiling is 'impossible' depends on how much emphasis one places on the innate ability of the profiler. If we do not discount the possibility that the instinct, the experience, the innate ability and insights of the profiler may yield 'results' and that the organised/disorganised typology fails only when cast adrift from the profiler then even a semblance of structure may be enough.

Concluding Remarks

The story of investigative psychology and offender profiling is unique because of its obvious pragmatism and the way in which fact and fiction interact so freely with the subject matter. Profiling is widely used and the organised/disorganised typology is the dominant typology despite a lack of empirical support within the academic investigative psychology literature. In empirically testing the organised/disorganised typology, investigative psychologists have highlighted some of the hypotheses and assumptions that underlie the application of the typology within a profiling process. One of these is what Canter and Youngs (2009) call a 'consistency principle'. There are two ways in which this may be interpreted. First, the organised offender brings an organised approach to his criminal activity (Canter and Youngs 2009, p.336). His criminal behaviour is consistent with his non-criminal behaviour. Second, the organised offender will *continue* to commit organised crimes *over time* (Snook et al. 2008). Organised offenders will not all-of-a-sudden start committing crimes that are disorganised. Both of these forms of consistency have been studied empirically. An optimistic assessment from the point of view of proponents of the organised/disorganised typology would be that the evidence is mixed. Investigative psychologists tend to be more pessimistic about the results that have been obtained so far. Snook et al. (2008) argue that the whole idea of an organised/disorganised typology is flawed because it relies on personality traits, which have been discounted heavily as explanatory factors for behaviour within the broader psychology literature. Nevertheless, offender profiling and the organised/disorganised typology continues to be applied by real law enforcement agencies to real crimes.

In the first part of this book, our aim was to delineate the lone wolf terrorist's opportunities and choices. Although this is applicable to the pre-emption of the lone wolf terrorist, pre-emption remains a very difficult challenge. Our delineation in terms of risk and reward of the lone wolf terrorist's opportunities and choices serves another purpose. Once the lone wolf terrorist strikes he reveals his place within the opportunity set or within the statistical structure that we have defined and developed. The outcomes of some attack methods are more variable or risky than others. An attack method choice or a series of attack method choices reveals something about the lone wolf terrorist's preferences for risk. Risk preference is something that enters into the profiling process and although they might not use the language of economics, offender profilers attempt to determine whether the offender may be risk averse or more risk seeking from the nature of the crime. It is this part of the profiling process to which we may be able to contribute the most. Our delineation of the lone wolf terrorist's opportunities in terms of risk or variability of outcomes is much more formal and allows us to separate the lone wolf's risk preference as revealed by his attack method choice from other aspects of his activity, including the planning he appears to have undertaken and the prudence with which he has deployed the particular attack method. The lone wolf's choice of attack method indicates an acceptance of a greater or lesser likelihood that the actual outcomes will diverge from what he was expecting. He might be equally extremely careful and cunning in undertaking either an assassination or an armed attack. However, his choice of assassination indicates a willingness to bear a far lower likelihood that the actual outcomes will diverge from those that were expected.

Chapter 11

THE ORGANISED/DISORGANISED TYPOLOGY AND OFFENDER RISK

> Implicit within the organised/disorganised typology is the assumption that serial killing activity can be conceptualised as being primarily about the completion of a task. The essential distinguishing feature is in the approach (organised or disorganised) taken to the achievement of this task——Canter and Youngs 2009, p.343.

As we have mentioned before, using aspects of the crime scene and other evidence to place unknown offenders into a category or typology is one of the cornerstones of offender profiling. The profiler aims to determine the 'kind of person' most likely to have committed a crime (Douglas et al. 1986). The person's patterns of thinking guides the person's behaviour (Douglas et al. 1986, p.405). The crime scene is a record of the person's behaviour. Aspects of the crime scene may allow the profiler to determine the motive and type of person who committed the crime (Douglas et al. 1986, p.405). The most prominent typology or classification scheme utilised by law enforcement sees two 'kinds' or 'types' of offender: organised and disorganised. Evidence at the crime scene is examined and used to place the offender in one of these two types. Once this has been accomplished, the profiler can use the typology to draw additional inferences about the type of person who committed the crime. A 'disorganised' crime scene places the offender in the 'disorganised type'. The disorganised type may be less likely to have a skilled job and may be more likely to be socially inept with an inability to maintain interpersonal relationships (Canter et al. 2004, pp.293-294). The FBI's organised/disorganised typology, developed from interviews with offenders, is by far the most routinely used typology (Snook et al. 2008, p.1259).

ORGANISED/DISORGANISED TYPOLOGY AND THE PROFILING PROCESS

Douglas et al. (1986, p.407) provide the most clearly expressed explanation of the profiling process. Here the authors describe a five-stage process followed by the criminal profilers working out of the FBI's Behavioural Science Unit:

1. Profiling inputs stage. Here, information about the crime is gathered. This includes physical information about the crime scene, the environment, economic, social or political factors particular to the crime scene, information about the victim and forensics.
2. Decision process models stage. This is the data analysis stage and may involve a complex information processing task. Not surprisingly, the development of decision support systems is an important part of investigative psychology (Canter and Youngs 2009, p.5). During this stage, the profiler is concerned with crime type and style, intent, victim risk, offender risk, escalation, time and location factors.
3. Crime assessment stage. This involves the reconstruction of the crime and classification of the crime as organised or disorganised. Aspects of organisation that are considered include victim selection, control of victim and the sequence of the crime. Other factors that are considered during this stage involve motivation and crime scene dynamics.
4. Criminal profile stage. This involves a description of the type of person who committed the crime and the individual's 'behavioural organisation' with relation to the crime. This is then validated against the information pertaining to the crime (collected at the earlier stages).
5. Investigation stage. Potential offenders are evaluated against the profile. The investigative process may end or further information may become available. The profile is re-examined and the investigative process continues until there is an apprehension.

The organised/disorganised typology obtains a place of prominence in this process and constitutes the cornerstone of the crime assessment stage of the profiling process. In the above process, the organised/disorganised typology emerges in steps three and four. According to Douglas et al. (1986, pp.412-413), in the context of a murder investigation, an organised offender is one who appears to plan his activities, target his victims, display control at the scene and act out a violent fantasy. The disorganised offender is one who appears not to have planned his activities precisely, selected victims by chance and behaves haphazardly during the crime. Behavioural and personality characteristics are associated with an organised or disorganised offender and can be determined from the crime scene (Canter et al. 2004, p.293). For example, Canter et al. (2009, pp.293-294) suggest that an organised offender may lead an orderly life. He will have at least average intelligence, be socially competent and in skilled employment. This organisation will be reflected in a crime that is planned, where the victim is restrained and the weapon carried to and from the crime scene. The disorganised offender leads a disorderly life. This disorganisation will be reflected in the crime scene which will exhibit disarray, evidence left at the scene including, possibly, the murder weapon, the body left in the open and no use of restraints on the victim. It is quite clear that within the profiling process as described, the organised/disorganised typology is the central 'inference generating' model. If the examination of the relevant factors leads to a classification of the crime scene as organised or disorganised, then inferences can be drawn about the offender's characteristics.

It is in the second step of the profiling process that the profiler assesses the *offender risk*. Douglas et al. (1986, p.411) explain:

> Data on victim risk integrates with information on offender risk, or the risk the offender was taking to commit the crime. For example, abducting a victim at noon from a busy street is high risk. Thus, a low risk victim—killers seek high-risk victims at locations where people may be vulnerable, such as bus depots or isolated areas. Low-risk types include those whose occupations and daily lifestyles do not lead them to being targeted as victims—snatched under high-risk circumstances generates ideas about the offender, such as personal stresses he is operating under, his beliefs that he will not be apprehended, or the excitement he needs in the commission of the crime, or his emotional maturity.

The approach that is described by Douglas et al. (1986) is a qualitative assessment of the risk that the offender took in carrying out the crime. Errors can enter into this approach because it is easy to conflate the steps that the offender took in carrying out a particular type of offense—the way he carried out the murder or robbery or kidnapping or assault—and the offender's choice to partake in that particular offense rather than some other type of legal or illegal activity. It is the latter that reveals the offender's preference for risk and not the former. By first defining the lone wolf terrorist's risk as the variability of the outcomes of particular types of attack methods and measuring that variability by the variance or standard deviation of the fatalities and injuries inflicted by particular types of attack methods over time, we have developed a way to order the riskiness of the lone wolf terrorist's opportunities. His choice of attack method or attack method combination rather than the precise way in which he carries out his attack using that attack method or combination becomes the basis for an assessment of how much risk the lone wolf terrorist was willing to bear and this, of course, is the basis for an assessment of his risk preference.

Leaving aside the question of the relative merits of qualitative and quantitative assessments of risk, a risk assessment that is drawn within a typology such as the organised/disorganised typology is subject to the shortcomings of the typology itself and so too are the inferences that are drawn about the offender on the basis of any such risk assessment. When we are talking about risk and risk preference, a particular shortcoming of the organised/disorganised typology is salient. This is what might be called the 'consistency principle'. Whether or not the risk preference of the lone wolf terrorist is determined by either a qualitative or quantitative approach, the organised/disorganised provides a particular interpretive framework for this piece of investigative information that may be overly restrictive and potentially misleading. As we have mentioned before, the organised/disorganised typology, along with other similar typologies, require that the offender will act consistently in the sense that if he is organised in his terrorism he is organised in his non-terrorism and, also, that his terrorism will continue to be organised over time. Risk preference, however, is unlikely to be consistent in the sense that it is unlikely to remain the same over time or across different activities. Rather, as the lone wolf terrorist progresses with his terrorist activities and as the amount of human tragedy that he inflicts accumulates his risk preference may undergo changes. The economic analysis of risk preference incorporates this from the outset.

As we shall explain, an individual's risk preference may be described both relatively *and* absolutely and both relative and absolute risk aversion can be expected to change over time. In this case, as the lone wolf terrorist accumulates victims during the course of a single attack—a spree—or over a series of attacks, we may expect his risk preference to change in the following ways. If the lone wolf terrorist is characterised by decreasing absolute risk aversion, for example, we expect that the *absolute* amount of time and other resources that he allocates to terrorism will increase as his victims accumulate. That is, he will become more specialised in terrorism. If he is also characterised by constant relative risk aversion, however, we should not expect to see his attack methods choices to alter. Rather, the allocation of his resources among the different attack methods at different levels of risk should remain more or less the same. Depending on whether we expect the offender to exhibit increasing, decreasing or constant relative and absolute risk aversion, we should expect increasing, decreasing or constant levels of specialisation and increasing, decreasing or constant allocations to more risky attack methods as the lone wolf terrorist's victims accumulate. This flexibility overcomes the inherent static of a typology such as the organised/disorganised typology and, as we shall see, allows us to make more nuanced predictions within an investigative context about what the UNSUB lone wolf terrorist is likely to in the future. This circumvents somewhat a major criticism of the organised/disorganised typology. This criticism we have called the requirement of a consistency principle.

A Consistency Principle

Profiling is widely used and the organised/disorganised typology is the dominant typology despite a lack of strong empirical support within the academic investigative psychology literature. In empirically testing the organised/disorganised typology, investigative psychologists have highlighted some of the hypotheses and assumptions that underlie the application of the typology within a profiling process. One of these is what Canter and Youngs (2009, p.336) call a 'consistency principle'. There are two ways in which this may be interpreted. First, and most basically, the organised offender brings an organised approach to his criminal activity (Canter and Youngs 2009, p.336). His criminal behaviour is consistent with his non-criminal behaviour. Second, the organised offender will *continue* to commit organised crimes *over time* (Snook et al. 2008). Organised offenders will not all-of-a-sudden start committing crimes that are disorganised. Both of these forms of consistency have been studied empirically. An optimistic assessment from the point of view of proponents of the organised/disorganised typology would be that the evidence is mixed. However, investigative psychologists tend to be more pessimistic about the results that have been obtained so far.

To empirically test the hypothesis that an organised individual brings an organised approach to his criminal activity and a disorganised individual brings a disorganised approach, Canter et al. (2004) examined the 'co-occurrence' of crime scene variables categorised as 'organised' and 'disorganised'[1]. The implication of the organised/disorganised typology is that organised variables should co-occur to a high degree whilst organised and disorganised variables should not co-occur. Canter et al. (2004) could find no distinct sub-sets of 39 variables in 100 serial killings committed by 100 serial killers in the United States. Some of the results might be interpreted as providing some support for an organised category within serial murder. A number of the 'organised' features do consistently co-occur but

[1] Davies et al. (1997), Mokros and Allison (2002) and Woodhams and Toye (2007) have examined consistency by undertaking studies aimed at determining whether criminals' criminal behaviour is consistent with aspects of their non-criminal behaviour. Some relationships were detected but the evidence is weak.

Canter et al. (2004) conclude that this is more likely to be evidence that organised features are part of the nature of serial murder rather than a function of an 'organised type'. Disorganised features were found to co-occur even less frequently. Consequently, the authors caution against relying on the organised/disorganised typology but, as we have mentioned before, do not rule out the possibility of some structure (other than the organised/disorganised structure) within co-occurrences of the complete list of crime scene variables.

A number of other empirical investigations have been undertaken in order to determine whether organised criminals continue to commit organised crimes over time whilst disorganised criminals continue in a disorganised fashion. Snook et al. (2008) argue that these assumptions, which underlie the organised/disorganised typology, are flawed. Snook et al. (2008) draw on the results extant within the broader psychological literature to argue that a reliance on traits or personality dispositions as the primary explanation for behaviour is mistaken. Indeed, we saw at the outset that this much was grasped by the economic theorists who developed the early expected utility models of crime and criminal behaviour, preferring instead to rely on responses to incentives rather than psychological idiosyncrasies and personality traits. Snook et al. (2008) cite the psychological literature that reports the importance of situational factors in the prediction of behaviour: Bowers (1973), Mischel (1968), Alison et al. (2002), Andrews and Bonta (2006), Bennell and Canter (2002), Gendreau et al. (2006) and Woodhams and Toye (2007).

The literature is not completely devoid of support for a hypothesis of consistency of a criminal's behaviour over time. For example, offenders appear to exhibit consistency in the choice of target in serial commercial and residential burglaries and for these and other types of crime, offenders will exhibit consistency in some characteristics and no consistency in others. It does seem, however, that the evidence for the very high level of consistency of the sort that appears to be required for an organised/disorganised typology to function effectively is weak. Of course, this is taking a purely empirical point of view and does not consider the possibility that the profiler's own judgement and experience somehow compensates for these weaknesses to permit a sound offender profile to be constructed. Snook et al. (2008) attack offender profiling on this front too by drawing on evidence that indicates that professional profilers are not significantly more accurate in the construction of profiles than people who are not profilers. Given the current state of affairs, it is possible that a typology based on economic theory and the economic models of crime and criminal behaviour that are extant in the economics literature may complement and perhaps even strengthen some aspects of the organised/disorganised typology and its application to the profiling process.

TOWARDS ECONOMIC PROFILING

Drawing inferences about the lone wolf terrorist from information about his attacks and his choice of attack methods where an economic theory or model enters under Canter's '→' is the next step for the economic analysis of terrorism. Given the multi-disciplinary nature of investigative psychology is it unlikely that investigative psychologists will object overly to the economist's presence and, indeed, an additional dimension will be added to the discipline that may prove to be useful. One point of contention must be cleared up immediately, however. Economics is inextricably linked to a 'rational choice' model of behaviour the nature and implications of which are widely misunderstood both within and without economic science. Rational choice should only be interpreted to mean that a person chooses to allocate his scarce means—time, money and other resources—towards the achievement of some end or ends. It does not mean that the person will never make a mistake or somehow makes an infinite number of calculations that never err both in terms of input and output. It simply means that people act *purposively*.

It is probably true to say that Gary Becker is the most well-known 'crime economist'. Of course, his reputation, among those familiar with his work, is built on his avant-garde applications of the orthodox (neo-classical) expected utility model of economic behaviour to everything from crime to marriage. Being neo-classical this work adopts the mathematical approach and casts all these sorts of behaviours in mathematical formulas. In his "Crime and Punishment: An Economic Approach" Becker (1968) argues that economics can be used to develop optimal public and private policies to combat illicit behaviour. Obviously, this is broader subject matter than the development of an economic view of criminal action, which is to be found in his Section 3, 'The Supply of Offenses.' The supply of offenses is some function of the probability of apprehension, the punishment if convicted and a mixture of other variables such as income from legal activities, income from illegal activities, willingness to commit an illegal act and so on. Within this context, which really defines the opportunities for illegal and legal actions and the costs and benefits of each, the person will choose among (legal and illegal) opportunities in a manner that maximises his expected utility. His expected utility depends on the utility of the monetary and psychic income from committing an offense and the disutility of costs of the punishment if he is caught. Each of these is weighted by the probability that the event (caught or not caught) will occur.

According to Becker (1968, p.176), this approach:

> "...follows the economists' usual analysis of choice and assumes that a person commits an offense if the expected utility to him exceeds the utility he could get by using his time and other resources at other activities. Some persons become 'criminals', therefore, not because their basic motivation differs from that of other persons, but because their benefits and costs differ. I cannot pause to discuss the many general implications of this approach, except to remark that criminal behaviour becomes part of a much more general theory and does not require ad hoc concepts of differential association, anomie, and the like, nor does it assume perfect knowledge, lightning-fast calculation, or any of the other caricatures of economic theory."

It is at the point where Becker 'cannot pause' that he references a work that is more important for our present subject matter and which more completely and painstakingly develops an economic view of criminal action. This is the work of Isaac Ehrlich. In 1967, his work was an unpublished manuscript. By 1973 part of this work and developments thereon had been published as "Participation in Illegitimate Activities: A Theoretical and Empirical Investigation."

If economics can be summed up in two words they would be: opportunities and choices. By and large, economic analysis first determines the opportunities that are available and then examines the choices that a person will make when confronted by those opportunities. In Ehrlich's (1973, p.522) work, this is very clear:

> "...Even if those who violate certain laws differ systematically in various respects from those who abide by the same laws, the former, like the latter, do respond to incentives. Rather than resort to hypotheses regarding unique personal characteristics and social conditions affecting respect for the law, penchant for violence, preference for risk, or in general preference for crime, one may separate the latter from measurable opportunities and see to what extent illegal behaviour can be explained by the effect of opportunities given preferences."

This passage also contains a clear statement of a key point of strength in the economist's view of criminal action. This is the non-reliance on particular personality traits to explain or analyse criminal behaviour. This being said, it is still easy to fall into the trap of thinking that a criminal or a terrorist must be a risk seeker and that economics has introduced a personality trait by sleight of hand. However, it is not necessarily true that a terrorist is a risk seeker. For one thing, risk seeking would see the terrorist engage only in the most risky terrorist activities. This is not observed. More importantly, even if it is the case that terrorists are on average more risk seeking (less risk averse) than law abiding citizens, risk seeking is not a personality trait that is particular to the criminal mind[2]. Rather, risk preference is something that is revealed by the choices that people make from the available opportunities. Given the adequate incentives structure, even risk averse people may be willing to take more risks. Opportunities that have much higher risks attached may be selected if there is an appropriate chance of a much higher reward than that which is available from the 'safer' option. This is, of course, the essence of the large number of articles on incentives structures that can be found in the economics literature. In the end, terrorists respond to incentives.

Ehrlich's carefully developed treatment of the nature of the incentives embedded within the opportunities available to engage in legal and illegal behaviour allows him to examine criminal action in a more complete theoretical context where costs and gains from legal and illegal behaviour are considered, rather than just the cost of punishment (Ehrlich 1973, p.522). The other interesting feature of Ehrlich's work is that it does not simply present the choice problem as one involving a choice of either a legal or an illegal activity as though these two things were mutually exclusive. Everyone has the option of doing legal and illegal things in some proportion. Many people who engage in criminal behaviour devote only some of their time to such illegitimate activities and spend the rest of their time doing legitimate things like holding steady employment. Over a life time, people may also drift in and out of criminal behaviour (Ehrlich 1973, p.524). The choice is an allocation of time and other resources to the available opportunities and the choices that are made need not be exclusively illegal or legal.

Ehrlich works in the neo-classical style of mathematically expressing the opportunity set and the (expected) utility that the person attaches to each choice. As such, a person has an expected utility function that is applied to the available opportunities which, in this case, consist of a set of legal and illegal activities each with a benefit and a cost. Ehrlich assumes that legitimate activities are safe because the returns that can be had from them are known with certainty. Illegitimate activities are risky because the returns that can be had from them

---

[2] The reason why economic analysis may conclude that a risk seeker will spend more time in criminal activity than a risk averter is because it is often assumed in the theory construction phase that legitimate activities provide a low risk or risk free return while criminal behaviour provides a risky return. If this assumption is not made, the risk seeker may allocate time and resources to risky activities, all of which may be entirely legal. It would just depend on the opportunities (payoffs and risks) involved.

are uncertain and depend upon whether or not the person gets caught and what punishment is imposed in the event of capture. The activities are not mutually exclusive and the person's choice problem is not to simply choose the activity (legal or illegal) that has the highest expected utility but to choose the legal activity, the illegal activity or a *combination* of both that has the highest expected utility. Since he cannot carry this 'market' activity on without pause, he must also spend some of his time in neither legal nor illegal activity. Ehrlich calls this 'consumption' or 'non-market' activity. As mentioned before, many mistakes may be made in this choice process and it is not the case that the person is assumed to choose perfectly and accurately.

Once set down mathematically, the choice problem can be solved. This usually means that 'first order' optimality conditions are determined and the equilibrium choices obtained. What can be said about the choices in equilibrium depends on the context that has been sketched or delineated. Within Ehrlich's analysis, the person is choosing to allocate time and resources to legal and illegal activities and 'consumption' activities such that his expected utility is maximised. Ehrlich is able to work out the optimal values for each of these times spent under different conditions, especially when the person making the choice has different types of risk preference, and determine a range of different possible combinations of illegal and legal activities. For example, whatever a person's risk preference may be, a *sufficient* condition for entry into illegal activity is, roughly, that the marginal expected return on illegal activity exceeds the marginal return on legal activity. If the person is risk averse, this is also a *necessary* condition. If this condition is not met, risk averters will never engage in illegal activity and will allocate all time and resources to legitimate activities (Ehrlich 1973, p.528). Ehrlich also determines under which conditions a risk seeker will specialise completely in illegitimate activity and when a risk averter can be expected to combine legal and illegal activities.

This theoretical framework can form the basis for an empirical study if estimates for the relevant variables (for example, probability of apprehension and return to illegitimate activity) can be found. Various predictions flow from the framework and these can be tested empirically. For example, Ehrlich finds that it is optimal for some offenders to 'repeatedly offend' and even increase the intensity of their illegitimate activity. Changes in the probability of apprehension or the cost of conviction will change the incentive structure. If these things increase and everything else remains the same, incentives for illegitimate activity are reduced. However, the response of the prospective criminal to this change in the structure of his opportunities depends on his risk preference. A one percent increase in the expected marginal costs of punishment will have a more than proportional effect on the decisions of the risk averter but a less than proportional effect for a risk seeker. In fact, Ehrlich (1973 p.530) shows that a risk seeker who allocates some time to legal activities and some time to illegal activities may actually be inclined to increase his allocation to illegal activities when the expected marginal cost of punishment increases. Similar results can also be worked out for situations where there is an increase in the expected marginal return to illegal activity.

Opportunities and incentives matter in explaining how a person allocates time between legal and illegal activity. The best choices that a person can make when confronted by these opportunities can be worked out and the ways in which the best choices change when opportunities are reshaped can be determined. An economic view of criminal action along the lines developed by Ehrlich and the generations of 'crime economists' that have followed in his and Becker's footsteps can tell us what to expect with regards to the conditions under which people will engage in criminal activity, the ways in which they divide their time between legal and illegal activity, the relevance of risk preference and the effect of changes in law enforcement strategies and penalties. Useful as this might be, we have come to the point where we must turn this theoretical work on its head. Once we observe an act of terrorism, what can the economic view of criminal action say about the offender? If we observe the use of a particular attack method, what can economics say about the person who committed the act of terrorism? The essence of these questions is an economic approach to offender profiling where the framework that permits evidence left at the crime scene to be used to draw inferences about the offender is one that is some offshoot of the economic view of criminal action.

Concluding Remarks

The organised/disorganised typology is the most widely used classification scheme within offender profiling and investigative psychology. Constructing an offender profile is a task that primarily involves the drawing of inferences about the offender from information about the crime and crime scene. This information is left behind by the offender in much the same way as he may leave behind any type of clue. The utilisation of the organised/disorganised typology involves classifying the crime into one of the two categories. Inferences about the offender are then drawn. Implicit within this inference drawing process is the assumption that the offender displays consistency between his non-criminal and criminal activities and between criminal activities over time. Given the absence of empirical support for this typology within the investigative psychology literature, one must conclude that contrary to the direction which the academic investigative psychology literature must take in order to develop firm scientific foundations, the practice of offender profiling places some degree—probably a very high degree—of positive value on the individual ability of the profiler to draw inferences about the offender from the crime scene. A mixture of pragmatism and scientific method characterises the field and the tension between the academic approach and the approach that is applied in the field quite clearly runs through the respective literatures.

Another problem or point of contention within the literature is the apparent reliance of the practice of offender profiling, particularly as it makes use of the organised/disorganised typology, on personality trait-based models of behaviour. The psychologists have long ago recognised the weaknesses of this approach. Within economic science, the trait-based approaches were rejected at the very outset by those economists responsible for constructing the first economic models of crime and criminal behaviour. The problem, of course, is that the rejection of a trait-based approach when combined with the possibility that successful offender profiling is in some part attributable to the skills, ability and experience of the profiler, the academic approach to investigative psychology and offender profiling is left to continue the task of working out the structure of criminal activity, criminal behaviour and crime scene evidence whilst the practice of profiling on the basis of the organised/disorganised typology continues to expand. Economic science enters the field in a somewhat better position. Having rejected trait-based models of behaviour and, in general, the collection of historical facts in favour of theoretical work, an approach to profiling based on the theoretical foundations of economic science is neither beset by the weaknesses that characterise the practice of profiling nor is it beset with the academic investigative psychologist's inclination to embark upon a tedious task of data analysis for the purposes of divining a structure that will form the basis for the drawing of inferences about offenders.

An approach to profiling individuals involved in illegitimate activity, including lone wolf terrorism, that is based on the theoretical-analytical frameworks of economic science would certainly not be weaker than the approaches currently being applied within investigative psychology and is likely to be significantly stronger, theoretically, than the practical approach that draws so strongly on an organised/disorganised typology. An economic approach to profiling would work in the same manner as the current approaches. Based on information available about the crime and the crime scene, the analyst would attempt to classify the offender into two or more categories. These would not be categories based on personality traits. On the basis of the classification, the analyst would utilise a broader economic analytical framework based on expected utility theory and mean-variance analysis in order to draw inferences about the offender. This requires drawing from the economic theoretical structure every last implication about the offender that can be drawn on the basis of the category into which he has been placed. Economic science can probably contribute more than would be expected of it in this regard. Whether this is used as a complement to the practical profiling of experienced law enforcement agents or the academic profiling of experienced investigative psychologists depends entirely on whether such individuals see value in it.

In developing an approach to offender profiling that is based on economic theory, it is certainly not the intention to replace or usurp investigative psychology as the scientific foundation for the development of offender profiles. This much has been said several times already. However, an approach to offender profiling that is based on economic theory would have very strong theoretical foundations and would be exempt from some of the limitations that have characterised the practical and academic approaches to offender profiling. Contrary to conventional wisdom or popular opinion, an economic approach to offender profiling would not require offenders to be perfectly rational calculating machines. On the contrary, offenders can make mistakes and their behaviour can change over time. Offenders do not have to perfectly weigh up the odds of success. Economic science may permit less to be said about the offender. It seems unlikely that the offender's type of motor vehicle or way of dressing or speech impediment would be among the inferences drawn about an offender by the investigative economist. Perhaps, though, what can be inferred about an offender on the basis of the sound theoretical structure of economic science is all that can be said.

Chapter 12

INVESTIGATIVE ECONOMICS AND THE ANALYSIS OF LONE WOLF TERRORISM

> The process used by an investigative profiler in developing a criminal profile is quite similar to that used by clinicians to make a diagnosis: data are collected and assessed, the situation reconstructed, hypotheses formulated, a profile developed and tested, and the results reported back——Douglas et al. 1986, p.405.

Opportunities and choices constitute the essential features of the analytical framework within which the lone wolf terrorist is encompassed. The lone wolf terrorist is encompassed by this analytical framework regardless of any individual personality traits that he may have and regardless of the 'uniqueness' of his particular activities. All of his potential or actual terrorist actions have a risk and an expected payoff. The opportunities are, in essence, pairs of risk and reward that are related to one another by the statistical-correlation structure of the payoffs to the attack methods that may be utilised in terrorist operations. We have called this the risk reward relationship or trade-off. In selecting an opportunity—a point of risk and reward—the lone wolf terrorist reveals his preferences for risk. This is not a personality trait that describes terrorists or criminals in the sense that it would be if we were to claim that criminals or terrorists are by their very nature seeking of risk. Rather, within a framework of opportunities and choices, the choices that lone wolves make reveal a risk preference to the investigator and law enforcement. There is no assumption that this is systematically higher or lower than non-criminals or that there is some criminal or terrorist personality trait systematically embedded within a type of risk preference. It is the effect of opportunities given preferences that occupies the attention of the economist, not personal predispositions towards risk, violence or law-breaking.

Lone wolf terrorists respond to incentives. An increase or decrease in the risk associated with a terrorist action may lead to an increase or decrease in the lone wolf's involvement in such activity depending on whether he is risk averse or risk seeking. In our delineation of opportunities and choices we were able to work theoretically on the types of choices that would be made by a lone wolf terrorist with a particular type of risk preference and level of risk aversion. Of course, unless we know what type of risk preference the lone wolf terrorist has, our ability to provide behavioural investigative advice is limited to narrowing down or delineating feasible opportunities and choices. This may be very useful in planning for different types of scenarios and if we could discover some level of risk aversion that characterises a 'typical' lone wolf terrorist we could identify which attack methods or combinations are most likely to be chosen by this 'archetype' lone wolf terrorist and which attack methods should be the focus of law enforcement agency preparations. However, we would like to go further than this. Like everyone else involved in the pursuit of offenders, the economist cannot reach any conclusions about a particular offender—an actual individual—until that offender engages in some observable activity. Once he does so and once we are sure we are more than likely dealing with a single individual—remember that law enforcement usually does not know this until a series of offenses have been committed—we may see that his risk preference has been revealed by his choice of attack method. Working from this point backwards through our economic analytical structure yields the inferences that will constitute our contribution to the profile of the UNSUB lone wolf terrorist.

THE ECONOMIC THEORETICAL FRAMEWORK: A SUMMARY

The complete theoretical structure that we draw upon in developing an 'economic' profile of the lone wolf terrorist consists of two main parts. First, there is the Becker (1968) and Ehrlich (1973) expected utility models of criminal behaviour and, to a certain extent, the applications of these models to the economic analysis of terrorism. The Ehrlich (1973) model is a rich theoretical framework that has the potential to function as an 'inference generator' once a criminal has engaged in some form of illegitimate activity and revealed his risk preference. For the Ehrlich model to function like this, however, it must rely on a demarcation of the riskiness of legitimate activity vis-á-vis illegitimate activity. Since Ehrlich only makes this 'two-category' distinction, the inferences that can be drawn are quite limited. If legitimate activity is free from risk or variability in the sense that its outcomes are known more or less with certainty and illegitimate activity is risky and its outcomes variable, then a criminal's risk preference reveals itself predominantly by the time he spends in illegitimate activity. The Ehrlich analysis may be interpreted as a 'portfolio'[1] model in the Markowitz sense. With this interpretation, the individual is seen to divide his time or allocate his resources to two 'assets': (1) a single legitimate risk free activity; and (2) a single illegitimate and risky activity. The distinguishing feature of the opportunity set would be that it would intersect the vertical expected payoffs axis at whatever certain payoff was associated with the legitimate activity. This is depicted in Figure 12.1.

Ehrlich's (1973) expected utility model of crime and criminal behaviour posits an individual who maximises the expected utility function by deciding allocations between what Ehrlich calls 'non-market activities', which could be anything that people spend their 'spare' time on, and 'market activities', which are either legitimate or illegitimate. Time is divided between things that have nothing to do with legitimacy and things that are either legitimate or illegitimate. A person who has 100 percent of his time available to him, say, might allocate three-quarters of it to non-market activities. The other one-quarter he might divide evenly between legitimate or illegitimate activities. In the end, all of his time is allocated and the

[1] In the literature dealing with the economics of criminal behaviour, 'portfolio models' has been the name given to models that describe this partitioning of time into different legitimate and illegitimate activities (see Eide 1994). Though the name is the same, these models are *not* based on the portfolio theory of Markowitz and have not been interpreted as such. The Markowitz approach was introduced into the economic analysis of terrorism in Phillips (2009).

proportions across these two areas, market and non-market, as well as the proportions within market activities, legitimate and illegitimate, will be determined in a manner that maximises expected utility. Key considerations are the pecuniary rewards available in both legitimate and illegitimate activities and the penalties associated with unsuccessful engagement in illegitimate activities. Of course, a law abiding citizen will divide his time between non-market activities and market activities but, as far as the latter are concerned, he will allocate all of his 'market activity time' to legitimate activities and no time at all to illegitimate activities.

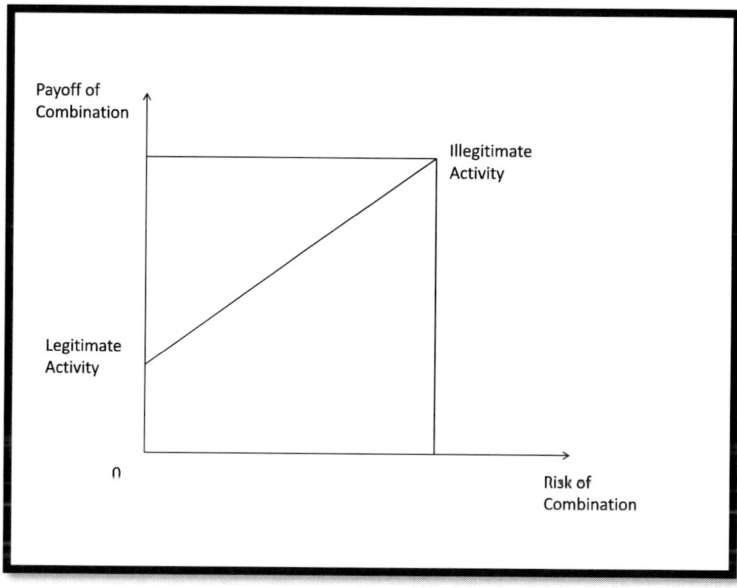

Figure 12.1. Risk and Reward when Legitimate Activity is 'No Risk'.

The problem, I think, with the illegitimate-legitimate dichotomy is that it seems to imply that only people who are less averse to risk or risk seeking will engage in illegitimate activity. This seems to introduce a personality trait into the analysis. The reason why this appears to be the case is because legitimate activities are made, at least in the first instance, to occupy the 'zero risk' position. Although in this model, risk averse individuals will engage in the illegitimate activity along with less risk averse individuals, it is the case that in this model more risk seeking individuals will be found to be more likely to devote more time to the illegitimate activity than risk averse individuals and the ways in which alterations in the incentive structure affect individuals' decisions will always be attended by similar considerations. This certainly clouds the fact that the actual engagement in the illegitimate activity is not something that characterises the decisions of only one 'type' of individual. If the Ehrlich model is 'inverted' from the start, we find that the confusion does not surface with the same intensity. A person who is observed to allocate a large amount of time to a risky activity—one whose outcomes are variable—when he could have chosen to allocate his time or resources to an activity with no risk or variability is revealing his preference for risk. As such, for our purposes, the Ehrlich model helps us to convey the fact that there will be a link between resource allocation—specialisation—and risk preference.

Keeping in mind that we expect a less risk averse lone wolf terrorist to devote more resources to terrorism—to exhibit a higher degree of specialisation—than a more risk averse lone wolf terrorist, we move on to our analysis of choice from among combinations of attack methods, all of which are risky. This is safer ground because we are, effectively, dealing with relative levels of risk aversion across different types of lone wolf terrorists rather than different types of risk preference across lone wolf terrorist and law-abiding civilians. A more risk seeking lone wolf terrorist will choose attack methods and attack method combinations that have higher expected payoffs and higher risk. A more risk averse lone wolf terrorist will choose attack methods and attack method combinations that have lower expected payoffs and lower risk. This analysis of choice under conditions of risk operates soundly even if we do not consider the issue of specialisation at all but assume that a person who makes the decision to be a lone wolf terrorist simply chooses to allocate all of his 'terroristic' resources to the attack methods. However, it is the case that some lone wolf terrorists devote some of their time and resources to other things, including the development of their ideology and even the writing-up of their manifestos. When we start from the point of attack and work backwards through the theoretical structure that we have developed, we are working on the basis of 'revealed risk preference'. A lone wolf terrorist who chooses a particular attack method or attack method combination reveals his preference for risk. Working through the implications of this revealed risk preference leads us to several other conclusions about the type of lone wolf terrorist who may have been responsible for the attack that has been observed. Our complete theoretical structure is a mean-variance expected utility analytical framework that allows the revealed preferences of the lone wolf terrorist to be identified more precisely. This is complemented by the more traditional full expected utility analytical framework of Ehrlich and Becker which provide us with a theoretical rationale for expecting a greater degree of specialisation in or resource allocation to the attack methods. Together, these frameworks are used to draw inferences about the lone wolf terrorist on the basis of his terroristic criminal actions, the crime scene and other relevant information.

An Alternative or Complement to the Organised/Disorganised Typology

The classification scheme or typology that emerges from a logical extension of Ehrlich's (1973) economic theoretical framework and the Phillips (2009; 2011) mean-variance approach to the analysis of terrorist choice is one based on the revealed risk preferences of individual lone wolf terrorists, especially by their choice of attack method or attack method combination, and their resource allocations to terrorism. Risk preference is revealed explicitly by choice of attack method. It is implied that a choice of a very risky attack method with more variable outcomes, which indicates a lower level of risk aversion, will be attended by a higher likelihood of a higher resource allocation to or specialisation in terrorism. A profile of a lone wolf terrorist is constructed within the theoretical frameworks of economic science by 'working backwards' (drawing inferences) from the lone wolf's terrorist activities through the typology or classification scheme. Once the lone wolf's activities have been linked with a particular 'type', the logical-economic theoretical framework should permit conclusions to be reached about the characteristics of the unknown lone wolf and his likely future actions. The 'type' of lone wolf terrorist that we shall be able to identify is one with a particular 'type' of risk preference.

There are two categories or types of risk aversion that form the foundation for our profile: (1) more risk averse or less risk seeking; and (2) less risk averse or more risk seeking. We also leave open the option of allocating the lone wolf terrorist to an intermediate category of risk aversion that we shall call something like, 'moderately risk averse'. These categories should encompass the actions of most our serial lone wolf terrorists. Later we shall introduce a special type of risk seeking lone wolf terrorist in order to provide a category in which to place those lone wolf terrorists who have engaged in spree shootings or other types of 'time concentrated' attacks. Whether the lone wolf terrorist is more risk averse or less risk averse will be determined on the basis of his choice of attack methods. As mentioned in the previous chapter, we are providing a more structured and quantitative approach to that part of the profiling process that focuses on the determination of how much risk the offender took in undertaking an attack. After one attack, just like the investigative psychologists and law enforcement agents, we are best advised to be tentative about the type of risk preference that has been revealed by the UNSUB. At this point, we might not even know that we are dealing with a lone wolf terrorist rather than a terrorist group. It will be after the second or third attack that we shall be in a position to be much more confident about our analysis of the level of risk aversion that has been revealed by the lone wolf and we shall be confident in classifying the lone wolf terrorist as being of either more risk averse or less risk averse.

The More Risk Averse Lone Wolf Terrorist and the Inferences We May Draw

Let us keep in mind two pictures as we proceed through this discussion. The first is the set of opportunities that we have determined from the RAND-MIPT data concerning attack methods and the fatalities and injuries inflicted by them. This set of opportunities, when sketched, is concave in shape. If we allow different levels of specialisation in terrorism then we find that we have a 'set of sets', one inside the other, ultimately encompassed by the complete specialisation opportunity set which is both the 'optimal' opportunity set and the boundary between feasible and infeasible attack method combinations. The second is the contents of each opportunity set or, put another way, each individual point on or within the opportunity set. These points are the positions of each feasible attack method or attack method combination. It is the second picture that will be most important and relevant to the determination of the lone wolf's risk preference because it is his position among the different attack methods and combinations that reveals his risk preference and it is this that he reveals by his choice of attack method. His level of specialisation—the first picture—may be revealed by evidence additional to the attack method choice or inferred from the attack method choice. A choice of assassination, for example, may lead us to the conclusion that the lone wolf terrorist is more risk averse and we may infer from this that he is less likely to be allocating all of his resources to terrorism. We should expect to find him engaged in other activities. Perhaps these will be alternative non-violent methods of expression, if his motivation is amenable to such a course of action.

A lone wolf terrorist signals that he is more averse to risk if he chooses attack methods or combinations of attack methods which are characterised by relatively less variability. Attack methods or combinations that have less variable outcomes have more certain outcomes. These types of attack methods will attract the more risk averse lone wolf terrorist who is unwilling to bear larger 'swings' in the possible outcomes of his terrorist attacks. Once we have defined risk as variability and found a way to measure it, it is a relatively simple matter to decide which attack methods are riskier than others. Of course, one of our key points throughout those chapters where we attempted to delineate the lone wolf terrorist's opportunities is that opportunities do not simply consist of the individual attack methods. Not only may the lone wolf terrorist decide on different levels of specialisation or engagement in terrorism but he may also combine attack methods over time. When combinations are considered another aspect of the statistical structure that underlies the lone wolf's opportunities is uncovered. This is the concavity of the opportunity set and the fact that low risk opportunities may be combined with medium or higher risk opportunities to produce a combination of attack methods that sits in the low-moderate range of risk. The result is that we have a more nuanced view of the risks and rewards associated with the terrorist's feasible choices and a more complete framework within which to locate his choices once he makes them. If these choices involve attacks such as kidnapping, assassination or arson or combinations of assassination and bombing, then the lone wolf will revealed a preference for attack methods or combinations with a lower but more certain payoff. He will reveal his high level of risk aversion.

This conclusion could complement the offender profiler's assessment of the offender's risk. The profiler could, if he or she so wished, take our assessment of the UNSUB lone wolf terrorist's risk preference and use it as another piece of data in the construction of his or her offender profile. If this is viewed as a worthwhile contribution, then economic analysis would have contributed positively to the investigative process. Although the experienced profiler may draw a number of inferences from his or her or our assessment of the offender's risk preference, it is the case that economic analysis may provide additional insights or inferences of its own. These inferences are drawn from working through the economic logic that underlies and runs through the frameworks that we have been developing. Several inferences may be drawn that might prove to be of some utility within the investigative process. These include inferences relating to the location of the lone wolf terrorist relative to his attack target and the possibility that he will 'drift' from location to location, his level of specialisation or engagement in terrorism rather than alternative activities, his reactions to press or media attention and the attention of law enforcement and, most importantly given what we have said about the 'consistency principle' of the organised/disorganised typology, we may draw inferences relating to the intensity of his attacks and his engagement in terrorism over time as his successes accumulate. All of these are derived from the economic logic upon which our analysis has been constructed.

If the lone wolf terrorist, through his choice of attack method, reveals that he has a relatively higher level of risk aversion we may infer that he will not be a complete specialist in terrorism. We would not expect a lone wolf terrorist who is more risk averse to allocate 100 percent of his time and resources to terrorism. We would not expect the opportunity set associated with complete specialisation to apply to him. Rather, one of the interior opportunity sets, perhaps associated with 10 or 25 percent resource allocation to terrorism, will be relevant in thinking about this type of lone wolf terrorist. If his motivation lends itself[2] to some other form of expression—for example, rallies, demonstrations, the writing of pamphlets or longer 'manifestos' and miscellaneous online activity—then we should expect that the more risk averse lone wolf terrorist will be engaging in these sorts of legitimate or semi-legitimate activities. In fact, given what we have inferred about his level of specialisation in terrorism and his level of resource allocation to attack methods, we expect that the more risk averse lone wolf terrorist will spend the majority of his time engaged in legitimate or semi-legitimate activities. For the serial lone wolf terrorist, this type of activity will likely continue during his engagement in terrorism. With perhaps less than 25 percent of time and other resources allocated to terrorism within each period, the serial lone wolf terrorist must fill up his time. If his motivation lends itself to some form of expression, then this will be how he spends some of his time.

The more risk averse lone wolf terrorist will not be found in the vicinity of his target location and he may drift from place to place in order to continue his terrorist activity. This seems like a rather logical conclusion and, in fact, it seems like a conclusion that does not have anything much to do with our formal definition of risk and our quantitative measurement of it. This is not the case. We must think about the lone wolf terrorist in terms of the opportunities that are available to him and the risk-reward trade-off that characterises these opportunities. The more risk averse lone wolf terrorist requires a higher 'risk-reward ratio'. He occupies the relatively steeper part of the opportunity set and his indifference curves are also relatively steep. If his absolute risk aversion increases as his successes accumulate, we would expect this type of lone wolf terrorist to attempt to find opportunities that, at the very least, maintain the risk reward ratio that he found to be sufficient to entice him to undertake his initial act of terrorism. Although our opportunity sets are static when drawn on the printed page, they are dynamic over time. An attack will attract the attention of law enforcement and may be expected to decrease the risk-reward ratio in a manner that renders a further attack incompatible with the lone wolf's risk preference. He will either withdraw from terrorism for a period of time or he will go to another location where his tried and proven attack method yields the desirable risk-reward trade-off. This type of inference relates to the first to the extent that a need to 'drift' will undermine the lone wolf terrorist's ability to spend time in steady legitimate employment. The relationship between risk aversion, 'drift' and employment is something that must be considered by law enforcement agencies in pursuit of the more risk averse serial lone wolf terrorist.

A serial lone wolf terrorist engages in a series of attacks over time. A serial lone wolf terrorist who is more risk averse will continue to engage in terrorism as long as there are appropriate opportunities available. By 'appropriate' we mean attacks that have an expected payoff that is commensurate with the risk or variability involved. It is not necessarily the case that a more risk averse lone wolf terrorist would strike and withdraw. If there is limited law enforcement response or if the attack attracts limited media attention, the lone wolf may perceive the risks not to have been enhanced and may engage in another attack soon after his first. We cannot rely on risk aversion to limit the number of attacks in the serial lone wolf terrorist's series. This being said, it is a fundamental result of the economic analysis of terrorism that the terrorist may be deterred from undertaking an attack by the imposition of

[2] It may not. For example, the underlying motivation may some non-directed anger or narcissistic rage. As such, there may be no other way for the lone wolf terrorist to express himself except through violence. In this case, the non-specialist lone wolf terrorist will fill his days in employment (or unemployment).

various security initiatives. He may also feel as though media or press attention has increased the chances that the outcomes of his attacks will be more variable. With more vigilant local law enforcement agents, ongoing investigation by other security agencies and a more wary populous, there is a greater chance that he may be detected or observed whilst carrying out an attack or his bombing device might be discovered or his parcel bomb might not be opened by a suspicious recipient or it might be opened by someone other than the intended recipient. The more risk averse the lone wolf terrorist happens to be, the more these sorts of increments in the real or perceived potential variability of the outcomes of his attacks will deter him from following his first attack quickly with a second and a third.

There are two ways in which the lone wolf terrorist might engage with a 'wider audience' other than by engaging in acts of violence. If his motivation lends itself to some form of written expression or articulation, the risk averse lone wolf terrorist might be inclined to engage with the traditional media or social media in order to disseminate his point of view. For the risk averse lone wolf terrorist, this will be undertaken carefully and with a good deal of consideration. Engagement with the media also involves risk for the lone wolf terrorist and the amount of publicity or attention or following that he receives as well as the other outcomes that might derive from such an engagement are variable and, therefore, risky. It was engagement with the traditional media that led to the identification of the Unabomber but it was engagement with the media that enable other lone wolf terrorists to invoke additional terror. This type of 'expression' or 'activism' must not be confused with the second type of non-violent engagement that may characterise the actions of the lone wolf terrorist. This is the 'taunting' of law enforcement. Serial offenders, including lone wolf terrorists, have been known to do this from time to time. However, unlike non-violent expression, taunting is less likely to characterise the actions of the more risk averse lone wolf terrorist. Taunting is designed to provoke the interest of law enforcement and increase the real or perceived variability of the outcomes of the next terrorist action. Variability is not something that is desired by the more risk averse lone wolf terrorist. While he may spend a considerable part of his time and resources on non-violent expression and while he might tentatively seek dissemination for these expressions, we are unlikely to see taunts from him directed towards law enforcement, either directly or indirectly through the media.

The picture or sketch of the lone wolf terrorist that we have constructed is one in which his choices reveal his risk preference and his other responses *with reference to risk and reward* are consistent with this revealed risk preference. We always try to think of anything else that the lone wolf may do in terms of risk and reward where risk is the variability of the outcomes. The types of terrorist attacks (or combinations of terrorist attacks) that reveal a higher degree of risk aversion are combinations of assassination and bombing. If the lone wolf cannot combine attack methods, kidnapping, assassination or bombing activity reveals a higher degree of risk aversion. Since he is unlikely to be a specialist in terrorism, a large part of his time will be occupied by activities other than terrorism. Potential suspects may include those who have engaged in some form of political or non-violent activism if the underlying motivation lends itself to such forms of expression. Law enforcement must be careful not to confuse contact made with them by the lone wolf UNSUB with the lone wolf's attempts to disseminate his ideas or message. The more risk averse lone wolf will not be compelled to make contact with law enforcement merely to taunt them and enhance the risk that he faces. Such a risky activity that increases his chances of being apprehended is not likely to be a behaviour exhibited by the very risk averse lone wolf UNSUB. Although we will not go back through the mean-variance calculations here, law enforcement will be able to place the lone wolf in expected payoff-risk space, particularly after the serial lone wolf has engaged in two or three terrorist actions. At such a time, the lone wolf UNSUB has revealed his risk preference and other inferences may then be derived by thinking about how the UNSUB will be assessing the variability and average payoffs of his actions and the opportunities available to him.

THE LESS RISK AVERSE LONE WOLF TERRORIST AND THE INFERENCES WE MAY DRAW

In most respects, everything that we have said about the more risk averse lone wolf terrorist is 'inverted' for the less risk averse lone wolf terrorist. It must be remembered that all of our serial lone wolf terrorists are risk averse to some degree. One might think of them as less risk seeking (more risk averse) or more risk seeking (less risk averse) but none of our serial lone wolf terrorists has shown a tendency to plunge all of his time and resources into the single most risky attack method. Within the mean-variance framework that we have constructed, a lone wolf with lower risk aversion and the opportunity to combine attack methods will drift towards combinations that are predominantly characterised by higher weightings to bombing, hostage taking and unconventional attacks. When combination is not possible, the lone wolf UNSUB with a lower level of risk aversion will allocate more and more resources to armed attacks and may even come to specialise in them. If he desires even more risk, hostage taking and unconventional attacks will entice him. Since he is likely to be a more of a specialist, most of his time will be allocated to terrorism. Potential suspects are less likely to include those who have engaged in political or non-violent activism to any substantial degree and the less risk averse lone wolf terrorist is less likely to attempt to disseminate his ideas through traditional or social media. However, the more risk seeking or less risk averse lone wolf terrorist might be compelled to make contact with law enforcement. Such a risky activity increases the real or perceived variability of the outcomes of his terrorist activities and provides the additional risk that he desires.

The less risk averse lone wolf terrorist will choose attack methods or combinations of attack methods that are characterised by a higher expected payoff but which have more variable outcomes. As such, he will be seen to occupy the 'flatter' section of the opportunity set and his indifference curves will also be relatively flat when compared with the steeper indifference curves of the more risk averse lone wolf terrorist. Once he reveals his risk preference by the choice of a more risky attack method, we may draw a number of inferences. As mentioned before, these will be the inverse of those that were drawn for the more risk averse lone wolf terrorist. The less risk averse lone wolf is more likely to be found in the vicinity of his target locations and he is less likely to move from place to place. The reason for this is simply that the increase in variability that may attend enhanced law enforcement efforts and enhanced public vigilance is an enticement rather than a deterrent. He does not need to seek locations where his chosen attack method yields the required risk-reward ratio because he is more willing to accept variability. As a result his day-to-day activities might display more stability than the fragile, drifting more risk averse lone wolf terrorist. His attacks might be more concentrated together in time and, at the limit, extremely time concentrated[3]. He is more likely to taunt law enforcement and less likely to engage in forms of legitimate expression. The defining characteristic of this type of lone wolf terrorist is that he does not require a large increase in his expected payoffs to entice him to bear additional risk.

THE SERIAL LONE WOLF TERRORIST'S BEHAVIOUR OVER TIME

In our discussion of the organised/disorganised typology that dominates offender profiling practice, we noted the investigative psychologists' concerns regarding the 'consistency principle' embedded within this typology. The behaviour of the serial lone wolf terrorist over time is critically important. The economic models of decision-making under conditions of risk and uncertainty contain embedded within them the possibility that risk aversion will change over time, especially as the individual's payoffs accumulate. Risk aversion is not static over time. Most investigative psychologists and offender profilers probably know this intuitively. It would be reflected, for example, in qualitative judgements such as, "The offender is becoming bolder with each passing attack." The way in which economic analysis treats risk aversion over time or in relation to accumulated payoffs may augment this qualitative approach. Economic analysis recognises two ways in which risk aversion may be thought about: (1) absolutely; and (2) relatively. In our context or analytical framework, absolute risk aversion refers to the absolute allocation of resources to terrorist activities as the lone wolf terrorist's payoffs accumulate. Relative risk aversion refers to the percentage allocation of resources to more or less risky terrorist activities as the lone wolf's payoffs accumulate. Both absolute and relative risk aversion may be increasing, decreasing or constant over time. If we choose to define the lone wolf terrorist's preferences by the quadratic expected utility function, then we will define both his absolute and relative risk aversion as *increasing*. This will mean different things depending on where within the opportunity the lone wolf starts and whether he is more or less risk averse at the outset of his series of attacks.

The less risk averse or more risk seeking lone wolf terrorist who is characterised by increasing absolute and relative risk aversion may be expected to do two things as the victims of his attacks accumulate. First, his level of specialisation in terrorism may reduce gradually from near complete specialisation to some lower level. He will gradually commit less time and resources to his terrorist activities. Second, his initially quite risky attack methods combinations—armed attacks, bombings, hostage-taking and unconventional attacks—may gradually be replaced by less risky attack methods or combinations. He may gradually transition into bombings and assassinations as the payoffs to his more risky initial attacks accumulate. The more risk averse lone wolf, likewise, may reduce his already low level of specialisation and, if one of the riskier attack methods had made up any part of his attack method combinations, he may transition away from it to focus on those attack methods with the least variable outcomes. Both types of lone wolf terrorists may become satiated after a successful attack or series of successful attacks. Law enforcement should expect either type of lone wolf terrorist to strike and then withdraw for a period of time. Satiation or complete

[3] A completely time concentrated terrorist attack will be a 'spree' of violence and spree offenders will be found to occupy a special place in our typology. This is discussed in a subsequent chapter.

satisfaction with his terrorist activities may occur after an attack that yields relatively few victims. It would not be unusual for a more risk averse lone wolf to be easily satiated and withdraw from terrorism completely for an extended period of time. This would not be a response to risk but a response to the outcomes and accumulated outcomes of his terrorist activities. The economic logic that underlies our analysis leads us to expect a 'strike and withdraw' pattern and, furthermore, leads us to expect that the period of withdrawal could be lengthy and the lone wolf terrorist may enter upon it after a single successful attack which need not necessarily be one that inflicted a very large amount of human tragedy. The lone wolf terrorist is more easily satiated than we might expect.

Concluding Remarks

A typology or classification scheme that emerges from an economic analytical framework is one based on revealed risk preference. This type of economic analysis does not assume that any particular type of risk preference is exhibited by criminals or terrorists or lone wolf terrorists and that this distinguishes them from 'normal' people. Rather, risk preference is a quality that all people exhibit in some form or other. The revealed risk preference typology that we have developed may be taken to a very high degree of analytical precision. Every point in expected payoff-risk space can be defined and the precise location of the lone wolf terrorist within that space can be identified. We noticed, however, that fine-grain analysis may not be necessary to obtain useful results. At very low levels of risk particular attack methods dominate the attack method combinations. The same is true at intermediate and high levels of risk. A lone wolf UNSUB who is observed to engage in combinations of assassination and bombing, for example[4], has revealed a risk preference that is characterised by a higher level of risk aversion. A lone wolf UNSUB who is observed to engage in hijacking, hostage taking or unconventional attacks reveals a preference that is characterised by a lower level of risk aversion. Just as law enforcement faces problems initially in the association of different crimes with a single serial killer, the more terrorist activities that the lone wolf terrorist attempts or undertakes, the more he reveals about himself. With each attack, the investigator can place the lone wolf terrorist more precisely within expected payoff-risk space and more precisely determine the lone wolf's type of revealed risk preference.

Equipped with an idea about the lone wolf UNSUB's type of risk preference, the investigator and law enforcement can draw further inferences from the established economic theoretical frameworks that have long been applied to the analysis of criminal and terrorist behaviour. These inferences include aspects of the lone wolf's specialisation and, by implication, the extent of his involvement in both the violent attack methods of terrorism and other forms of expression, the lone wolf's geographical location relative to the location of the attacks (because of the necessity to move to find pockets of favourable risk-reward trade-off), the lone wolf's likely propensity to engage in communication with law enforcement and the behaviour of the lone wolf terrorist over time, particularly as injuries and fatalities accumulate. The opportunities available to the lone wolf terrorist may be delineated and his

[4] If combination is not possible, then a very risk averse lone wolf UNSUB may be observed to attempt to assassinations.

choices from those opportunities reveal his preferences. By developing the mean-variance framework and encompassing the lone wolf terrorist's opportunities and choices within it, it is possible to use the lone wolf's terrorist actions, especially his choice of attack method, as a starting point for the drawing of inferences that may be operationally useful as investigative advice.

Chapter 13

METESKY, KACZYNSKI AND FUCHS

> BOMB BLAST IN TERMINAL. An explosion from a small homemade bomb startled many commuters during the rush hour at 5:22 P. M. yesterday in Grand Central Terminal, but no one was injured and there was no panic[1].

From the crime scene and the nature of the attack method or attack method combination that the lone wolf has deployed, inferences are drawn about the lone wolf UNSUB. This is the nature of offender profiling. An approach to offender profiling that is based on economic analysis involves the drawing of inferences from an economic theoretical framework using the risk preference revealed by actions or choices as the starting point. The lone wolf's choice of terrorist action reveals a preference. Like the choices and patterns of behaviour exhibited by serial killers, the lone wolf's preferences will become clearer to the investigator following two or three attacks. It will be very difficult to draw any solid conclusions on the basis of information revealed by just one terrorist attack. Because a mean-variance analytical framework yields computable results and provides a clear indication of the relative risk of each attack method and combination, we have used this as the theoretical foundation for an analysis of the opportunities and choices of the lone wolf in expected payoff-risk space. His choice places the lone wolf in a particular region of expected payoff-risk space and this placement reveals a particular type of risk preference. Revealed risk preference becomes the starting point for the drawing of inferences about the offender.

FBI profilers will not usually want to know anything about any potential suspects when forming a profile and prefer to work solely from the facts about the crime scene (Douglas and Olshaker 1996). Therefore, constructing profiles of known offenders is likely to be fraught with difficulty and we might draw conclusions that we would not have drawn at the time in the midst of a real investigation. Nevertheless, for the purposes of illustration we will work through the activities of some of the notable lone wolf terrorists and sketch some outlines of their profile as it would emerge from the economic analysis that we have developed. Starting from the types of attacks that the lone wolves undertook, we shall follow the process that we have described to construct an economic profile. First, the risk preference revealed by the type or nature of terrorist attack will be determined. For this we shall rely on the mean-variance analytical framework which allows us to avoid making qualitative judgements about the riskiness of particular terrorist activities. Once the risk preferences are revealed, we draw

[1] Excerpt from the New York Times, March 1951.

inferences about the lone wolf from the economic theoretical frameworks that have been set down in previous chapters. We then compare the sketched economic profiles with the actual characteristics of the offenders (example, location, engagement in other activities besides violent terrorism and so on). We envisage that, as time passes and specialised empirical investigations are undertaken into economic profiling, the level of sophistication deployed in constructing economic profiles will be enhanced significantly.

THE MAD BOMBER

George Metesky a.k.a. 'The Mad Bomber' was responsible for a series of bombings that were, initially at least, motivated by his grievance with Consolidated Edison. Metesky had been injured in an industrial accident in 1931 but was denied workers' compensation. Consolidated Edison was the direct target of his first bombing attempt. In November 1940, he left a bomb on a window sill at the Consolidated Edison building. It was discovered before it exploded. About a year later, a similar device was found in the street not too far from Consolidated Edison's building. It too failed to explode because the fuse had not been set. It is possible that the device was discarded by Metesky on the street because he had second-thoughts or perceived the risk too great, perhaps after seeing a police officer on street patrol in the area. This aborted bombing attack was Metesky's last attack for almost ten years. He did not completely disappear. During this period Metesky sent a number of letters to the police, the press and Consolidated Edison. In March 1951, Metesky commenced his re-engagement in terrorism and launched a new campaign of bombing. This time, however, Metesky's bombing devices were much more sophisticated and his targets much more diverse.

Metesky's new bombing campaign began with a bomb placed in the Grand Central Terminal. It exploded without causing any injuries. Until his eventual capture in 1956, Metesky placed a further thirty devices at various locations around New York City. He placed bombs in phone booths, storage lockers and public restrooms at Grand Central Terminal, Pennsylvania Station, the Radio City Music Hall, the New York Public Library, the Port Authority Bus Terminal, the RCA building and in the subway. Metesky also bombed movie theatres where he secreted the bombing devices in the upholstery of the seats. His bombs injured fifteen people. Ten of these injuries were the outcome of two attacks on theatres and music halls. In 1954, a bomb Metesky had planted in the upholstery of a seat in the Radio City Music Hall exploded with a capacity audience of 6,200 people in attendance. There were four injuries. In 1956, a bombing at the Paramount Theatre injured six people. Again, there was a large audience in attendance when the bomb exploded. Metesky did not target out-of-the-way places where the chance of injury or fatality was small. He targeted crowded places and would certainly have expected a bomb placed in the upholstery of a movie theatre seat to cause some level of injury. The injury toll could have been higher. Not all of Metesky's bombs exploded, including a bombing attempt at the Times Square Paramount where a device was discovered inside a seat's upholstery, apparently some months after it was planted. Metesky was arrested in early 1957.

The case of 'The Mad Bomber' is often recounted within the investigative psychology and offender profiling literature because his was one of the first cases to which the technique of offender profiling was applied. Based on the nature of the crimes, a Dr James Brussell produced a detailed profile of the type of individual the bomber might be (cited by Canter and Youngs 2009, p.68):

- Male (because most bombers are male)
- Has knowledge of metalworking, pipefitting and electricity
- Suffered an injustice by Consolidated Edison, which had rendered him chronically ill
- Suffers from an insidious disorder, paranoia and has a persistent and chronic disorder
- Is pathologically self-centred
- Has no friends, male or female, is a loner
- Symmetric athletic body type, neither fat or skinny
- Is middle-aged (due the onset of illness and duration of bombings)
- Good education, likely high school education but not college
- Unmarried, possibly a virgin
- Distrusts and despises male authority, hates father
- Never progressed past the Oedipal stage of love for his mother due to her early death or separation from him
- Lives alone or with female mother-like relative
- Lives in Connecticut, is of Slavic descent, Roman Catholic and attends church
- Neat, tidy and clean-shaven
- Quiet, polite, methodical and prompt
- Has chronic illness, either heart disease, cancer or tuberculosis, most probably heart disease
- Would be wearing a buttoned double-breasted suit when caught

A number of aspects of this profile are correct, including the last point about the style of dress the offender would be wearing when caught. However, some of the aspects of the profile appear to be more the product of 'profiler intuition' than the scientific drawing of inferences from evidence left at the crime scenes. It is just this type of profile that has driven such intense interest in both offender profiling as a process and the offender profiler as a 'Mind Hunter'. To be able to sketch such a precise picture of the individual is fascinating but it cannot rely solely on the detached application of a scientific framework. There must be guess-work involved, which sometimes produces correct results, or there really is a special intuition possessed by successful offender profilers. The academic investigative psychologists prefer to conclude that it is the former. Canter and Youngs (2009) point out that some of the strikingly correct features of the Mad Bomber profile lose their impact upon closer analysis. The fact that Metesky was indeed wearing a buttoned double-breasted suit when arrested is explained not by the special insight of the profiler, they say, but by the fact that such style of dress was the typical style of the day. Furthermore, despite its detailed nature, Canter and Youngs point out that the profile of Metesky was of little use in apprehending the offender. Rather, evidence gathered from other sources eventually led law enforcement to Metesky.

A profile of Metesky built on the basis of the type of economic analysis that we have developed throughout this book would be quite different from the one produced by Dr Brussell and probably quite different from that which would be produced by a modern profiler using the organised/disorganised typology. We would not have anything to say about the potential offender's relationship with his mother, his style of dress, marital status or feelings towards his father and other authority figures. Inferences of this nature cannot be drawn from the economic theoretical frameworks that we have developed. In the case of 'The Mad Bomber' the investigative economist would work from the attack method choice and the risk preference revealed in that choice to develop a small number of additional insights into the profile of the offender. These inferences will be a smaller number of 'degrees of inference' from the crime scene evidence than offender profiles the kind we have seen produced by investigative psychologists and professional profilers. According to the investigative economist or economic profiler, 'The Mad Bomber' might have the following characteristics:

- Low-to-mid—neither very high nor very low—risk aversion can be concluded on the basis of the offender's choice of bombing as an attack method. In addition, the bombs were placed at rather than mailed to the target locations. Placing bombs at the target is archetype indiscriminate bombing and may be contrasted with parcel or letter-bombing which is far more targeted. The variability associated with the former is higher than the variability of the possible outcomes that we would expect from assassination-type targeted parcel bombing.
- A relatively high degree of specialisation is to be expected with the offender allocating a considerable percentage of his time and other resources to terrorism. Bombing is not the riskiest attack method and we might expect that the offender will be engaged in some attempts to disseminate a message.
- The offender will not need to traverse large geographical distances. With low-to-mid level risk aversion, the offender will find opportunities for generating expected payoffs with his chosen attack method while bearing an appropriate level of risk. He will be found relatively close-by.
- He will be deterred if the risk becomes too great (or too small). For this reason, he will feel a need to control the situation. Police and press attention may be important to this offender. When the attention is not sufficient, when the risk is too low, he will taunt them or make contact with them. If police attention becomes too great, if he feels them closing in on him, his taunts will cease. These actions should not be mistaken for non-violent expression or an alternative to violence.
- Until he is apprehended, the offender will most likely to continue his attacks. He is yet to inflict significant amounts of human tragedy and he is unlikely to have been satiated by the payoffs that he has managed to secure.
- There will not necessarily be an escalation in the intensity of the attacks but if he is ignored by law enforcement or the press, if he does not feel as though his actions are characterised by a sufficient level of risk, he may increase the number and intensity of his attacks. In all of this, he will not be reckless and may even abandon an attack in mid-course if he feels that following through with the terrorist action will increase his chances of apprehension to a significant degree.

The first point is the clearest and most direct inference. From the attack methods that the offender has chosen, it can be concluded that the offender has a middle range level of risk aversion. This is particularly the case for Metesky after the renewal of his bombing campaign in 1951. This revealed risk preference forms the basis for the drawing of additional inferences. With a level of risk aversion that is revealed as being neither extremely low nor extremely high, the offender can be expected to specialise in terrorism to relatively high degree and to remain in relatively close proximity to the location of his targets. This inference flows logically from economic theory. If the offender were very risk averse, he would need to drift away in order to find a location to deploy his chosen attack methods such that they generated their expected payoffs with an appropriate level of risk. The less risk averse the offender is revealed to be, the less need he has to do this. However, unless the offender has a very low level of risk aversion, he will begin to feel uncomfortable if risk increases too much. With a low-to-mid level of risk aversion it follows that the offender will have some compulsion to control events such that his perceived level of risk remains within tolerable bounds. Initiating or withdrawing from contact with law enforcement and press is one way to manage this risk.

We know that offender profiling, especially when undertaken within an organised/disorganised typology, experiences difficulty in describing or accounting for changes in offender behaviour over time. Economic analysis is not troubled to the same degree. Each of the functional forms that could be used to represent the offender's expected utility has implications for the *relative* risk aversion of the offender. In the theoretical framework that we have developed, relative risk aversion refers to the percentage of resources that the lone wolf terrorist allocates to risky attack methods as the injuries and fatalities caused by his terrorism accumulate. If the lone wolf terrorist has an expected utility that can be described by the quadratic functional form, he will be characterised by increasing relative risk aversion. That is, the percentage of his resources that he allocates to terrorism will decrease as the injuries and fatalities that he has caused accumulate and his choice of attack method may show signs of transition from attack methods with more variable outcomes to attack methods with less variable outcomes. The more risk averse the lone wolf, the greater will be the tendency to reduce the amount of resources allocated to terrorism as the list of injuries and fatalities increases and the greater will be the tendency to transition to less risk attack methods. If the revealed risk preference of the lone wolf indicates a lower level of risk aversion, this tendency will not be as strong. In conjunction with what we know about satiation and the lone wolf terrorist's successes or failures at obtaining payoffs from his acts of violence, we can infer in the case of 'The Mad Bomber' that the bombings will continue relatively unabated.

Relative risk aversion has implications for the lone wolf's satiation and the variations in the intensity of his attacks. Inferences are able to de drawn about both of these factors. If the lone wolf reveals himself to have a lower level of risk aversion and we apply the quadratic functional form to his expected utility function, then there will be a weak tendency towards satiation over time as injuries and fatalities accumulate. A lone wolf that becomes satiated or approaches satiation will reduce the intensity of his attacks and perhaps avoid terrorism for some period of time. This can occur over a relatively narrow range of injuries and fatalities and it may not necessarily take a very large number of injuries and fatalities to produce satiation. In the case of the 'The Mad Bomber', a low-to-mid level of risk aversion should produce a relatively weaker tendency towards satiation. This is why we can infer in the case of 'The Mad Bomber' that the attacks are likely to proceed without any significant period of abatement, especially given the failure of most of the bombing attacks to generate large numbers of injuries and fatalities. Relative risk aversion may also explain Metesky's hiatus throughout the ten year period preceding 1951. His first attack and aborted second attack indicate that the earlier Metesky was very much more risk averse. In the Metesky case, we would conclude that the attacks would continue with no abatement in intensity.

The Brussell profile contains a number of detailed points that rule in and rule out particular individuals. The profile that we have developed complements this type of 'traditional' profile. Furthermore, the possibility should not be overlooked that a professional offender profiler may be able to do more with the results of our analysis than we have been able to. Rather than contributing additional specific advice along the lines of the offender's education, relationships and so on, the behavioural investigative advice generated by the application of economic analysis to the construction of an offender profile is relevant to the overall investigation and the management of the hunt for a lone wolf suspect who is at large and potentially capable of engaging in further attacks. The economic analysis first of all provides some insights into the riskiness of the attack method or attack method combinations chosen by the lone wolf UNSUB. It does so without relying on qualitative assessments of the relative riskiness of different attack methods. The lone wolf's choice of attack method reveals a risk preference. Now we know what 'type' of lone wolf we are pursuing. If he is low-to-mid level risk averse, we expect him to remain close and continue to focus on targets within a relatively small geographical proximity. He does not need to find other places where his chosen attack methods will yield a higher or lower expected payoff. If the risk that he is bearing is not high enough he will taunt law enforcement or the press. If the risk becomes too great, his taunts will cease. He will not be easily satiated by injuries and fatalities and can be expected to continue his attacks unabated. Although these pieces of behavioural investigative advice are not as 'individual' as those provided by a traditional offender profile, they are important and relevant to the management of the manhunt.

THE UNABOMBER

> Mail Bomb Attack Leaves Yale Computer Scientist in Critical Condition: Explosion: Authorities are investigating to see if there are links to a blast that injured California genetics researcher earlier in the week[2].

Theodore (Ted) Kaczynski a.k.a 'The Unabomber' is an American lone wolf who engaged in a prolonged parcel or letter-bombing campaign which lasted for almost twenty years[3]. Between 1978 and 1995 Kaczynski, apparently motivated by his views about development and environmental degradation, mailed sixteen parcel and letter-bombs to various targets around the United States. The bombing devices caused three deaths and twenty-three injuries. Compared to Metesky, Kaczynski's attacks were far more effective though the bombing device used in Kaczynski's first attack was, like Metesky's, relatively crude. Kaczysnki's first attack occurred in May 1978. It appears as though Kaczynski left a parcel in the parking lot of the University of Illinois at Chicago. This in itself is interesting because at first it would seem as though Kaczynski delivered the bombing device to his target location. However, Kaczynski's target was actually the person whom he had identified as the

---

[2] Shogren (1993). Excerpt from the Los Angeles Times, June 25, 1993.

[3] A colleague and I developed a short profile of Theodore Kaczynski and Franz Fuchs, based on economic analysis, in Phillips and Pohl (2012).

'sender' of the parcel. This was a professor in materials engineering at Northwestern University at Evanston, Illinois. When the parcel was discovered at the University of Illinois in Chicago it was placed in the mail and returned to the 'sender'. The materials engineering professor alerted security when he received the parcel and a university security officer was injured when the parcel was opened. The parcel contained Kaczynski's first delivered pipe-bomb, a choice of attack method that would become the Unabomber's signature over the ensuing two decades.

Kaczynski targeted Northwestern University again the following year, causing minor injuries to the person who opened the parcel. By the late 1970s then, there was some indication that a bomber was targeting particular types of research at universities. In May 1979, Kaczynski became more than a 'university bomber' when mailed a parcel containing an explosive device from Chicago to a business in Washington. The parcel was placed on an airplane out of Chicago carrying passengers and cargo, including mail. Kaczynski's device ignited enroute and could have proven disastrous if it had exploded. As it happened, however, the device produced a lot of smoke—some passengers required treatment as a result of smoke inhalation—and the pilot was forced to make an emergency landing. Kaczynski's next target was also 'airline' related. The target was the chief of United Airlines, who suffered minor injuries when he opened a parcel sent to his home in Chicago. With these two attacks and his previous parcel bombings at Northwestern University, Kaczynski emerged as the university and airline bomber or 'Unabomber'.

His bombing campaign continued through 1980 to 1982. His targeted parcel bombs caused injuries to university staff at Vanderbilt University in Tennessee and at the University of California at Berkeley. After this period of frequent activity, Kaczynski was nowhere to be seen for several years. Then, in 1985, his bombing campaign resumed. A research student at Berkeley was injured in a May 1985 parcel bombing, a researcher and his assistant were injured in November and then, in December, Kaczynski inflicted his first fatality when a computer store owner opened a package that Kaczynski had left outside of his computer store in Sacramento, California. The intense period of bombing was concluded with a similar attack in February of 1986 which injured another computer store owner in Salt Lake City, Utah. The geographical distance between each of these is considerable but traversable by motor vehicle and, of course, within the 'range' of parcel bombs delivered by a postal delivery service. Chicago and Evanston in Illinois, Berkeley and Sacremento in California and Salt Lake City in Utah. Chicago, of course, is a long way from the west coast (about 2000 miles). Berkeley and Sacremento are about 100 miles apart from each other and Salt Lake City is about 700 miles from Sacremento. Kaczynski occupied a cabin in the wilderness in Montana, about 1000 miles from Berkeley.

Kaczynski did not engage in another attack for seven years. His final campaign, however, inflicted two fatalities and several severe injuries. His victims included a researcher at the University of California and a professor at Yale. The attacks took place within a few days of each other in June 1993. Like his other attacks, a large geographical distance separated Kaczynski and each of his two targets. Yale, in Connecticut, is about as distant as one can get from the west coast. It is nearly 3000 miles from Berkeley. Both of these university targets were injured. A year and a half later, Kaczynski struck again and again his attacks display the same 'distance' characteristics. This time, however, his attacks had fatal consequences. In late 1994 an advertising executive was killed by a parcel bomb he opened at his home in New Jersey and in early 1995 a timber industry lobbyist was killed when he opened a parcel delivered to the California Forestry Association. At this time, Kaczynski was entering the final stages of his terrorist actions. His final two attacks had been deadly and his attention was now focussed on the dissemination of his 'manifesto', which was published in two major newspapers. The ideas contained in the manifesto were idiosyncratic enough that Kaczynski's brother, David Kaczynski, was able to recognise that Theodore Kaczynski was more than likely one of the FBI's most wanted men. He informed law enforcement and Kaczynski was arrested in early 1996.

'The Unabomber' was the target of one of the largest manhunts in United States history. It is not surprising that F.B.I. profilers produced an offender profile of the UNSUB. Ultimately, of course, it was the offender's brother who provided the vital investigative breakthrough but law enforcement may still have obtained considerable utility from the profile in terms of the guidance and focus it provided to the ongoing investigation but regardless of how personally specific an offender profile may be, it may not lead directly to the offender. A profile based on economic analysis would generate different inferences about the suspect than a traditional offender profile and, once more, would represent a contribution to the overall investigation, including the management of potential targets and the anticipation of the suspect's future engagement in violent acts of terrorism. Profiling based on economic analysis of an unknown offender's choices and revealed risk preference is not just about the individual or personal characteristics of the UNSUB and will never be able to provide personal or specific details of the nature contained in some of the traditional offender profiles. A profile constructed on the basis of economic analysis and the process that we have developed would suggest that 'The Unabomber' would have the following characteristics:

- Although the suspect engaged in 'bombing', parcel or letter-bombing is much more akin to assassination. The suspect reveals his risk preference to be characterised by a higher level of risk aversion.
- We do not expect the offender to be a specialist or near-specialist in terrorism and he may engage in other forms of expression if his motives are political-ideological and lend themselves to other forms of expression.
- We should not expect the suspect to remain in close geographical proximity to his targets. He will need to drift in order to find 'pockets' where his chosen method of attack yields an appropriate expected payoff. The investigator would note, however, that parcel or letter-bombing enables the suspect to drift from target to target without actually changing his base of operations. He will not be close-by but he may not necessarily be 'on-the-move'.
- The suspect will be deterred if he perceives law enforcement or press attention as becoming too intense. Being far away protects him from this. He will not taunt law enforcement or the press. To do so would increase the risk of his activities. That is something he does not desire.
- He is more easily satiated within any single time period and his risk aversion is increasing from an already relatively high starting point. These two factors lead us to expect there to be significant periods of time in which the suspect ceases his engagement in terrorism. These are especially likely to occur after he inflicts some injuries or fatalities.

- The suspect is unlikely to increase the intensity of his attacks. His attacks may be more or less successful in terms of inflicting injuries and fatalities but the scale and frequency of his attacks is unlikely to show a significant increase. If anything, we would expect his increasing risk aversion to produce less frequent attacks and we might even expect there to be a gradual transition to even less risky attack methods.

Leaving aside the offender profiler's skills, the 'raw' application of a typology such as the organised/disorganised typology to the Unabomber case would be fraught with difficulties. Apart from the nature of the attacks themselves, which are quite obviously organised, there was very little except disintegrated bombing devices and parcels on which to base the drawing of further inferences. The contribution of economic analysis to the investigative process is very different from the personal characteristics that constitute most offender profiles. From the points that have been sketched, however, one can see that the aspects of the profile that we might be able to contribute to the investigative process are likely to be relevant to the *overall* manhunt operation including some insights about the offender's likely future actions. The mean-variance framework provides the quantitative framework within which to assess the relative riskiness of the various attack methods and attack method combinations. The lone wolf terrorist's choice of attack method reveals his risk preference. The implications of the lone wolf terrorist's revealed risk preference provide the basis for the drawing of inferences about his actions and choices.

A profile constructed on the basis of economic analysis is possible because of the structure that underlies both the opportunities to engage in particular types of terrorism and the choices that individuals make in pursuing these opportunities. A more risk averse individual such as the Unabomber must seek pockets where the expected payoff to his activities remains commensurate with the risk. Each enhancement in law enforcement attention makes this trade-off less desirable and the lone wolf terrorist must continue to 'drift' or cease his engagement in terrorism for an indefinite period. Kaczynski drifted by deploying the parcel or letter-bombing method of bombing assassination. This enabled him to target diverse locations and remain distant in terms of his own geographical proximity to any of the crime scenes. With a higher level of revealed risk aversion, we would expect the suspect to be more easily deterred by the attention of law enforcement. Given that he does not desire additional risk, he has no need to taunt law enforcement or the press. With a higher level of risk aversion, we would expect the suspect to be more easily satiated, particularly after a successful attack. This is why we expect that he may fade away for a period of time after inflicting only a small number of injuries and fatalities. Finally, with a higher level of risk aversion, he is less likely to specialise in terrorism. This is why we expect him to be active in pursuing other forms of expression. Kaczynski produced a manifesto and even promised to cease his engagement in terrorism if the manifesto was published. Beyond revealed risk preference, the profile constructed on the basis of economic analysis cannot produce a list of personal characteristics of the suspect. It can provide behavioural investigative advice that contributes to the formation of a more complete picture of the suspect.

Franz Fuchs

Most of our discussion throughout this book has been focused on American lone wolf terrorists or, at least, lone wolf terrorists who operated within the United States. As we noted a good many chapters ago, Europe has experienced a number of incidences of lone wolf terrorism. Franz Fuchs was an Austrian lone wolf terrorist. He was engaged in a bombing campaign that lasted several years from 1993 to 1997. Fuchs's chosen attack method combination was a combination of parcel or letter-bombing and conventional bombing. Fuchs sent or placed twenty-eight bombs, including five 'waves' of a total of twenty-five letter-bombs, that left four people dead and fifteen injured. The motivation for his engagement in terrorism appears to have been racial. Most of the targets of his letter-bombs were involved in some form of refugee or immigrant advocacy, directly or politically (Instituut voor Veiligheids 2007, p.26). Fuchs commenced his campaign against these types of targets in December 1993, with letter-bombs directed at several individuals, including a priest, a journalist and the Mayor of Vienna. Several of the targets suffered injuries. This wave of letter-bombings was followed in August of 1994 by the planting of an explosive device at a bilingual school in Carinthia, in southern Austria. The bomb was discovered but three police officers suffered injuries while attempting to diffuse it. Soon after this attack, Fuchs sent a letter to the Slovenian foreign minister in which he claimed responsibility for the attacks on behalf of a fictional terrorist organisation, 'Bajuwarische Befreiungsarme' (Instituut voor Veiligheids 2007, p.53). In this respect, his actions are reminiscent of both Kaczynski's 'Freedom Club' and Kurbegovich's 'Aliens of America'.

Fuchs resumed his letter-bombing campaign in late 1994 with a second wave of five letter-bombs. All of the devices failed to explode and no-one was injured. A few months later, in February 1995, Fuchs undertook his most deadly bombing attack. In the second instance of his deployment of conventional bombing attack methods, Fuchs attached an explosive device to a sign containing a racist slogan. Fuchs placed the sign in a public park. Four people from a nearby community were killed when the device exploded as they tried to remove the sign. A few days later, Fuchs planted another bomb in Stinatz, in eastern Austria. This device injured an environmental services employee (Instituut voor Veiligheids 2007, p.67). In June 1995, Fuchs undertook a third wave of letter-bombings. This time, several injuries resulted. In October 1995, Fuchs inflicted a further two injuries in a fourth wave of letter-bombings. Fuchs's fifth and final wave of letter-bombings occurred in December 1995. The bombs were either discovered or exploded prematurely and no injuries were caused. Fuchs struck once more, a year later, with a single letter-bomb sent to the stepmother of a prominent politician. It exploded during police attempts to diffuse it. Fuchs was arrested in October 1997. During the arrest he exploded a device in an apparent suicide attempt. He was badly injured and a police officer was hurt. Fuchs survived and was sentenced to life in prison (Instituut voor Veiligheids 2007, p.81).

Like the other lone wolf terrorists who we have discussed, Fuchs was also profiled by an investigative psychologist. Thomas Müller constructed a profile in which Fuchs was described as follows (Instituut voor Veiligheids 2007, p.81):

- An Austrian male and probably over 50 years old
- He lives in a family house, since he needs the space to keep his material.

- He possesses specialized tools and a hobby workplace.
- He is a Catholic and has knowledge of hierarchies and religious titles.
- He probably completed secondary school.
- He also has knowledge of chemistry and has an interest in history.
- He likes order and tidiness and is extremely precise

Again, the traditional offender profile concentrates on very individual, personal characteristics of the UNSUB. Some aspects of the profile are more or less correct. The accuracy of other aspects is debatable. Just like in the other cases that we have discussed, the offender profile did not play a direct role in the apprehension of the offender. The police officers who approached Fuchs on the day of his arrest did not know who he was and if he did not detonate an explosive device when the officers approached him, they might not have arrested him. The profile that we might construct on the basis of an economic analysis of Franz Fuchs' decisions and choices would have generated behavioural investigative advice relevant to the overall manhunt operation but would not have contributed anything with regard to the offender's religion, tidiness or predisposition for precision. Apart from the UNSUB's revealed preference for risk, economic analysis does not attempt to list a set of personal characteristics such as those contained in the profile constructed by Müller. Rather, the profile based on economic analysis provides behavioural investigative advice that is relevant to the management of the investigation and manhunt and insights that may be relevant to the offender's potential future actions. As we have said before, though, the experienced offender profiler may do more with our 'diagnosis' of risk preference than we are willing to do. Our profile for Franz Fuchs may have looked something like this:

- The offender reveals mid-level risk aversion. With regards to his attack methods, he is predominantly involved in assassination-type letter-bombing but combines this attack method with conventional forms of bombing. Such combinations produce levels of risk that are low-to-mid range.
- He is likely to allocate a relatively large portion of his resources to terrorism. He is unlikely to be engaged in other forms of activism.
- The offender might taunt law enforcement or the press if he feels as though the risk that he is facing has fallen below a desirable level. However, these are unlikely to be aggressive taunts. They will not reveal a significant amount of information to law enforcement.
- The offender will likely drift from place to place looking for 'pockets' where his chosen attack methods yield their expected payoff with a commensurate amount of risk. This drift may be simulated by letter-bombing or involve actual movement from place to place.
- It will be difficult, except by chance, to find him in close geographical proximity to his targets. However, he has indicated by his willingness to place explosive devices in public places that his risk aversion is not so high that he feels the need to operate at a great distance. He will be found to live or work within a relatively close proximity to his targets.
- He is unlikely to escalate the intensity of his attacks.

- He might become satiated and cease his engagement in terrorism for a period of time, especially after a series of very successful attacks. If his attacks are not successful, he will continue with them relatively unabated.

In some ways it may be best to simply say that Fuchs is less risk averse than Kaczynski but not so risk seeking as Metesky. This characterisation, which is reflected more precisely in the list of dot-points that constitutes the economic profile, explains much of Fuchs's behaviour. He sent letters to law enforcement and government officials but these letters could not be characterised as 'taunts' or 'dares' designed to dramatically enhance the risk he was bearing. He drifted from place to place to plant his bombing devices but he resided in Gralla, in southern Austria, not a great distance from the location of some of his targets. He faded away for brief periods after his more successful attacks, only to return some months later with new waves of letter-bombs. When his attacks failed, he was willing to try again very soon afterwards. Sometimes only a month or two separated his unsuccessful attacks and his re-emergence. The intensity of his attacks remained fairly constant for the duration of his campaign. He communications do not amount to a manifesto or treatise such as that produced by Kaczynski but his writings are more substantial than the very short warnings or taunts that Metesky sent to the press during his bombing campaign. Mid-level risk aversion is consistent with a relatively high but probably not complete specialisation in terrorism.

RISK AND REWARD

Apart from one letter bomb which targeted Consolidated Edison (and did not explode), Metesky may certainly be classified primarily as a lone wolf terrorist engaged in the deployment of the 'bombing' attack method. Kaczynski operated predominantly as a letter-bomber and his attacks appear to be specifically targeted assassination-type attacks rather than archetype bombings which are more public, more indiscriminate and characterised by much more variable outcomes than assassinations. Fuchs combined both letter-bombing and conventional bombing. After two or three attacks, the risk preference of the lone wolf is more clearly revealed. In the case of Metesky, law enforcement could begin to conclude after two or three attacks that 'bombing' was the lone wolf UNSUB's choice of attack method. This places the individual in at least the mid-range of risk and indicates a lower risk aversion (more risk seeking) type. In the case of Kaczynski, law enforcement could begin to conclude that 'assassination' or targeted letter-bombing was the lone wolf UNSUB's choice of attack method. This places the individual in the low-range of risk and indicates a higher risk aversion type. Fuchs is more complex and is an example of why it is necessary to gather evidence from two or three crime scenes before an accurate profile may be constructed. Fuchs started with targeted letter-bombs but quite quickly, within a year or so, became involved in conventional bombing as well.

In the Metesky case, the higher risk activity of specialised bombing would place the lone wolf in the category of lower risk aversion (more risk seeking) type. We would expect a lone wolf with this type of revealed risk preference to be enticed by the risk of the terrorist activity. He will not be averse to taunting law enforcement or the popular press. He will not be involved in other forms of political expression. He will not write a treatise, a manifesto or a pamphlet about his views. He will be more of a specialist in terrorism rather than someone who wishes to convey some sort of message via legitimate and illegitimate modes of expression. He will not be adrift in search of more favourable risk-reward trade-offs. He will be found close by. Until he is apprehended, the less risk averse or more risk seeking lone wolf will likely to continue his attacks relatively unabated. There will not necessarily be an escalation in the intensity of the attacks but if he is ignored by law enforcement or the press, if he does not feel as though his actions are characterised by a sufficient level of risk, he may increase the number and intensity of his attacks. In all of this, he will not be bold or reckless and may even abandon an attack in mid-course if he feels that following through with the terrorist action will increase his chances of apprehension to an undesirable degree.

In the Kaczynski case, the lower risk activity would place the lone wolf in the more risk averse type. We would expect a lone wolf terrorist of this type to drift. If he was close to the geographical location of the earlier attacks, he has likely drifted away to find more favourable risk-reward trade-offs. Attention from law enforcement and the popular press will unsettle him *if* he is listening or paying attention to it, particularly if he feels as though he has lost control of the situation and his chances of apprehension have increased as a result. In the case of a letter-bomber, of course, the lone wolf terrorist can drift from a stable 'home base' location by sending his bombing devices to a range of different locations. Except by chance, the more risk averse lone wolf will not be found in close geographical proximity to his targets. He will not live in the area that he has targeted. He will not be a local resident. If he was, he will be ready to move on. The more risk averse lone wolf will not be a specialist in terrorism. He will spend a relatively large part of his time on legitimate political activism or other activities if he is not politically motivated. He will write about his views or participate in forms of expression other than terrorism. At the right time, he may seek publicity but he will not taunt law enforcement as such. Following a successful attack or series of attacks, the more risk averse lone wolf may drift away and avoid engagement in terrorism for a long time.

Fuchs is an interesting and more complex case. At first, law enforcement would place him in the much the same category as Kaczynski. The letter-bombs that were sent by Fuchs do have characteristics that place them more in an 'assassination' or 'targeted' type category than in the conventional bombing attack method category, although their 'wave' nature is an important feature that distinguishes Fuchs's letter-bombing campaigns from Kaczynski's. This initial characterisation of Fuchs would change with Fuchs's decision to engage in conventional bombing attacks. He planted three bombs in public places and was responsible for the four fatalities that resulted. This certainly places Fuchs's attack method choices in a higher risk category than Kaczynski's. Being more risk seeking than Kaczynski, this lone wolf will be more inclined to communicate with, but not necessarily taunt, law enforcement. This type of lone wolf will drift in search of expected payoffs with commensurate risk but he will be found relatively near his targets. He does not need to drift as far. He will be relatively close by. The risk entices him to some degree and he is not as easily satiated. He will continue with his attacks unabated, particularly if they are less successful than he anticipated, and must be apprehended lest he continue to engage in terrorism. He may write about his motivations but is more likely to specialise in terrorism. This specialisation will limit the extent to which he engages in non-violent forms of expression. In everything, the trade-off between risk and reward is paramount.

CONCLUDING REMARKS

It is unlikely that economic analysis will be able to develop an approach to offender profiling that allows inferences to be drawn that approach the level of personal and individual specificity that characterises some of the profiles produced by the professional profilers. The inferences that are drawn within the frameworks of economic logic have to be worked out on the basis of an economic theoretical framework of opportunity and choice. All offenders, including lone wolf terrorists, face a set of opportunities from which they can choose. These opportunities are not limitless. From the set of opportunities, the lone wolf makes his choices. These choices can be analysed in a number of different ways. The traditional approach is to assume that the lone wolf will attempt to maximise his expected utility. In our mean-variance analytical framework this is equivalent to assuming that the lone wolf will choose the most dangerous attack method or attack method combination at the level risk that agrees with the lone wolf's preferences. Both the opportunities and choices of the lone wolf terrorist are encompassed within the economic theoretical framework.

When the lone wolf makes a choice of attack method or attack method combination he reveals his preference for risk. This revelation is the starting point for our approach to the offender profiling process. Each of the attack methods that are available within the opportunity set of the lone wolf are characterised by risk and expected payoff. We know which attack methods and combinations will be chosen by lone wolves with different preferences for risk. We know that more risk seeking or less risk averse lone wolf terrorists will choose attack method combinations with heavier allocations of resources to hostage taking or unconventional attacks. We know that more risk averse or less risk seeking lone wolf terrorists will prefer attack method combinations with heavier allocations of resources to bombing, armed attacks and assassination. And we know that very risk averse lone wolf terrorists will prefer attack method combinations with high resource allocations to assassination and bombing. This delineation of the lone wolf's opportunities and choices allows us to say a lot about the risk and reward trade-offs that confront the lone wolf and provides some insights into the lone wolf's opportunities and choices that may be useful for law enforcement in their efforts to pre-empt or prepare for terrorist actions. However, it is not until the lone wolf strikes that we know the 'type' of the particular lone wolf that we must now pursue.

The lone wolf's choices of attack methods allow us to identify the lone wolf's preference for risk. Based on this revealed risk preference, certain other features of the lone wolf UNSUB may be inferred from the underlying economic-theoretical models of criminal and terrorist behaviour. The types of inferences that can be made about the lone wolf concern the lone wolf's degree of specialisation in terrorism, his geographical location relative to the location of his targets, the likelihood that he will 'taunt' law enforcement and the popular press and the ways in which the lone wolf might be expected to behave following the success or failure of his earlier attacks. Part of the problem with the organised/disorganised typology is the inherent assumption of consistency that it contains. Economic analysis requires no such assumption[4]. If the lone wolf is of the more risk seeking type, he may be expected to escalate his attacks and his contact with law enforcement and the popular press in order to enhance the

[4] Do not confuse the von Neumann and Morgenstern axiom 'consistency' with an assumption of consistent behaviour over time. These things are quite different.

risk of his activities. It is the risk that entices him and he is not as easily satiated by the injuries and fatalities he has been able to inflict. If the lone wolf is of the more risk averse type, the lone wolf is more easily satiated and less likely to enhance the intensity of his attacks over time. Indeed, the more risk averse lone wolf might be expected to cease his activities for an indefinite period, particularly after he has tasted success.

The inferences that we have drawn are not exhaustive and, as we have said, may be complemented by the additional insights of offender profilers who may use our determination of the offender's risk preference as a starting point in their consideration of offender risk. Further study and more imagination will likely increase the number of things that can be plausibly said about an offender and the inferences that can be drawn about him from the nature of his crime and the crime scene. The inferences that can be drawn within an economic framework will not, by themselves, constitute a profile that is personal enough to guide law enforcement to the lone wolf UNSUB. This too may be beyond the scope investigative psychology. The things that have been inferred above on the basis of revealed risk preference and the economic logic of choice under risk and uncertainty are useful things to know about any UNSUB offender. The inferences that may be drawn on the basis of economic analysis provide advice to law enforcement about the type of offender they should be looking for and the type of behaviour they may expect from that offender in the future. Lone wolf terrorists may drift away or they may escalate the intensity of their terrorist attacks and they may move throughout the feasible regions of expected payoff-risk space. However, at all times the lone wolf faces opportunities and choices which may be analysed in terms of their expected payoffs and risk.

Chapter 14

'SPREE' SHOOTERS: COMPLETING THE TYPOLOGY OF AMERICA'S LONE WOLF TERRORISTS

What 'type' of lone wolf terrorist is the 'spree shooter'? Is he risk averse or risk seeking? The answer is that he is not easily classified as being of either type. Rather, he is a 'plunger' who suddenly and all-at-once plunges all of his resources into terrorism when before he had allocated none. The list of lone wolf terrorists contains a number of individuals who engaged in sudden sprees of violence characterised by intense time-concentration. The attack method of choice for these individuals has usually been 'armed attack' and the weapon of choice has usually been a firearm. The record of lone wolf terrorism in the United States is characterised by a number of spree shootings perpetrated by individuals such as Aimal Kansi, Colin Ferguson, Rashid Baz, Larry Shoemake, Ali Hasan Abu Kamal, Buford Furrow, Ronald Taylor, Richard Bauhammers, Hesham Mohammed Ali Hadayet, Naveed Afzal Haq and Nidal Malik Hasan. The 'spree' lone wolf is different from the serial lone wolf terrorist and represents a different challenge to law enforcement. The terrorist actions of the spree lone wolf are concentrated within a very short period of time. Law enforcement efforts directed towards the pursuit of the 'spree' lone wolf must be condensed and investigative efforts must proceed on the basis of either limited evidence or rapidly evolving and accumulating evidence. In some cases there may be no time for an investigative process at all. In order to complete our typology, we will need to encompass the opportunities and choices of the spree shooters within our economic analysis.

TIME CONCENTRATION AND 'PLUNGING'

The defining characteristic of the spree lone wolf terrorist—or any spree shooter—is the time concentration of his attacks. At the limit, a spree attack may be over in minutes and it will usually come without any perceivable warning. This type of action is far removed from the drawn-out serial offenses committed by serial lone wolf terrorists such as Metesky and Kaczynski. In order to encompass the spree shooter within our analytical framework we must add another 'type' of risk preference to our typology. All of America's serial lone wolf terrorists are risk averse to some degree. Some display low levels of risk aversion and others a relatively high level of risk aversion. By definition, none of the serial lone wolf terrorists allocated all of their time and resources to an act of terrorism undertaken within a 'moment' of time and they did not allocate all of their resources to the most risky attack method. They were not what we might call 'plungers'. As a result, the variability of the possible outcomes of their attacks was not as high as it could have been if different choices were made and the variability of the outcomes was given a chance to 'even out' over time as the averaging process worked through the outcomes of a series of attacks. The spree shooters are much different. Without warning they embark on a sudden spree of violence involving the plunging of all resources into a time-concentrated attack undertaken, usually, by the choice of 'armed attacks', an attack method with highly variable outcomes. These are not the actions of risk averse individuals.

It will be recalled that economics has a particular definition of risk seeking behaviour that does not simply mean a willingness to take risk. All of the lone wolf terrorists take risk or bear variability. Formally, risk seeking means a willingness to accept a 'fair gamble' but it also implies, within the risk-reward framework that we have been describing and developing, that a risk seeker will always choose the attack method with the highest risk. In fact, in this formal sense, risk-seeking is not observed at all to characterise America's lone wolf terrorists. None have engaged in the riskiest attack methods: hostage-taking and unconventional attacks. There is, however, a special type of risk-seeking risk preference on display among the lone wolf terrorists. This is a type of risk seeking behaviour that Tobin (1958) calls 'plunging'. As Phillips (2012) explains, this type of behaviour is characterised by the sudden plunging into terrorism in a time-concentrated attack. Whereas this type of terrorist was not involved in any terrorism before, he suddenly and all at once plunges into a spree of violence. This type of risk preference and behaviour has characterised the actions of almost half of America's lone wolf terrorists. It is also a type of behaviour that is especially worrying given the potential for large numbers of fatalities within a concentrated period of time; such a short period of time, in fact, that law enforcement may not be able to respond quickly enough to stem the violence.

Like the serial lone wolf and the transnational terrorist, the spree lone wolf is faced with opportunities and the necessity to make a choice. The RAND-MIPT categories of attack methods, each with their expected payoffs and risks and the possibility that they may be combined, represent his opportunities. Fundamentally, his opportunities are expected payoff-risk 'pairs'. A serial lone wolf, a transnational terrorist or a spree lone wolf, if he chooses optimally, chooses the most dangerous attack method or combination of attack methods at his chosen level of risk. One important difference, perhaps the most important difference, between the spree lone wolf and the serial lone wolf is the time-concentrated nature of the spree lone wolf's engagement in terrorism. Within the expected utility model of choice that we have been developing, a spree lone wolf's most distinct characteristic is his willingness to suddenly and all at once 'plunge' all of his resources, including time, into terrorism when he had not previously been engaged in terrorism. Only a lone wolf with a particular type of risk preference will be observed to suddenly and completely 'plunge' all of his resources into terrorism. What is more, the spree lone wolf who is willing, under certain circumstances, to plunge all of his resources into terrorism will be extremely sensitive to changes in the expected payoffs to terrorism. Even a small adjustment to the risk-reward trade-off may precipitate a spree of terroristic violence.

The spree lone wolf terrorist presents special challenges to law enforcement. The time-concentrated nature of the spree lone wolf's terrorist actions is the most distinct feature of his behaviour. Unlike the serial lone wolf, the spree lone wolf all at once 'plunges' all of his resources, including time, into terrorism. Where before he was not engaged in risky terrorist activity he is now suddenly fully engaged in terrorist actions. What is more, he shuns the 'time diversification' that characterises the serial lone wolf's actions and directs all of his resources towards a time-concentrated spree of terrorist violence. Within a mean-variance expected utility framework, the type of behaviour that characterises a spree lone wolf is reflected by a utility maximising individual whose utility maximisation problem is solved by devoting either zero resources to terrorism or, following an innovation in the risk-reward structure that characterises the available attack methods, suddenly plunging 100 percent of his time and other resources into terrorism. This sudden change is unique to the 'plunger' and will not be exhibited by either a risk averse lone wolf or an (ordinary) risk seeking lone wolf.

THE SPREE: OPPORTUNITIES AND CHOICES

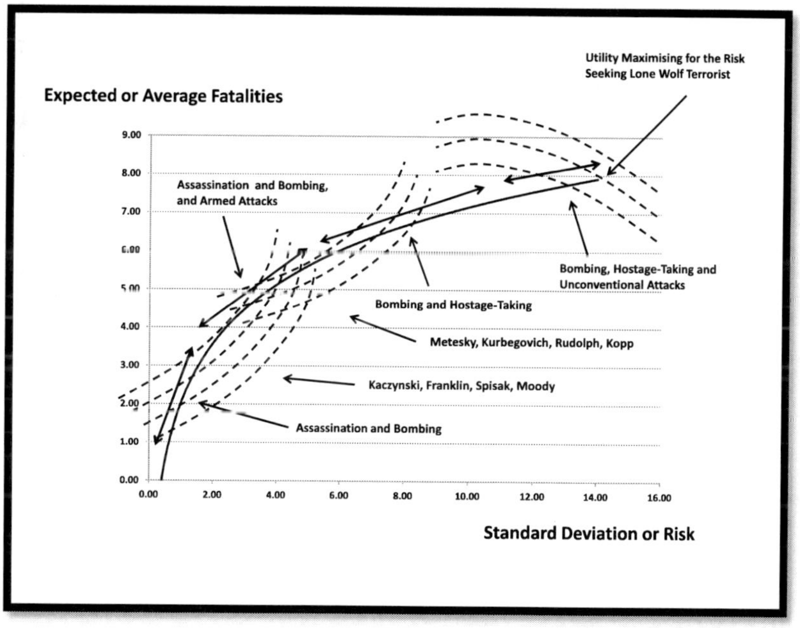

Figure 14.1. Risk Preference, Attack Methods and Lone Wolf Terrorism.

America's lone wolf terrorists have chosen armed attacks—some targeted and serial, others less discriminate and time-concentrated—and bombings—again, some targeted and serial and other less discriminate. The serial lone wolf terrorists have been, as we have explained, risk averse to some degree. Figure 14.1 identifies the approximate location of some of the more risk-averse and some of the less risk-averse lone wolf terrorists[1]. As before, risk aversion is depicted by the steepness of the indifference curves. The more risk-averse lone wolf terrorists are depicted by a set of relatively steep indifference curves located in the low-expected-payoff-low-variability region of the opportunity set. The less risk-averse lone wolf terrorists are depicted by a set of relatively flat indifference curves located in a region of the

[1] The diagram does not contain the location of all of the lone wolf terrorists simply to avoid crowding the diagram.

opportunity set characterised by higher variability. Each of the serial lone wolf terrorists could be represented by a set of convex indifference curves indicating that an increase in the variability of the possible outcomes of a particular type of terrorist attack must be accompanied by an increase in the expected outcomes. By contrast, a risk seeking lone wolf terrorist would be represented by concave indifference curves indicating a willingness to give up payoffs in order to bear more risk. Whereas the risk averse lone wolf's optimal choice could be anywhere where the uppermost indifference curve is tangential to the opportunity set, the risk seeking lone wolf's optimal choice will be the point of intersection between his uppermost convex indifference curve and the opportunity set. Invariably, this point of intersection must occur at the highest possible level of variability or risk.

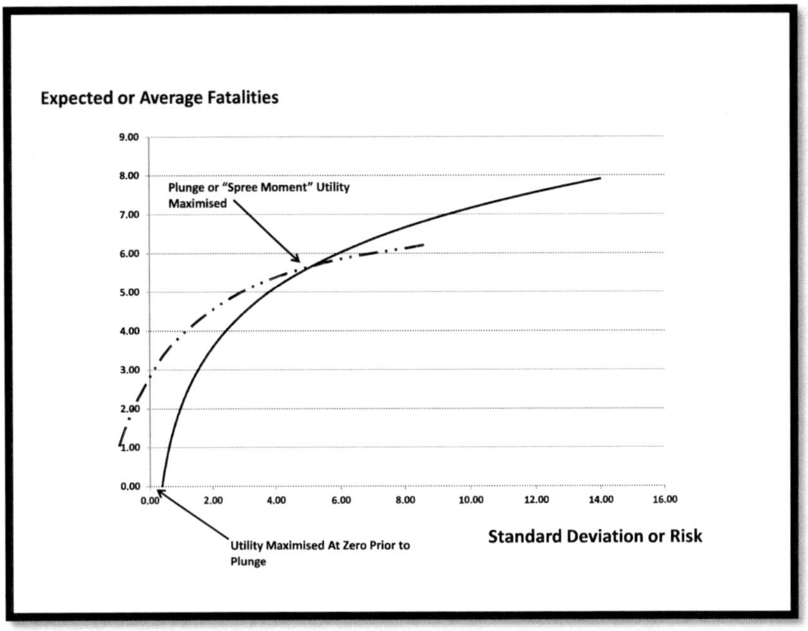

Figure 14.2. The 'Plunging' Spree Shooter.

The spree shooter who suddenly plunges all of his resources into a time-concentrated spree of violence stands apart from both the risk averse lone wolf terrorist and the as-yet-unobserved risk seeking lone wolf terrorist. Figure 14.2 depicts the preferences of the risk seeking plunger across the same opportunity set. This particular type of behaviour is more dynamic and is not completely amenable to static depiction in a single diagram. The plunging lone wolf terrorist is not involved in terrorism at all and then suddenly plunges all of his resources, including time, into a concentrated spree of violence. Prior to this event, the utility maximising point is zero. This could be represented by a set of concave indifference curves (not shown) where the highest indifference curve intersects the origin and encompasses but does not touch or intrude into the opportunity set. A spree is precipitated by either a perceived change or real change in the opportunity set such that a the highest indifference curve now cuts or intrudes into the opportunity set at some point or the indifference map changes shape in a manner that brings about the same outcome. The point at which the highest indifference curve intersects the opportunity set will represent the attack method into which all resources will suddenly be plunged. Such time-concentrated sprees of violence have usually been shooting sprees. As such, we would expect a utility maximising plunge point to be associated with a 100 percent resource allocation, including time, to armed attacks. Phillips (2012) provides further analytical development of this particular point. All that we need to note here is that there is a risk preference category that encompasses the behaviour of the 'spree shooters' and the opportunities and choices of spree lone wolf terrorists can be analysed within the economic analytical framework that we have developed.

Arranging the Lone Wolf Terrorists in Our Typology

The lone wolf terrorist's choices reveal something about the lone wolf terrorists' preferences for risk. By choosing attack methods that may be expected to inflict a particular number of fatalities but which are attended by a greater or less possibility that the actual outcomes will diverge from those that were expected and by concentrating their attacks into a very short period or by diversifying across time by slowly and serially accumulating victims, the lone wolf terrorists reveal a preference for risk. Some lone wolf terrorists have chosen to deploy attack methods that are expected to inflict only a small number of fatalities, perhaps just one, but which are characterised by a very low possibility that the actual outcome will diverge from that which was expected. The lone wolf terrorists who engaged in attacks whose outcomes are more certain than those associated with other attack methods are our most risk-averse lone wolf terrorists. These lone wolves require much larger increments in expected payoffs to entice them into more risky modes of attack. In the absence of these enticements, these more risk-averse lone wolves will engage in targeted assassination-style attacks mostly directed towards individual victims. Assassinations, arsons, targeted bombings and targeted armed attacks usually of a serial nature will characterise the modus operandi of the more risk-averse lone wolf terrorists. In contrast, the less risk-averse lone wolf terrorist will engage in less targeted armed attacks and bombings aimed at groups of individuals or indiscriminately selected targets, such as when a bomb is left to detonate in a public place. Low or high risk aversion or behaviour characterised by at least some unwillingness to accept a higher amount of variability in the possible outcomes without an increase in the expected or average outcome encompasses America's serial lone wolf terrorists. The special case of risk-seeking or 'plunging' encompasses the spree lone wolf terrorists. A complete typology of America's lone wolf terrorists is presented in Table 14.1.

A natural or obvious classification of terrorists and terrorist groups emerges from the economic analysis of choice under uncertainty. The way in which people choose from among risky opportunities depends on their risk preference and risk preference can be partitioned into three categories: risk aversion, risk seeking and plunging each with its own levels or degrees. In order to allocate actual lone wolf terrorists to such a typology or classification scheme it is necessary to determine the risk that they have chosen to bear in undertaking particular types of terrorist activity and in order to do this a definition and measurement of risk is required. If one accepts the particular definition of 'risk as variability' that underlies mean-variance analysis and the analysis presented herein, then one may accept a classification of lone wolf terrorists according to the variability that they could have expected the outcomes of their attacks to exhibit. The details of the measurement of this variability of the outcomes of terrorist attacks then become the central issue and point around which debate may be entered into. There are different ways in which this might be done and different payoffs that might be chosen. Fatalities and injuries, however, are the immediate outcome of terrorism and lone wolf terrorists who decide upon particular attack methods must expect some level of human tragedy to result. Furthermore, fatalities and injuries are the most immediate subject of news reports concerning terrorism and if any information disseminates to terrorists through the media the fatalities that have been inflicted and the variability of these outcomes across different types of attacks is one such piece of information.

Table 14.1. Risk Preference Typology and the Classification of America's Lone Wolf Terrorists

More Risk Averse	Less Risk Averse	Risk Seeking and Plunging
Byron De La Beckwith	George Metesky	Mark Essex
Sirhan Sirhan	Muharem Kurbegovich	Neal Long
Theodore Kaczynski	Michael Griffin	Mir Aimal Kansi
Joseph Paul Franklin	Rachelle Shannon	Colin Ferguson
Joseph Christopher	Eric Rudolph	Rashid Baz
Frank Spisak Jr.	Paul J. Hill	Larry Shoemake
Walter Leroy Moody Jr.	John Salvi	Ali Hasan Abu Kamal
Mohammed Reza Taheri-azar	James C. Kopp	Buford Furrow
		Ronald Taylor
		Richard Bauhammers
		Hesham Mohamed Ali
		Naveed Afzal Haq
		Nidal Malik Hasan

Concluding Remarks

The most important question that might be asked is, "What use at all is a typology or classification scheme?" Apart from its utility in simply facilitating the arrangement of complex phenomena into a more organised form, typologies have two important uses in the terrorism context. The first is more theoretical and involves the ways in which typologies and the assignment of individual terrorists within a typology makes use think more carefully about the *essence* of the actions of the terrorist. The second is more practical and verges on the uses to which typologies are put in investigative psychology and offender profiling and law enforcement. The typology that has been developed and worked out throughout the last few chapters of this book highlights certain aspects of the lone wolf terrorists' choices that might sit in the background in other types of analysis. It is possible to depict the lone wolf terrorist as choosing from among different attack methods or combinations of attack methods on the basis of the fatalities that are expected to be inflicted by those attack methods. It is also possible to depict the variability of the outcomes, of those expected fatalities, as a risk that the lone wolf terrorist trades off against higher or lower average outcomes. Not everyone will agree, of course, on all the details but it should be noted that the theoretical-analytical framework as such 'works' with any payoff to which the terrorist might attach importance and which the analyst may measure.

The broad outlines of such an approach as this serve to separate the 'riskiness' of the actions themselves from the lone wolf terrorists' actions to manage that risk. All terrorist attacks involve risk because the outcomes are not certain. Whatever payoff the terrorist expects to obtain, the actual outcome may vary to a greater or lesser degree from that which was expected. This may happen for a multitude of reasons. Careful planning, careful timing, combining different attack methods over time and so forth serve as means to reduce the variance of the outcomes but the positive relationship between average payoffs and variability remains inherent in the statistical structure of the terrorism context. Whatever payoffs series may be chosen as the basis for an analysis, a definition of the risk of those payoffs that separates that risk from whatever steps the terrorist may take to manage those risks is essential if there is to be any classification of the riskiness of different types of terrorism. This is the case because the choice itself incorporates such steps. A particular attack method is chosen, for example, because, in the terrorist's judgement, it has a more appropriate risk-reward trade-off. Like the attack method that it was substituted for or 'ranked' higher than, it will be characterised by risk—perhaps more, perhaps less—but if we do not have a clear definition and measurement for risk, the relative risk of a particular attack comes to be assessed not against the ex ante possible divergence of the actual outcome from that which was expected but against the ex post outcomes themselves which incorporate the terrorist's approach to that ex ante variability. Risk is a concept that cannot be separated from an 'unknown' (but imaginable) future.

The lone wolf terrorist confronts the possibility that the actual outcomes to his planned attack may vary from that which he expected. This will be more or less the case depending on the type of attack he chooses. The essence of the economic analysis of choice under risk is an individual assessing the available opportunities on the basis of this variability. When a lone wolf terrorist chooses a targeted assassination-style attack, it is a risky thing to do. However, the outcomes are not as variable on average as those associated with a less targeted bombing attack but neither is the potential impact as large. Only a clear definition and measurement of risk can make this distinction between the levels of riskiness that characterise what are all very risky activities. The terrorist's approach to a particular attack may involve countless planning and preparation factors such that the 'narrative', if one could be constructed, of the choice process may be both complex and relatively idiosyncratic. If it is accepted that a trade-off between average outcomes and the variability of those outcomes is a salient feature of a terrorist's salient payoffs and that the terrorist is aware somehow that he confronts this trade-off, the essence of the choice process can be depicted clearly as a choice between attack methods or targets or times or locations on the basis of a trade-off or ranking of each opportunity's risk and reward. All of the other factors that may characterise the planning process may then be viewed separately as steps taken to manage the risk that characterises the attack method or target or time or location that has been chosen. The result of these steps may be an actual payoff that is somewhat above the average or expected outcome. This, in turn, is reported upon and absorbed into the terrorism context perhaps altering slightly the expected payoffs and risks to the particular attack type and its alternatives.

Investigative psychology and offender profiling 'work' by classifying the unknown offender to a place within a typology on the basis of evidence left at the crime scene and other information that is known about the crime. Because a certain 'type' of individual is assumed to commit a certain 'type' of crime, broadly speaking, law enforcement can be given a profile of the unknown offender that may be used to guide their operations. Typologies of offenders can be useful to law enforcement. Despite debates that tear at the fabric of the emerging discipline of investigative psychology, offender profiles are in strong demand from law enforcement agencies. A risk preference based typology may one day develop into a useful tool for law enforcement agencies to use, in combination with other investigative tools and other typologies, particularly in pursuit of serial lone wolf terrorists. A more risk-averse terrorist will act in ways that are distinct from a less risk-averse terrorist. These distinctions, including the need to seek out opportunities with a desirable risk-reward trade-off, may be the source of insights that law enforcement might find useful and, ultimately, a terrorism studies focussed on the development of operationally relevant analysis.

Chapter 15

THE CONCLUSION

Pre-emption and pursuit of the lone wolf terrorist are the two things that we have been focussed on throughout this long discussion. There are many pre-requisites for the effective pre-emption of the lone wolf terrorist. One of these is some way of delineating the lone wolf terrorist's opportunities. The terrorism context is complex but it is not intractable. It depends on how one looks at it. One way to view the terrorism context is through the analytical lens of orthodox economics. The result of this has been the derivation of several important insights about terrorist behaviour. However, the perspective provided by orthodox economics, especially the application of full expected utility analysis, does not yield results that may be classified as directly operationally relevant. The results provided by orthodox economic analysis of terrorism are relevant to policy and policy may guide the operations of law enforcement and security agencies in a general sense but the results of orthodox economic analysis are not operationally relevant in particular cases involving particular individuals. It is not surprising that some of the first research that applied economic analysis to the phenomenon of lone wolf terrorism did not take a completely orthodox approach.

Our approach has been to minimise the use of complex mathematical economic theory and concentrate instead on the application to the problem of lone wolf terrorism of an approach to the economic analysis of choice under risk and uncertainty that yields computable rather than strictly logical results and, what is more, does so on the basis of information that is just as readily available to the analyst as it is to the lone wolf terrorist. Mean-variance expected utility analysis is based on more restrictive assumptions than some of the more complex mathematics that might be applied to the theoretical analysis of terrorist behaviour but what is 'lost' by dealing with restrictive assumptions is gained in content. In any case, our first step required no assumptions at all. Terrorists in word and deed have indicated that their objective is to inflict human tragedy. They have done this through the utilisation of about ten attack method categories. Each attack method has inflicted some average number of fatalities when deployed and for each attack method this series of outcomes exhibits some amount of variability over time. Although some other series of outcomes might be identified as being salient to the terrorist's decision-making, human tragedy is the most direct outcome of the discriminate or indiscriminate use of attack methods that each must be expected to inflict some amount of harm. None of the attack method categories is associated with zero human tragedy.

Each attack method is an 'opportunity' to inflict harm. Fundamentally, the set of all opportunities associated with all of the attack methods and combinations of attack methods is a set of mean-variance 'pairs'. There is a mean level of human tragedy associated with an attack method or combination and there is a level of risk or variability measured by the variance or standard deviation of the outcomes. Looking at the terrorist's opportunities in this way provides a stark and clear picture that completely contrasts with the more complex image provided by orthodox full expected utility analysis in which the opportunities are an array of potential outcomes and probabilities, the latter being unobservable directly by either the terrorist or the analyst. Our picture of the lone wolf terrorist's opportunities is a concave set that encompasses all of the optimal and sub-optimal opportunities that are feasible given the historical record of terrorism. The opportunity set is computable on the basis of information that we could reasonably expect the prospective lone wolf terrorist to possess and consider. Not only is it computable but the complete opportunity set can be drawn as a concave set in expected-payoff-risk space. This is critically important for our later task of locating a particular lone wolf terrorist within the opportunity set in order to identify the risk preference that his choices of attack methods have revealed. The clarity with which we are able to identify for law enforcement the shape of the risk-reward trade-off that confronts the lone wolf terrorist and the significance of the correlation structure in determining the concavity of the risk-reward trade-off distinguish our approach from the full expected utility analysis.

When it comes to making choices from the opportunity set, we first of all work under the possibility—though not necessarily under the assumption—that the lone wolf terrorist will attempt to choose optimally or rationally. In our framework, this also means that we are working under the possibility that he will choose most dangerously. The lone wolf terrorist's objective is to inflict some amount of human tragedy. His means of doing so are the attack methods that have been used by all terrorists over the past five decades or combinations of those attack methods. His optimal choice of attack methods will be his most dangerous choice. Even a stern critic of rational choice and economic analysis would not venture to argue that we should ignore these opportunities on the grounds that no terrorist is rational enough to choose them. This might be the case if we were talking about some complex intangible payoff such as political influence and an array of probabilities associated with each possible outcome but we are working on the basis of information that the lone wolf terrorist has and could reasonably be expected to consider. Our determination of the lone wolf's choices requires us to assume that he need only have some idea about the expected or average number of fatalities that a particular attack method may inflict and the variability of those possible outcomes. We may then picture the lone wolf terrorist as deciding upon his attack method on the basis of the average outcomes he associates with it and the variability of those outcomes. That is, reward and risk.

A mean-variance expected utility analysis is obviously much more 'visualisable' than full expected utility analysis. There is no need for an array of probabilities for every possible outcome and when the terrorist's opportunities and choices are examined in the context of a measureable objective such as the outcomes of the deployment of particular attack methods, probabilities are not explicit in the analysis or in the terrorist's thoughts at all. The terrorist chooses by weighing up the likely outcomes against the possibility that the actual outcomes may diverge from what he expected. It is true that mean-variance expected utility analysis is based on one or two restrictive assumptions but it can hardly be argued that a full expected utility analysis or equilibrium-type analysis is based on more realistic assumptions.

Furthermore, many of the main objections related to the use of mean-variance analysis within an entirely different context:

Criticism: In order for a preference ordering formed on the basis of mean and variance to be consistent with the von Neumann and Morgenstern axioms, it is necessary to assume that the decision-maker is described by quadratic utility. The substance of this particular criticism is that quadratic utility implies increasing risk aversion and, more problematically, satiation.

Reply: First, as Tobin (1969, p.14) notes, "The von Neumann and Morgenstern axioms will not by themselves tell us anything about how an individual chooses among combinations (portfolios). Some restrictions must be placed on the utility function to obtain useful results." Second, satiation is not necessarily a problem in our analytical context. Third, as later research pointed out, the quadratic utility function approximates a wider class of utility functions and mean-variance preference orderings closely approximate preference orderings formed on the basis of full expected utility.

Criticism: Mean-variance expected utility analysis requires a normal distribution and the outcomes of terrorist attacks are not normally distributed.

Reply: First, the 'raw' outcomes may not be normally distributed but the outcomes per attack per year are a different matter. Second, it is *not true* that mean-variance expected utility analysis *requires* a normal distribution. If one wants to guarantee that a mean-variance preference ordering is consistent with the von Neumann and Morgenstern axioms, then one needs *either* quadratic utility or a normal distribution. However, we now refer back to our reply to the first criticism. Mean variance preference orderings closely approximate a full expected utility analysis *without* quadratic expected utility or normally distributed payoffs and, fundamentally, the axioms are not sacrosanct, particularly if we want to know how the terrorist will choose.

The literature is overflowing with equilibrium analysis, game theory and other context-specific full expected utility analysis. A lot of the results that have been obtained from the economic analysis of terrorism over the past three or four decades have practical or strategic implications. There is no doubt that they are relevant to the operations undertaken by defence and security agencies. But in the context of lone wolf terrorism, characterised as it is by a single lone offender, the economic analysis of terrorism must extract more from the economic theoretical frameworks than it has been able to up til now. A purely logical economic theory of lone wolf terrorism will not suffice. The building blocks of economic theory must be used in new ways and made to yield results that are operationally relevant as well as logically consistent. The lone wolf terrorist must be encompassed within an economic theoretical framework that is capable of producing more than purely logical results. When the lone wolf's opportunities and choices have been encompassed within such a framework, the 'investigative economist' emerges as a new actor in the pursuit of the lone wolf terrorist. Even though the opportunities and choices confronting the lone wolf may seem to be intractable in scope, economic analysis can delineate those opportunities and identify the lone wolf's most dangerous choices. This can be accomplished because of the structure that characterises the payoffs that can be expected from the deployment of the various attack methods and combinations of attack methods.

THE ECONOMIC LOGIC OF MEANS AND ENDS

Economics says that the individual has some objective or end that he wants to achieve and that he uses his scarce means in order to achieve it. This is not an assumption. Everyone has 'ends' and everyone acts on them every day. Ends may differ in order of importance. Some are more pressing than others and individuals 'rank' or prioritise their ends. Everyone does this every day too. If they did not, nothing at all would get done. Either no plans would get underway or they would get underway and then fall apart. If ends were never prioritised there would be nothing keeping a person's focus on even the most trivial objective. New objectives would displace the old in a completely unstructured manner. People do prioritise their ends. To achieve an objective or end requires 'means'. Unfortunately, means are scarce and must be apportioned among the ends. Not all of the ends may be able to be achieved. In pursuing his ends, the individual makes choices about how to allocate his scarce means to the attainment of his ends. It is this choice that is studied in economics. There is nothing to say that the individual will not make mistakes in choosing the means that he applies to his ends. He may choose a completely inappropriate, wrong, overly expensive or muddle-headed set of means to achieve an objective. People also do this every day but they also get things done.

In order to generalise beyond each of the multitude of ends that are pursued by different individuals, the economist makes use of the more general concept of utility. This is just the 'satisfaction' or 'payoff' that the individual attains from achieving his objectives, whatever they may be. The different ends produce different amounts of utility and scarce means are arranged so as to obtain this utility. Within some schools of economics, this arrangement is studied with the help of the mathematics and within some schools of economics it is studied almost solely in terms of mathematics. As such, use is made of the concepts of functional form and maximisation and minimisation. Orthodox economists will speak of the maximisation of utility. This refers to the optimal allocation of means to ends. An optimal allocation is one that generates the maximum utility. A complete and logically consistent mathematical framework has been developed to facilitate the analysis of choice when the objective or end being aimed at by the individual is the maximisation of utility. This mathematical framework, which contains assumptions required for the mathematics[1] to work, highlights in a very extreme way the logical structure of choice. Although extreme, even this representation of the logical structure of choice does not preclude the possibility that individuals may make mistakes and fail to 'maximise utility'.

At bottom, the choices studied by the economist are simply the ways in which means are allocated in pursuit of ends. The critics have not usually studied economic science carefully enough and the orthodox economists have clouded the economic logic with too much mathematics. Operationally relevant and computable results flow most freely from economic theoretical frameworks that capture the logic of choice without abstracting so much that the frameworks become mere mathematical formalisms. The mean-variance approach to the analysis of choice under risk is an economic framework that is characterised by the appropriate balance in this regard. When an individual makes choices under conditions of risk, the outcome or utility of those choices may diverge from that which was expected or hoped for. An individual aiming to maximise his utility under conditions of risk confronts the possibility that the choices of means he directs towards the achievement of this end may not

[1] Vis-à-vis the economic logic...

produce the outcome he expects. He must consider both the expected payoffs and the risks when making his choices. The utility that he expects to result from a particular choice is a function of the expected payoff and risk associated with that choice. The mean-variance approach is an analytical framework within which these choices can be analysed.

Unlike full expected utility analysis, mean-variance analysis is tractable computationally without the need for further intermediate assumptions. A full expected utility analysis is a purely logical depiction of the choice process. In this depiction, the individual weighs up the possible outcomes from the various ways his 'means' can be arranged and arrives at a conclusion concerning the expected utility of that arrangement. In pursuit of the maximum expected utility, the individual ranks each of his opportunities and picks the one that has the highest ranking or highest expected utility. Under conditions of risk and uncertainty, each of the utilities of each of the outcomes is weighted by the probability of occurrence. Although this can be depicted logically, it cannot easily be subjected to computation. Doing so would require a consideration of all of the relevant factors and their associated probabilities. Mean-variance expected utility analysis on the other hand is embedded within the same overall logical structure of choice under risk but it depicts the individual as ranking his preferences solely on the basis of the reward (mean) and risk (variance) of the outcomes. When the mean and variance of outcomes can be computed, mean-variance analysis can be applied to the analysis of choice in a manner that yields computationally tractable results. Despite being far less abstract, the results of a mean-variance analysis approximate those of a full expected utility analysis of choice. That is why Tobin and Markowitz argued so strongly for a mean-variance approach to analysing choice under conditions of risk.

The lone wolf terrorist confronts a set of opportunities and he makes choices. The lone wolf's opportunities can be delineated within risk-reward space. Each of the attack methods has an expected payoff and a risk and the expected payoffs associated with each attack method exhibit some type of correlation with the expected payoffs of the other attack methods. This statistical structure of risk and reward allows us to rule in particular opportunities and rule out others. The risk-reward relationship confronting the lone wolf is a concave set that provides him with the opportunity to increase his rewards by bearing more risk as well as the opportunity to increase his rewards at each level of risk by combining attack methods. Within the complete set of opportunities that are available to the lone wolf, there is an 'efficient' set of opportunities. These are the attack methods and combinations of attack methods that dominate all of the others. At each level of risk, the efficient attack method combinations have the highest level of expected payoff. This is the set of attack methods and attack method combinations from which the lone wolf will choose if he is maximising his expected utility. In our framework, the lone wolf who maximises his expected utility is also the most dangerous lone wolf terrorist. Even if the criticisms directed towards the logic of choice and 'rationality' were valid, those criticisms would surely not apply in this particular case because we would surely not ignore the possibility that the lone wolf terrorist will choose in the most dangerous manner.

In making his choices, the lone wolf terrorist considers the risk and the reward associated with the attack methods and combinations. His choice depends on the risk and reward trade-off and his preferences for risk. A lone wolf who is not very risk averse or who is more risk seeking will choose attack methods or combinations dominated by hostage taking, unconventional attacks and bombing. The more risk seeking lone wolf will allocate more resources to the riskier attack methods of hostage taking and unconventional attacks. If the lone wolf has a more moderate preference for risk he will be interested in combinations of attack methods that have lower allocations of resources to unconventional attacks and hostage taking. He will prefer to reduce the amount of resources allocated to these very risky attack methods and instead allocate more resources to bombing and armed attacks. When the lone wolf is very risk averse and not at all risk seeking, he will prefer attack method combinations dominated by assassination and bombing. These choices are consistent across all levels of specialisation in acts of terrorism. More risky attack methods are chosen by less risk averse lone wolves. Less risky attack methods are chosen by more risk averse lone wolves.

If the lone wolf terrorist cannot combine attack methods but must choose only a single attack method, his choice will depend on the risk that he is willing bear. At each level of risk, there is a single attack method and degree of specialisation in terrorism that produces the highest expected payoff. Assassination dominates the lowest levels of risk. Then bombing, then hijacking, then armed attacks, hostage taking and unconventional attacks. The very risk averse lone wolf will choose assassination but is unlikely to specialise in terrorism. A slightly less risk averse lone wolf will choose bombing but is also unlikely to specialise in terrorism. At a lower level of risk aversion, the lone wolf will choose bombing at increasing levels of specialisation. His resource allocation to bombing may approach 100 percent. As risk aversion falls further, the lone wolf will engage in hijacking. A 100 percent allocation of resources to hijacking may not satisfy an even more risk seeking lone wolf. He will engage in armed attacks. Beyond this, at very high levels of risk, the very risk seeking lone wolf will choose hostage taking or unconventional attacks. The lone wolf terrorist's preferences for risk shape his choices of attack methods and the degree to which he specialises in terrorism.

Once the lone wolf strikes, he reveals his preference for risk. The mean-variance expected utility framework that we have built around the lone wolf's opportunities and choices gives us a way of gauging the riskiness of the lone wolf's choices. Once the lone wolf has made two or three choices of attack methods, we will be able to say with some confidence what type of risk preference the lone wolf has revealed. At such time, we are no longer dealing with various types of lone wolves. At such time we are dealing with a particular lone wolf with a particular type of revealed risk preference. At such time we are dealing with a lone wolf occupying a particular position in expected payoff-risk space. Like the investigative psychologist or offender profiler, we can draw inferences about the offender from evidence left at the crime scene. In the context of lone wolf terrorism, the attack method or combination of attack methods deployed by the lone wolf terrorist is the starting point for the investigative economist who is using the analytical framework that we have developed. Having delineated the lone wolf's opportunities and choices in expected payoff-risk space, we can locate the lone wolf by his choice of attack method. This location is consistent with a particular type of risk preference. The lone wolf can be identified as being very risk averse, very risk seeking or somewhere in between. On the basis of this revealed risk preference we can say some more things about the lone wolf UNSUB. We can say whether the lone wolf UNSUB is likely to be close-by or moving in search of locations where his chosen attack methods yield an expected payoff that is commensurate with the risk he wishes to bear. We can say whether the lone wolf is likely to be a specialist in terrorism or whether he will be found engaged in other forms of non-violent expression. We can say whether the attacks are likely to continue unabated or whether a hiatus is to be expected or whether there will be an increase in the intensity of the attacks. Each of these things contributes to the investigative process and the management of the pursuit of the lone wolf.

THE NEW HORIZON FOR THE ECONOMIC ANALYSIS OF TERRORISM

The contribution to the construction of offender profiles, investigative economics, is the new horizon for both the economic analysis of terrorism and the economics of crime. The logical structure of choice and the statistical structure of criminal and terrorist activity provide a sound theoretical-analytical foundation that can be made to yield inferences about actual UNSUB offenders. The nature of a crime or terrorist attack reveals something about the offender that is reflected in the economic theoretical frameworks. In turn, these economic theoretical frameworks can tell us something about the type of behaviour the offender may exhibit and the type of individual that he is. The assessment of offender risk is a core component of the offender profiling process. When offender risk is assessed qualitatively, it is possible that aspects of the lone wolf terrorist's risk management processes, prudence and risk preference are conflated with the riskiness of a particular choice. By defining risk as variability and measuring risk by variance or standard deviation we can clearly define the riskiness of particular attack methods and obtain a clearer insight into the risk preference of a lone wolf terrorist who chooses a particular attack method without having our perspective clouded by the ways in which he approaches its deployment. Because of this and the other aspects of the analytical framework that we have developed, we may expect the analytical framework within which we have encompassed the opportunities and choices of the lone wolf terrorist to contribute operationally relevant investigative advice that is not misleading and which may be used to complement the behavioural investigative advice contributed by the academic investigative psychologists and the offender profilers.

References

Alison, L. J., Bennell, C., Mokros, A., and Ormerod, D. (2002). The personality paradox in offender profiling: A theoretical review of the processes involved in deriving background characteristics from crime scene actions. *Psychology, Public Policy, and Law*, 8, 115-135.

Alison, L., Goodwill, A., Almond, L., Heuvel, C. and Winter, J. (2010). Pragmatic solutions to offender profiling and behavioural investigative advice. *Legal and Criminological Psychology*, 15, 115-132.

Andrews, D. A., and Bonta, J. (2006). *Psychology of Criminal Conduct.* Anderson, Cincinnati, Ohio.

Associated Press (2011). Napolitano: lone wolf terror threat growing. http://www.cbsnews.com/8301-201_162-57336080/napolitano-lone-wolf-terror-threat-growing/

Becker, G.S. (1968). Crime and punishment: an economic alternative. *Journal of Political Economy*, 78, 169-217.

Bennell, C. and Canter, D. V. (2002). Linking commercial burglaries by modus operandi: Tests using regression and ROC analysis. *Science and Justice*, 42, 153-164.

Bowers, K. (1973). Situationism in psychology: An analysis and a critique. *Psychological Review*, 80, 307-336.

Canter, D. (1989). Offender profiles. *The Psychologist*, 2, 12-16.

Canter, D. (1994). *Criminal Shadows*. Harper Collins, London, UK.

Canter, D. (2004). Offender profiling and investigative psychology. *Journal of investigative psychology and offender profiling*, 1, 1-15.

Canter, D. V., Alison, L. J., Alison, E., and Wentink, N. (2004). The organized/disorganized typology of serial murder: Myth or model? *Psychology, Public Policy and Law*, 10, 293-320.

Canter, D. and Gregory, A. (1994). Identifying the residential location of serial rapists. *Journal of the Forensic Science Society*, 34, 169-175.

Canter, D. and Youngs, D. (2009). *Investigative Psychology: Offender Profiling and the Analysis of Criminal Action*. John Wiley and Sons, Chichester, UK.

Caproni, V. (2005). Statement of Valerie Caproni General Counsel Federal Bureau of Investigation before the Senate Select Committee on Intelligence. Federal Bureau of Investigation, United States Federal Government, Washington D.C. http://www.fbi.gov/congress/congress05/caproni052405.htm

Caruso, R. and Schneider, F. (2013). Brutality of jihadist terrorism: a contest theory perspective and empirical evidence in the period 2002-2010. *Journal of Policy Modelling*, forthcoming.

Caruso, R. and Locatelli, A. (2008). Deadly contests: an economic note on Al-Qaeda's reward system. *Economics of Peace and Security Journal*, 3, 62-67.

Crenshaw, M. (2000). The psychology of terrorism: an agenda for the 21st century. *Political Psychology* 21, 405-20.

Davies, A.,Wittebrood, K., and Jackson, J. L. (1997). Predicting the criminal antecedents of a stranger rapist from his offence behaviour. *Science and Justice*, 37, 161-170.

Dickey, C. (2003). T is for terror. *Newsweek*, July 9, 2003. http://www.msnbc.msn.com/id/3070093/t/t-terror/

Douglas, J.E., Ressler, R.K., Burgess, A.W. and Hartman, C.R. (1986). Criminal profiling from crime scene analysis. *Behavioural Sciences and the Law*, 4, 401-421.

Douglas, J. And Olshaker, M. (1996). *Mindhunter: Inside the FBI Elite Serial Crime Unit*. Heinemann, London, UK.

Dubner, S.J. (1999). I Don't Want to Live Long. *Time Magazine*, 154 (16), October 18, 1999.

Duyne, van P. (1999). Mobsters are human too. In *Profiling in Policy and Practice*, David Canter and Laurence Alison (editors), Ashgate Publishing, Aldershot, UK.

Ehrlich, I. (1973). Participation in illegitimate activities: a theoretical and empirical investigation. *Journal of Political Economy*, 81, 521-565.

Eide, E. (1994). *Economics of Crime: Deterrence and the Rational Offender*. Elsevier Science, Amsterdam, The Netherlands.

Elton, E.J., Gruber, M.J., Brown, S.J. and Goetzmann, W.N. (2003). *Modern Portfolio Theory and Investment Analysis*. John Wiley and Sons, New York.

Enders, W. and Sandler, T. (2002). Patterns of transnational terrorism 1970 to 1999: alternative time series estimates. *International Studies Quarterly*, 46, 145-165.

Fama, E. (1970). Multiperiod consumption-investment decisions. *American Economic Review*, 60, 163-174.

Fonda, D., Cuadros, P., Fulton, G., Land, G., Richards, C. and Sikora, F. (2003). How luck ran out for a most wanted fugitive. *Time Magazine*, 161 (23), September 6, 2003.

Gendreau, P., Smith, P., and French, S. (2006). The theory of effective correctional intervention: Empirical status and future directions. In F. Cullen, J. Wright, and M. Coleman (Eds.), *Taking Stock: The Status of Criminological Theory* (pp. 419-446). Transaction Press, Piscataway, NJ.

Gibbs, N. and Allis, S. (1996). Tracking down the Unabomber. *Time Magazine*, 147 (16), April 15, 1996.

Gibbs, N. and Blackman, A. (1993). Up in arms. *Time Magazine*, 142 (26), December 20, 1993.

Gibney, F., Dawson, P., Grace, J., Jackson, D., Krantz, M., Tartakovsky, F. and Thompson, D. (1999). The kids got in the way. *Time Magazine*, 154 (8), August 23, 1999.

Gladwell, M. (1997). Damaged. *The New Yorker*, February. http://www.gladwell.com/1997/1997_02_24_a_damaged.htm

Instituut voor Veiligheids en Crisismanagement (2007). *Lone Wolf Terrorism*, Instituut voor Veiligheids en Crisismanagement, The Netherlands.

Jenkins, R. (1994). The kind of man who sends bombs by mail. *Baltimore Sun*, December 16, 1994.

Kroll, Y., Levy, H. and Markowitz, H. (1984). Mean-variance versus direct utility maximisation. *Journal of Finance*, 39, 47-61.

Lacayo, R. and Cole,W. (1996). A tale of two brothers. *Time Magazine*, 147 (17), April 22, 1996.

Landes, W.M. (1978). An economic study of U.S. aircraft hijackings 1961–1976. *Journal of Law and Economics*, 21, 1-31.

Levy, H. and Markowitz, H. (1979). Approximating expected utility by a function of mean and variance. *American Economic Review*, 69, 308-317.

Mischel, W. (1968). *Personality and Assessment*. John Wiley, New York.

Mokros, A., and Alison, L. (2002). Is offender profiling possible? Testing the predicted homology of crime scene actions and background characteristics in a sample of rapists. *Legal and Criminological Psychology*, 7, 25-43.

Mueller III R.S., (2003). Testimony of Robert S. Mueller, III, Director, FBI Before the Select Committee on Intelligence of the United States Senate February 11, 2003. Federal Bureau of Investigation, United States Federal Government, Washington D.C. http://www.fbi.gov/congress/congress03/mueller021103.htm

Nelson, P.S. and Scott, J.L. (1992). Terrorism and the media: an empirical analysis. *Defence Economics*, 3, 329-339.

Neumann, J. Von and Morgenstern, O. (1944). *The Theory of Games and Economic Behaviour*. Princeton University Press, Princeton, NJ.

New York Times (1951). Bomb Blast in Terminal. Homemade Device Explodes in Grand Central. No One Is Hurt. *New York Times*, March 30. http://select.nytimes.com/gst/abstract.html?res=F50C1FFB355A1A7B93C2AA1788D85F458585F9

New York Times (1953). A homemade bomb rips station locker. *New York Times*, May 7. http://select.nytimes.com/gst/abstract.html?res=F00A14F73C5B157A93C5A9178ED85F478585F9.

New York Times (1957). 15 were injured by bomb blasts. *New York Times*, January 23. http://select.nytimes.com/gst/abstract.html?res=F30F1EF63C5F147B93C1AB178AD85F438585F9.

People v. Kurbegovic (1982). Crim. No. 39123. Court of Appeals of California, Second Appellate District, Division Five, December 29. http://law.justia.com/cases/california/calapp3d/138/731.html

Phillips, P.J. (2009). Applying portfolio theory to the analysis of terrorism: computing the set of attack method combinations from which the rational terrorist group will choose in order to maximise injuries and fatalities. *Defence and Peace Economics*, 20, 193-213.

Phillips, P.J. 2010. Terrorists' Equilibrium Choices When No Attack Method is Riskless. *Atlantic Economic Journal*, 39, pp.129-141.

Phillips, P.J. (2011). Lone wolf terrorism. *Peace Economics, Peace Science and Public Policy*, 17, Issue 1, Article 1.

Phillips, P.J. (2012). The lone wolf terrorist: sprees of violence. *Peace Economics, Peace Science and Public Policy*, 18, 1-11.

Phillips, P.J. and Pohl, G. (2011). Terrorism, identity, psychology and defence economics. *International Research Journal of Finance and Economics, 77*, 102-113.

Phillips, P.J. and Pohl, G. (2012). Economic profiling of the lone wolf terrorist: can economics provide behavioural investigative advice? *Journal of Applied Security Research*, 7, 151-177.

Rasch, W. (1979). Psychological dimensions of political terrorism in the Federal Republic of Germany. *International Journal of Law and Psychiatry*, 2, 79-85.

Rohner, D. and Frey, B.S. (2007). Blood and ink! The common-interest-game between terrorists and the media," *Public Choice*, 133, 129-145.

Salfati, C.G. and Canter, D.V. (1999). Differentiating stranger murders: Profiling offender characteristics from behavioural styles. *Behavioural Sciences and the Law*, 17, 391-406.

Sandler, T., Tschirhart, J.T. & Cauley, J. (1983). A theoretical analysis of transnational terrorism. *American Political Science Review*, 77, 36-54.

Sandler, T. and Enders, W. (2004). An economic perspective on transnational terrorism. *European Journal of Political Economy*, 20, 301-316.

Shogren, E. (1993). Mail bomb attack leaves male computer scientist in critical condition. *Los Angeles Times*, June 25. http://articles.latimes.com/1993-06-25/news/mn-7044_1_mail-bomb.

Smith v. Spisak (2009). On writ of certiorari to the United States Court of Appeals for the Sixth Circuit. The Supreme Court of the United States, No.08-724.

Snook, B., Cullen, R.M., Bennell, C., Taylor, P.J. and Gendreau, P. (2008). The criminal profiling illusion: what's behind the smoke and mirrors? *Criminal Justice and Behaviour*, 35, 1257-1276.

Spaaij, R. (2010). The enigma of lone wolf terrorism: an assessment. *Studies in Conflict and Terrorism*, 33, 854-870.

Tobin, J. (1958). Liquidity preference as behaviour towards risk. *Review of Economic Studies*, 25, 65-86.

Tobin, J. (1969). Comment on Borch and Feldstein. *Review of Economic Studies*, 36, 13-14.

Victoroff, J. (2005). The mind of the terrorist: A review and critique of the psychological approaches. *Journal of Conflict Resolution*, 49, 3-42.

Webster, W.H., Winter, D.E., Steel, A.L., Baker, W.M., Bruemmer, R.J. & Wainstein, K.L. (2012). *Final report of the William H. Webster Commission on the Federal Bureau of Investigation, counter-terrorism intelligence and the events at Fort Hood, Texas, on November 5, 2009*. Federal Bureau of Investigation, Washington D.C.

Woodhams, J., and Toye, K. (2007). An empirical test of the assumptions of case linkage and offender profiling with serial commercial robberies. *Psychology, Public Policy, and Law*, 13, 35-58.

INDEX

D

E

F

G

H

I